CHOOSE MEXICO

RETIRE ON
$600 A MONTH

CHOOSE MEXICO

John Howells & Don Merwin

Illustrated by Noni Mendoza

Maps by Carlos Rodriguez Robles

GATEWAY
BOOKS

Gateway Books
Distributed by Publishers Group West

Library of Congress Cataloging-in Publication Data

Howells, John, 1928-
    Choose Mexico : retire on $600 a month / John Howells & Don Merwin
    illustrated by Noni Mendoza : maps by Carlos Rodriguez Robles
        p.   cm.
    Includes bibliographical references (p.   ) and index.
    ISBN 0-933469-12-8
    1. Mexico—Guide- books. 2. Retirement, Places of—Mexico.
I. Merwin, Don, 1928-   . II. Title.
F1209.H78   1992
972.08'35—dc20   92-14248
                                                                    CIP

12 11 10 9 8 7 6 5 4 3 2 1

Contents

This book is dedicated to the people of Mexico.
They, above all, are the reason for our choice.

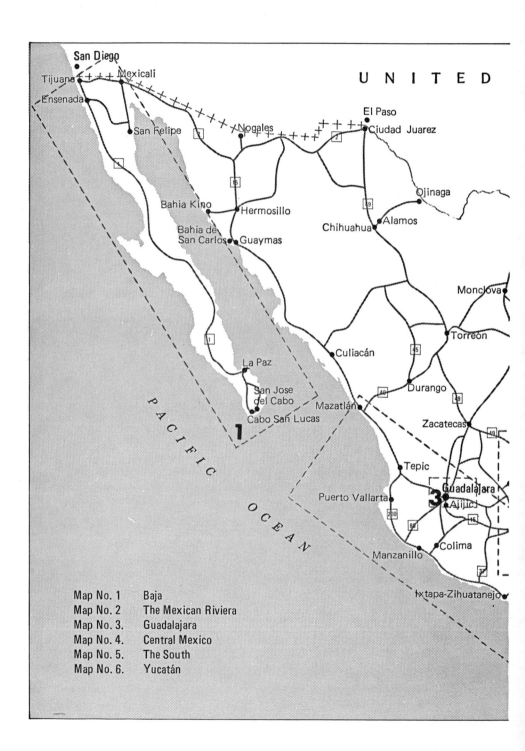

MEXICO

GULF OF
MEXICO

Piedras
Negras

Nuevo Laredo

Reynosa

Monterrey
Matamoros

Saltillo

Ciudad Victoria

San Luis Potosí **4** Tampico

Guanajuato
San Miguel Allende
Querétaro
Tequisquiapan
Pachuca

Morelia
Mexico City
Valle de
Bravo
Cuernavaca
Taxco
Puebla
Veracruz
Coatzacoalcos

Acapulco
5
Oaxaca
Villa Hermosa

Puerto Escondido
2
Puerto Angel Huatulco
Salina Cruz
San Cristobal
las Casas

Tapachula

6
Merida
Cancún
Cozumel

Campeche
Chetumal

CARIBBEAN SEA

C E N T R A L
A M E R I C A

GUANAJUATO, MEXICO...coai mendoza 1992

CHAPTER ONE

Why Mexico?

Many people look forward to retirement as an exciting change in lifestyle, not just a break from the workaday world. They want a complete change, perhaps in an exotic foreign country. (If you are reading this book you probably fall into that category.) Most people dream of a warm, temperate climate, surrounded by natural beauty and friendly people. Life is uncomplicated, easy, yet never boring. Somewhere in the background, music is playing and delicious food is never far away. From the picture window in the living room or from your tree-shaded patio, picturesque mountains form a hazy green backdrop, or is it the gentle swell of the ocean's surf? Maybe you can see wide boulevards and handsome buildings of a cosmopolitan city—we don't all have precisely the same dreams.

Unfortunately, for most of us the reality of retirement will bear little resemblance to this ideal. Fantasies are free, but comfortable living normally requires greater means than Social Security or other retirement benefits, given the high cost of living in the United States or Canada today.

While places such as California and Florida offer semitropical climates with warm summers (and chilly winters), only Hawaii can fill the bill as a tropical location in the United States or Canada. Hawaii is a lovely place to live, for those who can afford it.

As for foreign countries, many think about Europe, which is neither tropical nor exotic and is prohibitively expensive. Warm, tropical countries abound elsewhere in the world, that's true, but most of them are not places where you would want to visit, much less try on for retirement. For a foreign country to be a practical place for most North Americans to live—in addition to a nice climate—it should meet four conditions:

1. *It should be affordable.* Mexico certainly fills its promise in this respect. As you will see later on in this book, a budget of as little as $600 a month permits one to live an interesting life in comfort and dignity.

2. *A foreign country should be easily accessible,* so you can return and visit the grandkids occasionally, and they can visit you once in a while. (It goes without saying that it should be a place where they *want* to visit.)

3. *Your new home should be a safe place to live,* a place where local people like and respect North Americans. From the authors' perspective, Mexico is one of the safest retirement places we know of.

4. Finally, *a foreign retirement location should have large numbers of English-speaking residents*—preferably fellow North Americans—and a well-developed society that welcomes newcomers with warmth and genuine friendliness.

This last item is perhaps the most important of all. Without an extensive and friendly population of English-speaking compatriots, life would be absolute boredom. Unless you speak a foreign language fluently, odds are you wouldn't last long in a setting where you had no idea of what was going on around you, no matter how exotic or lovely the setting.

Clearly, Mexico fulfills all these requirements. What is more, unlike most foreign retirement situations, trying Mexico doesn't involve a deep commitment. You needn't bother with complicated visa requirements; a simple tourist card will do. You can drive anywhere in the nation in a matter of days. Should you decide that Mexico is not for you, it's a simple matter to pack up and return home for another look at your retirement menu. This book points out how it can be tried on a no-risk, experimental basis.

Furthermore, more and more people are discovering that Mexico is an ideal place for *part-time* living. Uncounted thousands spend pleasant winters there and return to their homes north of the border every spring. When we first started writing about retiring in Mexico, we tended to underestimate this phenomenon. "Wintering" in Mexico—or anywhere else for that matter—seemed like something you read about on the society pages, something that only rich people could do. The more we travel in Mexico in winter, the more people we meet who are neither tourists nor full-time residents. Their homes are in Burlington, Vermont, or Duluth, Minnesota. They are enjoying a month (or two, or three) in Mexico's sunshine and will rejoin their neighbors, children and grandchildren in the spring.

The opposite side of this coin is the great influx of "summer Mexicans" who flee from the heat and humidity of the Southern states, especially Texas, to enjoy the moderate climate of Mexico's central plateau. Some are retirees, others are teachers and others whose jobs leave their summers free. They, too, develop strong ties to the country, returning to the same places year after year, but their real homes continue to be up north.

Choose Mexico

Nine years ago we undertook the task of assembling facts and advice for those wishing to know about retirement in Mexico. Retirees and residents of all parts of the country were interviewed in person, by telephone and by questionnaire. "How much do you pay for rent? For food?" Medical care, insurance?" The authors covered every conceivable facet of U.S. and Canadian citizens living in Mexico.

When the book first appeared on the market, it was an instant success. *Choose Mexico* captured an important readership: those who seek dignified and interesting retirement at affordable costs. However, the authors were deluged with further questions from the readers, questions that the authors hadn't anticipated. A new, revised edition came out in 1988 to satisfy this demand. Like the rest of the world, Mexico is constantly undergoing change, and readers are again writing to ask how much change has taken place over the years and how it affects their retirement plans. Therefore, we present still another revision, the story of retirement in Mexico in the 1990s.

The question most frequently asked: "Is Mexico still the bargain it was in 1985?" The answer is a qualified "almost." Prices have risen gradually in Mexico, just as they have risen in your home town. But since Mexican prices started from such a ridiculously low level, the changes are much less significant than those we've seen in the United States or Canada. In the final analysis, Mexico is still a wonderful place to retire, and its low cost of living cannot be matched anywhere else in North America. This new edition should prove invaluable to the reader in making decisions about retirement living in Mexico.

Not Just for Retirees

This book isn't only for people who are already retired. Retirees who are thinking about changing their lifestyles will, of course, find this book useful in considering alternatives to their present situation. They may well decide that Mexico is the place to try. According to the U.S. State Department, more than 150,000 U.S. citizens now live there.

The greatest value of this publication, however, is for folks still in the planning stages, those casting about for retirement alternatives. By doing some planning now, you can avoid confusion and disappointment later.

The lifestyle we describe in Mexico is equally feasible for many others, particularly those engaged in seasonal work. They find Mexico a great place to live for *part* of each year. Why not escape winter by relaxing on a tropical beach or enjoying a sunny mountain village? For those planning to retire "at home," a part-time retirement in Mexico is an excellent idea. Reasonable prices in Mexico make early or partial retirement possible on an income far smaller than you might imagine.

Obviously, retirement in Mexico isn't for everyone. (Thank goodness for that, or the country would soon be overrun with North Americans.) Most retirees decide not to move away for retirement. Others feel that a total change of scenery is called for. To some, the chance to start a totally new life with new friends and experiences can be an adventure in itself. Still others need to move away from the high-cost areas where they presently live, looking for some place more affordable. Fortunately, Mexico is an alternative—for both full-time and part-time retirement—that doesn't involve a total severing of ties. This book points out how it can be tried on a no-risk, experimental basis.

When the original *Choose Mexico* was written, the only books available were ten or more years out of date. Many aspects of national character, scenery and customs change slowly, but practical details of living such as prices, regulations and the availability of foods and medications tend to change rapidly. Because we offered up-to-date information not available elsewhere, the original book was a success. However, we repeat the advice we gave in our first edition: when you pick up this book, should you find that the date on the copyright page is more than a few years old, treat many of the specifics in it with caution, or look for a more recent edition.

Mexico on $400 a Month?

When our first edition hit the bookstores back in 1985, $400 a month was a perfectly adequate income for retirement living in Mexico. Even today, $400 is more than the overwhelming majority of Mexican families earn. Mexican school teachers recently went on strike nationwide, demanding that their $200 a month salaries be increased. That's right, $200 a month. While it's true that most families would do just fine in Mexico on a $400 budget, realistically, few North Americans could adapt to living on such a low income. Not today. It would require a drastic change in diet, housing standards and daily living habits.

According to our latest research efforts, we find that $600 a month, judiciously spent, will provide a couple with comfortable and attractive housing, meals out when you like and possibly a part-time maid. This budget allows not merely for subsistence in Mexico, but for enjoyment of what the country has to offer. More money will enable you to live even more comfortably and will widen your choices of retirement sites and provide more travel opportunities. Even if your income is unlimited, this book will be useful to you; most of its sections are invaluable to anyone wishing to live in Mexico.

One note: the $600 figure does not cover the cost of an automobile. Public transportation is adequate and cheap, no matter where you live in Mexico, so a car isn't essential as it is back home. Furthermore, there is no way to estimate anyone's car expenses. We know people who spend $600 a month just to make payments on their Jaguar or Mercedes. On the other hand, our 1991 research trip to Mexico was in a 1967 Volkswagen bug, which gave us great gas mileage and convenience. (VWs are everywhere in Mexico, everybody knows how to repair them and repairs are inexpensive. We highly recommend them to retirees in Mexico.)

Although estimates of living costs are framed in terms of couples, there is no community of retirees in Mexico that does not have a large number of singles, both men and women.

In general, women alone seem to feel more comfortable where there are concentrations of their compatriots. Single men, however, can and do go anywhere in Mexico their fancies take them and find that they can live quite well on $600 a month.

The Good Life is Within Your Reach

What excites us about this book isn't adding to the literature of "Mexico on-the-cheap," but rather helping people who feel they are doomed to another decade of unsatisfying work, because they think they can't afford to retire, or those who look forward to retirement without enthusiasm. Above all, we want to communicate our conviction that the good life is within their reach *because*, not despite the fact that, it is in Mexico. If what you're looking for is a cut-rate Palm Beach or Palm Springs, flawed only by the presence of the natives, we urge you to look elsewhere. Most residents love being in Mexico; that country doesn't need foreigners who would rather be somewhere else.

Making a Choice

Most people are ruled by their jobs. They live where they do because they need to make a living. But once you don't have to go to work every day, you suddenly find that for the first time in many years, you are free to make some choices about where you can live. A job no longer rules you. Do you stay where you are, or do you move?

This is the first crucial question. For some, the thought of leaving their family, relatives and friends of a lifetime is unthinkable. They're willing to brave the winters, ice, slush and high heating bills or suffer summer heat and humidity and expensive air conditioning bills. For them it's worth it. Others who disagree will be reading this book. For the money many families spend just for utilities, they could rent a lovely house near the beach and stock the refrigerator with cold drinks. Think about *that* next winter when you're chipping ice off your windshield!

For many, simply moving to a warmer climate isn't the entire answer, not unless you adore hot summer weather. Florida summers, with 75 percent humidity and 90-degree days, make outdoor living all but impossible. Mosquitoes and cockroaches don't help, either. Arizona is dry, that's true, but even with low humidity, 110-degree summer days can keep you next to the air conditioner.

Happily, Mexico has a range of climates that are as nearly perfect as you can reasonably expect. "eternal spring," is a descriptive phrase often applied to parts of Mexico. There, you can choose your own climate (as you will learn later on in the book), and you'll find that most places where Americans live need neither air-conditioning nor furnaces.

Living on Social Security?

Trying to make ends meet on Social Security in the United States is a constant struggle in most urban settings. Even those with comfortable incomes find they spend a great deal of their money each month on basics and sometimes have to dip into their savings to get by. Most people who struggle with retirement finances don't realize they have any alternatives. They don't realize that on the average Social Security payment for a couple (almost $900 a month) they could retire on a $600 monthly budget in Mexico, and *save* money each month!

Now, please understand, the charm of living in Mexico is not just living inexpensively. Although the low cost of living is important, it's simply a happy side benefit. Friendly neighbors, picturesque villages, modern cities, breathtaking panoramas, cultural adventures and an atmosphere of peaceful living in a truly foreign country, all make Mexico a great place to be. Therefore, even if it were *expensive* to live there, it would still be worth it!

Another Mexico

The Mexico we describe in this book is *not* the country known by tourists on a two-week vacation. It isn't the Mexico visited by affluent vacationers who move from one luxury hotel to another, seldom coming into contact with the people. We present you with the Mexico known by *residents*—the real Mexico. It is the Mexico enjoyed by North Americans—particularly those of middle age and beyond—of moderate means, who desire economical yet comfortable places to live, food that is nutritious, enjoyable and affordable, medical care that is accessible and reliable and, above all, activities that define the difference between stagnation and vitality.

We must emphasize that the biggest attraction isn't inexpensive living. If you aren't one of those who appreciate Mexico and respect its people, please don't even think about going. Furthermore, we aren't encouraging impoverished people to move there (make sure you have some money as a backup, because someday you may want to return.) The affordable cost of living is just the icing on the cake. Mexico would be a delightful place to live even if prices were much higher than they are now.

Location

Another advantage of selecting Mexico for foreign retirement is its location. Unlike Spain, Italy, Australia or other foreign countries, Mexico is readily accessible. For relatively little time and expense, you can go there by airplane, train, bus or automobile. Mexico makes you feel that friends and family are not too far away. This physical closeness is one reason for choosing Mexico. You can drive home in a few days to spend the holidays with the grandchildren, or they can fly to visit you at reasonable fares anytime the urge strikes.

The close proximity of Mexico has yet another advantage for those who want to experience foreign retirement. Most Americans tell us they feel a need to renew their contact with home once or twice a year. They miss friends and relatives, and need a "culture-fix." This is easy when living in Mexico; home is just a few hours away. With your tastefully decorated house in Mexico as an attraction, your family and friends will be tempted to visit; you will have frequent opportunities to play the gracious host. If you live in Europe, the visits will be few and far between.

Is Mexico a Stable, Safe Place to Live?

First, let's look at the financial side. We hear people protest, "But Mexico must be a risky place to live, what with all that inflation! The country is going to collapse!" What about this?

The value of the peso, at the time we wrote the first edition of *Choose Mexico*, was around 150 to the dollar. Eight years later, the peso is more than 3,000 to the dollar. Now, that's inflation! As the value of the peso drops, prices and wages climb, trying to keep things even. Just what does this mean for you, as a resident of Mexico? The answer is: when the value of the peso drops, the value of the dollar *increases* in relation to the peso. For a time, the increase was very favorable to North Americans. Finally, in 1988, the currency was stabilized, with an official depreciation of the peso at a much slower rate than before. At first it was set at a rate of one peso per day. Then the official slide gradually fell to .4 pesos per day against the dollar. This official control on the rate of inflation has kept the peso rather flat for the past couple of years. This means that the peso is slightly over-valued. There are those who say this is a temporary measure, that eventually the values will fall to their true levels. In the meantime the almost-free prices of a few years ago are memories. However compared to prices here in the United States, Mexico is still bargain-land!

What about the Mexicans, whose savings were in pesos? Didn't they experience a horrible loss of purchasing power? Yes, but it wasn't as bad as you might think. At one time, banks in Mexico were paying interest well over 90 percent a year. You read correctly, *90 percent!* As the government got inflation under control, the interest rates dropped—gradually down to 60 percent, 45 percent and still dropping. At the time of writing, a bank account in pesos is paying 20 percent interest. This rate is, of course, much higher than possible in this country, and we'll talk about taking advantage of this later on in the book.

What's the bottom line? Mexico is still a bargain! We've simply had to raise the minimum ante to $600.

Political Stability

What is the danger of the country "collapsing," as some people claim? These people talk as if a country is like a large corporation; if it goes bankrupt, it will have to close its doors and go out of business.

The fact is, countries don't "collapse." They can't close their doors and send everybody home! They simply recognize that they can't pay their foreign debts, and continue business as usual. A Mexican economist once told me, "You Americans worry too much about whether or not we're going to repay the money we owe your banks. We aren't going to pay, so stop worrying about it!" We worry about the few billions owed by foreign countries, but think little of the *trillions* of dollars that our country is racking up in debts!

What about the danger of a revolution? We hear about revolutions in Central American republics, why not Mexico? From time to time one reads hysterical statements from politicians that "Mexico is next!"

Anyone who knows Mexico and its political processes knows how absurd these prophecies are. Mexican democracy is far from perfect, but it is a democracy in its own way. Mexicans enjoy a free exchange of ideas and a multiplicity of political parties, running the gamut from the extreme right to the extreme left. They campaign hard and pull no punches. While it's true that the same political party wins most elections, it does so by shrewdly adopting as its own, any ideas the other parties use to attract popular support. Thus, depending upon the political climate at the moment, the platform changes to draw voter support. That means, even when opposition candidates lose, their goals win and become policy by being adopted by the next government. Furthermore, since the close election of President Salinas Gortari, many government-backed candidates are being replaced by opposition party candidates.

Importantly, change does take place at the ballot box—peaceful change. In every revolution ever recorded in history, we find one essential point: *revolutions can occur if and only if the overwhelming majority demands a change, and there is no possibility of lawful, peaceful change.* Extremists exist in Mexico, of course, but they have great difficulty in attracting followers. Extremist parties are legal and quite active, but garner few votes. Mexican voters are very skeptical about politicians in general, and don't fancy taking chances with radical candidates. There is a general feeling that all politicians are scoundrels. (We won't argue the point.) The very thought of the people supporting a revolution to replace known scoundrels with unknown scoundrels is funny. When they want to change scoundrels, they can do it at the ballot box.

What About Crime?

If you live in North America, particularly in an urban area of the United States, you don't have to be told about crime and violence. A major incentive for many city dwellers to move is to escape the violence, robbers, muggers and youth gangs in their disintegrating neighborhoods. Unfortunately, we live in one of the most violent societies in the world. Is Mexico different, and if so, why?

Mexico does, of course, have crime. There has never been a society where there isn't crime, where laws are not broken. You wouldn't need laws if no one broke them. However, crime in Mexico is of a different nature than in the United States. Clearly, there are more crimes like burglaries and pickpockets (crimes which can be prevented by precaution and awareness). But one thing is obvious: the level of *violent* crime is much lower south of the border. Holdups and violent robberies are so unusual in Mexico that they make front page news all around the country, whereas in Cleveland or Phoenix, armed robbery and muggings seldom even make the back section of the local newspapers.

For example, in Guadalajara, Mexico's second metropolis, the homicide is reported at a rate of less than 8.5 per 100,000. Compare this to Chicago's 22 per 100,000, New Orleans' rate of 21.9 or Miami's rate of 33.2 per 100,000! Let's not mention New York. Thus, Guadalajara's murder rate is similar to Louisville's 8.81 or Albuquerque's 9.3 per 100,000 population. In nearby Lake Chapala, a very popular retirement spot for North Americans, one resident reports, "The Lake area has only four recorded murders of foreigners in 16 years and two were committed by Americans.

Just as small-town Iowa is about the safest place in the U.S.A., small-town Mexico is similarly safe. Big cities everywhere, as you well know, are crime-plagued. Leave something valuable on the front seat of your car in Mexico City, and its life expectancy is about the same as in New Orleans or Chicago. You should know better.

One type of crime that is rather rare in the United States, but very common in Mexico, is pickpocketing. There are many skilled practitioners who have developed it into a fine art. But the wary are rarely taken. North American residents who answered our questionnaires emphasized that they generally felt safer in Mexico than in similar places in the United States. They also noted that they have to be on their guard against pickpockets and burglars. Fortunately, common sense precautions usually prevent both pickpocketing and burglary.

Philosophy of Law and Order

The point is that there is a big difference between crime north and south of the border. Violent, audacious crimes such as hold-ups, muggings and rapes are simply not common in most of Latin America. Why? These countries have a different philosophy of law and order. Law in Mexico is based on what is commonly known as the Napoleonic Code. That is, instead of referring to past decisions of other courts to determine guilt and punishment (as our system does), all laws and crimes are codified, with procedures and punishments clearly spelled out.

Under this system it isn't the burden of the state to prove beyond a reasonable doubt that the accused is guilty, to convince a jury of 12 to vote unanimously for guilt. Rather, it's the accused's job to prove to a judge that he is *not* guilty. As a result, few criminals go free to repeat their crimes. In addition, when a person is convicted a second time, he is automatically labeled an "habitual criminal" and upon the third conviction, routinely receives a 20-year sentence.

Incidentally, parole, probation and time off for good behavior are not part of the Mexican system of justice. Crime doesn't pay in Mexico. The end result is that people try to conduct themselves at all times in a circumspect way in all their social and business transactions, always concerned that their behavior is above question. After all, you only get two strikes; then you're out!

Because of this harsh treatment of criminals, the streets are generally calm and safe, even late at night. Juvenile delinquency is practically unknown, particularly in smaller towns. Youth gangs and graffiti simply aren't tolerated. Drug use is looked upon with utmost seriousness. Although much marijuana is grown in Mexico, it is for export only; smoking it is dangerous!

This approach to law may be slightly repugnant to those of us raised in the tradition of "innocent until proven guilty beyond a reasonable doubt," but it is difficult to ignore the fact that our system doesn't seem to be particularly effective when it comes to dealing with habitual criminals. Mexican cities and towns seem to be escaping the wave of violent crime and drug addiction that so threatens us in the United States.

A second factor is that Mexico's family and community-oriented society effectively discourages juvenile crime and delinquency. Few visitors fail to notice how well behaved almost all Mexican teenagers are. If a kid were to get into trouble, he'd have to face his grandmother and his godparents, not to mention his uncles and aunts and cousins. In smaller towns, when a person goes to jail for a minor offense, he sometimes isn't fed for three days. He must suffer the humiliation of having his family come to the jail and push food through the bars as if he were some kind of animal. It's far easier to be a law-abiding citizen than have to face an irate grandmother. On weekends, instead of drinking beer and driving about the countryside, Mexican youths go to the town square with their parents and family. With the whole town watching, they walk around and around the square, talking to schoolmates and flirting with members of the opposite sex while their parents gossip and socialize with their friends and relatives. The family is all-important in Mexico.

Driving in Mexico

One of the most offbeat rumors you hear about Mexico, is: "You have to be very careful about driving in the cities, because someone is likely to run into your car and then sue you for damages!" This is really absurd, and whoever passes these rumors along obviously doesn't know the first thing about the Mexican legal system.

First of all, protection against liability is why you have insurance. If someone's car is injured, the insurance company pays. There isn't any such thing as a lawsuit in front of a jury as we have here. You can be sure that the insurance company isn't going to pay any more than the actual amount of damages. You don't see huge settlements for damages and punitive assessments in Mexico; the payments are limited by the actual losses. Suppose a person is injured and is off work for a few weeks? The insurance company simply figures out how much money he would have made if he were working and pays. If the injured party isn't satisfied with this, he can appeal the insurance company's decision. But that's the insurance company's problem, not yours.

However, you can get into real trouble by driving *without* insurance. If you have an accident *without* insurance, you are likely to be arrested until you can post a bond to assure the police that you can pay for the damages. Otherwise, you might simply skip across the border. We talk about this further later on in this book.

Choosing a Climate

A great reason for moving from your home town is to escape the rigors of winter or steamy summers. Mexico has such a wide variety of climates that most people have no problem finding just the right place. Of course, Mexico has its share of places that are unbearably hot or bone-chillingly cold, too humid or too dry. But not by coincidence, the places where most Americans (and most Mexicans, too) choose to live are either at high enough altitudes to enjoy "eternal spring" or on the Pacific Coast where the temperatures are higher but tempered by continual ocean breezes. Later in the book, you'll find detailed information to help you select the perfect climate for your purpose.

Gorgeous beaches flank both sides of the country, some crowded with sun-drenched tourists happy to escape from northern winters, some beaches silently inviting you to explore miles of untracked sand. From the picturesque desert panorama of Baja California to the tropical jungles of the Yucatán, the country abounds in breathtaking scenery. This draws a multitude of Canadians and Americans who spend billions every year taking in the beauty of Mexico.

Cities with modern buildings and elegant restaurants, flowing with excitement thrill many North Americans, while others prefer villages with cobblestone streets and band concerts in the town square. Each part of Mexico has its particular character. Each city and village is distinct; its personality differs dramatically from all others, in contrast to North America, where so many towns attempt to be carbon copies of each other down to identical restaurants, identical signs and mass-produced architecture.

We've heard people state that they think Mexico is ugly, because they've visited Tijuana or some other border town and weren't impressed. This is about as fair as a European visitor flying into the middle of Nevada then claiming that the United

States is a desert, with almost no one living there. (As you might suspect, this book doesn't particularly recommend border towns as choice places to retire.)

Something that impressed the Spanish Conquistadors, and also today's visitor to Mexico, is the Indians' love of flowers. There was something almost religious about blossoms, and they were to be found everywhere, in gardens, along roads, painted on walls. Almost five hundred years later this hasn't changed. No home is complete without some tenderly cared-for potted plants in the windows and perhaps bougainvilleas blooming over the door. In fact, the inhabitants probably don't think of beauty as a luxury. So much of it, provided by nature, is all around them and what requires a pot, some earth, some seeds, a brush and some paint is considered as much a necessity as food and shelter.

Making Friends

A big problem for people who choose to move to another location upon retirement is leaving friends they've made over the years. If you move to another American city, you'll find that making new friends is often a slow, difficult process. Unless you opt for a retirement community where people have age in common, or some other situation where people have similar interests, you often don't "fit in." People's friends tend to be mostly work-related or special-interest related, rather than simply neighbors. Unless you have special talents for accumulating friends, you could be lonely in a new setting for a while.

However, Americans living in a foreign setting are a different breed. They quickly learn the necessity of acquiring a network of friends. They welcome strangers into their social groups, and often actively seek out newcomers with invitations. Why should an English-speaking colony in Mexico be different from an ordinary neighborhood in the United States or Canada?

The answer is that few gringos (the colloquial Mexican term for Americans and Canadians) work in Mexico, and the few that do aren't part of a large work force. Their friends must come from their neighborhood and their English-speaking compatriots. People who, in their neighborhoods at home, barely knew their next-door neighbors (and certainly not those three doors away) will now band together in closely knit groups. New arrivals are therefore eagerly sought as valuable additions to the community.

Because the total North American population isn't very large to begin with, you usually find that age, occupation, religion, financial status and educational levels have little to do with the composition of the group. This makes for a stimulating and refreshing circle that is seldom found in social situations in North America. Artists and bricklayers, authors and housewives, hippies and yuppies, Baptists and Jews, youthful and elderly, conservative and liberal, all mix together, perhaps for the first time in their lives, and discover their horizons widened through a stimulating exchange of ideas and philosophies. This "instant friendship" is surely a major consideration in many retirees' decision to select Mexico as a retirement spot.

You'll find a clear bond of unity among English-speaking residents, yet it isn't unity *against* the Mexicans. Quite the contrary. Many discover that volunteering for public service projects to help local people is a rewarding way to become involved with other North Americans and to make friends with local people. Many a warm friendship between Mexican and American families has been forged through working in community projects.

Trial Living First

It would seem superfluous to urge anyone considering retiring anywhere to visit first and stay for several months before deciding anything. Yet, we have been surprised at the number of people who make snap judgments and want to start packing their furniture before they even know where they want to go. Mexico isn't very far away, and a six-month test retirement can be done without pulling up stakes at home or without going through a lot of legalities with the Mexican government. A simple tourist card, at no cost, will get you into the country for half a year.

Certainly, if promptness and efficiency are important to you, it would be essential to find out whether you can adjust to a country where those commodities are in short supply. When they say Mexico is "the land of mañana" they aren't kidding. Don't think you're going to change anything, either; the mañana concept is as much a part of Latin American culture as efficiency is part of ours. The same is true to some degree of sanitation and environmental protection—control of air and water pollution—which aren't up to the standards Americans are used to. Would you find that intolerable? There's only one way to find out. Try living in Mexico for a while before you make a commitment to living there permanently.

Although this book may be of use to a casual traveler in Mexico, it's basically intended to help prepare you for a journey of exploration. We've not presented a list of hotels, restaurants or side trips of sightseeing. This is best left to books like *Let's Go Mexico*, Frommer's *Mexico On $45 A Day*, or any of the other excellent, up-to-date travel guides available in your book stores. Carl Franz's *People's Guide to Mexico* presents an outstanding overview of the country, its people and its customs. We include maps in this edition, in response to many readers' requests, but for good, detailed driving information you can't beat a road map. American Automobile Association maps are excellent.

How Have Things Changed?

Obviously, prices and conditions in Mexico have changed since our last edition. Therefore, in the spring of 1991, we conducted another research project to bring things up to date for this edition. We needed to do another "test retirement" to see just how much it costs to live in Mexico in the 1990s.

One author and his wife traveled to a popular retirement area, rented an apartment for a month and kept scrupulous track of their expenditures. This time their budget came in at $601. Not bad, considering inflation both in Mexico and at home. They found a comfortable two-bedroom, two-bath apartment renting for $200 a month (with a one year-lease). Utilities (electricity and cooking gas) cost another $28. While their monthly food budget in California runs over $250, in Mexico they ate just as well on $175. They could have "bought into" the national health insurance program (free medicine, hospitals and doctors) for less than $20 a month, or chosen private insurance for $45 a month. A doctor's house call was only $13.33! Since they rarely visit doctors in the 'States, they didn't bother with the medical insurance. They observed, however, that if they were staying year-round in Mexico, they probably would have opted for the $20 a month coverage. As always, medical expenses are reasonable. A typical dentist charges $100 for a porcelain crown and teeth cleaning costs $10.83 a visit.

They spent $81 dining out. Laundry and a part-time cleaning lady accounted for an additional $30. Not counting their car, their basic expenses came to $601. A major expense was buying the *Mexico City News*, 60 cents a day, for a $18 a month. (Some residents read the *News* at the local library and save.)

Rent	$200
Food	175
Utilities	21
Bus and taxi transportation	21
Cleaning lady	30
Newspaper	18
Cable TV	13
Dining out	81
Miscellaneous (clothing, postage, etc.)	42
Total	**$601**

With few exceptions, they didn't drive their automobile during this test month. However, they suspected that, like most Californians, they would feel lost without a car for long-term living. This would mean adding a few items onto this budget. Full-coverage Mexican auto insurance for one car costs $240 for the year ($20 a month), which includes road service and legal representation. Gasoline costs about $1 a gallon for no-lead, so if you figure on occasional trips into the countryside, you'd have to add about $8 gasoline money for a 100-mile trip every other week. $20 a month would be reasonable for maintenance, given the inexpensive cost of Mexican mechanics.

Another expenditure which they didn't list was a catered cocktail party which cost $41. Obviously, this isn't an essential that everyone would spend. Since cocktail parties were an integral part of the social scene, they gave one of their own to repay the invitations they'd received during that month

Therefore, when the car expenses are added to this extra entertainment cost, the monthly total comes to $722. Many couples could then bank almost $150 a month out of their Social Security payments! If they did away with the car and catered parties, on their budget of $601 they would have nearly $275 every month to blow on travel, luxuries or to deposit in the bank.

The other author and his wife visited several other cities in early 1992. They, too, observed that economical living was still possible and were particularly impressed by the wide gap between what tourists and residents were spending on accommodations, food and transportation. They found comfortable hotels for less than $30 a night within a couple of blocks of the big international hostelries that were charging more than four times as much. Clean, enjoyable restaurants still offer full-course meals for as little as three or four dollars, they reported. But they backed out of some, obviously for the wealthy tourist, where prices were similar to those in the United States.

True, many things have risen over the years. Taxi drivers now want $1.25 instead of the 75 cents they charged for the same trip three years ago. Dinner in an upscale restaurant costs $9.00 instead of $6.00. Hotels that formerly charged $18 dollars are now $26. Remember, Social Security payments have also risen from a 1985 average of around $600 per couple to 1991's average monthly benefit of almost $900. Therefore, compared to the United States, living in Mexico is still a bargain.

Cesar Meniers — 1992

CHAPTER TWO

Living in a Foreign Country

On the United States' southern border is Mexico, a truly foreign country. The other two North American countries, Canada and the United States, have too many similarities—in language, world views and customs—to be considered "foreign." Therefore, for millions of North Americans, Mexico is the only foreign country they will ever visit.

Mexico appreciates these visitors, for they pour billions of dollars into the economy; the Mexican government refers to tourism as its "green pipeline." Tourists carry away—besides good memories of a vacation well spent—uncounted tons of curios, weavings, stuffed iguanas, lavender pottery and a host of other bizarre items as presents for their unfortunate friends back home. They enjoy the beaches, mountains and the interesting countryside and cities, yet they often miss the most charming part of Mexico: its uniquely foreign culture. Underlying the tourist traps, American-style restaurants and curio shops is a truly *foreign* country.

When we talk of foreign travel, we quite naturally think of Europe. Europe is far away, true, but is it really so *foreign*? After all, most of our ideas, customs and beliefs originally came from Europe. People there think pretty much as we do, behave similarly and see the world in the same terms. Mexico, however, is very different, much more foreign than any European country you're likely to visit.

To be sure, Mexico has European roots, beginning with the Spanish Conquistadors. Yet underlying this is a rich tapestry of customs and beliefs dating from the Aztecs, the Mayas and even before. Folk beliefs, legends, manners and other cultural artifacts are colored by this Indian heritage just as most Mexicans' skins are colored by the Native-American past. This blended culture is neither European nor Indian; it is *Mexican*. Once you begin to understand the country and its peoples, you discover an exciting new world.

Why the Differences?

At first glance, it doesn't stand to reason that Mexico should be so different from the United States or Canada. After all, the only thing that separates us is an artificial line we call a *border*. Sometimes a high fence or deep ditch, but sometimes just a shallow river or an imaginary boundary that can only be plotted on a surveyor's map, the border is nevertheless real. Once you step across that line, you enter a profoundly different world. In some respects, you step backward in time by half a century or more.

To understand the reasons why Mexico is so different from the rest of North America, we need to take a quick glance at history. The United States and Canada experienced their heaviest waves of immigration beginning in the early 1800s and lasting for about a century and a half. For the most part, these settlers were unemployed workers, displaced farmers and others who looked toward the abundant lands of America, seeking a chance for a new start in life. They brought traditions of individualism and valued hard work. They knew how to till land, how to build houses, to work in factories. They brought the technology of the Industrial Revolution which was sweeping Europe at that time.

The new immigrants discovered that the choice lands were occupied by Indians. They solved this problem by moving the original owners ever westward, or often, by slaughter. Small, family-operated farms sprang up in the forests and prairies. In the towns, small mercantile or manufacturing enterprises arose. The United States and Canada thus began as a working-class and middle-class society which more or less has retained these traditions through the centuries.

But Mexico was settled much *earlier*, in the 1500s. This was long before the Industrial Revolution wrought its changes upon the world. The original Spanish in Mexico were the *hidalgos*, or the minor nobility of Spain, that warrior class which had just defeated the Moors in Spain. Eager for adventure, they leaped at the chance of conquering new vistas, of becoming lords in a new world.

These soldiers brought with them the ideas of feudalistic Spain with its notions of nobility. Traditionally, European nobles *don't* work with their hands; they oversee others who do. The hidalgos' ideas of farming weren't small farms, but huge estates operated by serfs, just as was the custom in Spain.

The conquerors came as an army, without women or wives. But, instead of killing off the Indians, as their northern counterparts were to do two centuries later, the early Spanish *married* Indian women, and merged their European genes with the native American ones. Cortés himself started the ball rolling by marrying Malinche (or Marina) the Aztec girl who had been a Mayan slave, who guided the Spaniards to the Aztec emperor.

From the Spanish point of view, it would have been pointless to kill Indians; they were needed to operate the huge farms or *haciendas*. Indians there simply changed from having Aztec overlords to Spanish ones, and went on tilling the same lands their ancestors had for centuries. As they intermarried with the Spanish, a new race was created. The *mestizos*, with their darker skins and slightly Indian features have become the racial touchstone for the overwhelming majority of Mexicans. Spanish customs, traditions and folklore blended with Indian customs to create a new cultural synthesis, uniquely Mexican.

With the conquest, Spain quickly divided Mexico among the nobility and within a few decades the country had new owners. Then immigration all but stopped for several centuries. All of this occurred a hundred years before the Industrial Revolution got underway in Europe. Instead of building factories to manufacture goods, Mexico shipped rich agricultural and mineral bonanzas back to Spain in return for the manufactured goods they needed. Immigration—instead of flowing heavily, over long periods of time as in the north—went rather swiftly in Mexico. With few immigrants, modern European traditions were slow in reaching Mexico. While the United States and Europe were undergoing industrialization and modernization, Mexico remained an agricultural country with world views formed by feudal Spaniards of the 1500s.

To this day, Americans are puzzled at the upper-class Mexican's apparent lack of interest in things mechanical, and their attitudes toward labor. Up north, for example, being able to repair a car or perhaps to turn it into a "hot rod" is prestigious for American youngsters, no matter how wealthy their families. In Mexico, only low-income, working-class people bother with fixing their own cars. Often, upper- or middle-class drivers have no idea of how to change a flat tire, and often wait until someone comes along who knows how. Mexican businessmen will buy expensive equipment, and instead of scrupulously maintaining it, as one might expect, will run it until it stops, and then buy a replacement. All of this is understandable if you are aware of the historical perspective.

Many Different Mexicos

As you travel about the United States and Canada, you'll find a remarkable similarity between one section and another. To be sure, the scenery in Maine is different from Alabama or Nevada, but many, many things are the same. Meals served in Denny's or Howard Johnson's are indistinguishable, for example. People read the same books, watch the same TV shows, discuss the same current events, and generally speak the same dialects of English, using common slang words, sharing common humor, likes and dislikes.

Mexico is not so homogenized, and this is part of its charm. It is divided into many physical segments, each separated by geography and history. Each section has its own traditions, its unique cuisine, a climate of its own, and often, even language differences.

If you take a look at the map of Mexico, you'll begin to see why. You'll notice a long, narrow country, with several mountain chains running north and south, splitting the country and forming barriers against east-west communications. In pre-Colombian times, trails across these sierras were few in number and difficult to travel. Indian tribes living in the valleys developed different languages and different civilizations. You'll also notice that most highways and railroads run north and south. This is not only because of the mountain barriers, but because most of the highways and railroads were built years ago by U.S. manufacturing and mining interests, with the goal of getting raw materials out of Mexico to feed northern factories, and to ship goods into Mexico for sale.

Furthermore, the country is sliced laterally with rivers and deep canyons, sometimes thousands of feet deep, making north-south communication difficult in olden days. It's still not easy. Each of these sections, over thousands of years of settlement, developed its own variants of culture, food, housing and style. The early Spanish settlers adapted these foods and customs into their inventory of likes and dislikes. Today, even though TV and radio have bridged many of the gaps, these differences still persist and are a source of local pride. Almost any Mexican you meet will inform you that his particular section of the republic is universally recognized as the very best place in the whole world!

A Selection of Climates

The country is a checkerboard of valleys and plateaus, often with different climates from neighboring sections. In the tropics, for every 300-foot increase in altitude the temperature drops one degree Fahrenheit. While the Gulf coast cities like Villahermosa or Veracruz might swelter at 95 degrees, Mexico City enjoys temperatures of 70 or 75 degrees. There is a difference between living on the Pacific Coast and the Gulf Coast in that the constant breeze blowing off the Pacific keeps summer and winter temperatures pleasant, while the Gulf of Mexico coast can suffocate in the summer, and can catch chilly northern winds that whip down from Canada in winter.

What this means for the resident or retiree is that you can choose from an amazing variety of individual cultures and climates, each one distinct and a delight to discover. Each is a microcosm with its own cooking techniques, dress styles and sometimes different accents of Spanish. When you get away from the big towns, you often hear people conversing in *Nahuatl* or *Quechua*, the languages of the ancient Aztecs and Mayas.

The Indians themselves often look different from section to section. The physical barriers kept them apart for thousands of years, so the tribes tended to marry within the group, keeping bloodlines relatively pure, and developing tribal differences in appearance. There are at least 40 distinct racial and language groups in Mexico.

On the eastern coast around Veracruz, home of the Huastecan tribes, typical clothing is tropical white, with the men wearing shallow straw hats. The women love bright embroidery trim on their dresses. On the west coast around Tehuantepec, where the temperature is equally tropical, for some reason, women tend to wear ankle-length skirts. A bit farther north around the Costa Chica area, the Indian women wear long woven skirts of cochineal-dyed yarn, and occasionally go topless. Yes, you read correctly, *topless*. The early missionaries weren't able to completely wipe out the custom, although they did convince most women to wear a white, flouncy kind of overblouse. This is worn today; however, a few women still insist on going topless. It's only the very old women who still observe the custom, the younger set long ago replaced the purple woven skirts and white tops or bare bosoms with blue jeans and designer blouses.

In the Yucatán, women prefer to wear a loose dress of light cotton, called a *huipil*, and the men often work bare-chested, wearing lightweight white muslin trousers. Because temperatures and humidity can become difficult, this kind of dress is very practical. On the other hand, the northern part of Mexico is influenced by the "western" clothing of Texas and Arizona. There the climate is similar to Texas, Arizona and New Mexico, so it isn't surprising that clothing styles should be influenced by those states.

In the southern part of Mexico, nearby Guatemalan tribes affect styles with bright, colorfully woven garments. Depending upon the particular tribe, men may wear woolen mini-skirts or knee-length trousers. The patterns of the weavings denote which village the wearer is from, and the color of the ribbons in the hair indicate whether the person is married or single.

While each section of the country has its own clothing styles, styles from New York, London, Paris and Mexico City invade younger fashions, particularly in the larger, more cosmopolitan cities. The smaller the town or village, the more likely you are to find older, more traditional dress.

Different Diets

Mexican food varieties are another joy to the authors of this book. Each section of the country has its own kind of dishes, its own style of cooking. Part of the fun of traveling in Mexico is sampling menus from section to section.

Most tourists think in terms of tacos, enchiladas and chili rellenos. To them, that's Mexican food. This is understandable, since that's just about all that's served in Mexican restaurants in the United States. Similarly, most foreigners think that typical American cuisine is hamburgers and hot dogs. Just as you can find hamburgers in the United States, you can find your fill of tacos in Mexico, if that's your dish. Most restaurants that cater to Americans include them on the menu, but a really *good* restaurant would no more offer tacos and enchiladas than would a gourmet San Francisco restaurant offer hamburgers and hot dogs on its dinner menu. There is so much more to Mexican cooking!

In the Yucatán you discover such treats as venison cooked with a vinegar-cream sauce, or smoked *jaibali* (wild peccary), *cochinito pibil* (roast suckling pig, cooked in a pit with a delicious sauce). In the mountains you'll find succulent quail, delicately flavored with herbs and grilled over a charcoal fire, or eggs cooked with a dry cheese that transforms them into a delightfully textured breakfast. The seafood near the ocean is fabulous. Some of our favorite dishes are: *huachinango al mojo de ajo* (red snapper grilled, with garlic-butter sauce), *langostinos* (char-broiled fresh-water lobsters), and a bewildering variety of clams and shellfish. As an example of the menu varieties, one Mazatlán restaurant offers almost 20 shrimp dishes! One of the authors even tried iguana stew on a recent trip to Mexico. It tasted a little like chicken, but very bony and not much meat. Not recommended if you're hungry.

One of the delights of living in Mexico is being able to cook some of these regional dishes at home, to experiment and learn. (See Appendix for an excellent cookbook.) A trip through a typical market, with its variety of fresh fruits, vegetables and meats makes shopping and menu planning a pleasant adventure rather than a chore. With their tropical climates, many parts of Mexico have year-round growing seasons for items that are unavailable in the north for much of the year. Just about any time of the year is good for incredibly sweet strawberries or luscious melons.

Tropical fruits such as mangoes, pineapple, avocados and bananas are picked for the Mexican market when they are *ripe*, not days or weeks ahead to allow for ripening in a boxcar en route as they must be when destined for the United States.

Shopping is also fun because the foods are not only fresh but are there in a profusion and quality that most of us barely remember. In time, Mexican agriculture may become sufficiently mechanized, and chemical fertilizers cheap enough, to mass-produce the tasteless fruits and vegetables that we have learned to settle for in the United States, but for now, fruits, vegetables, eggs, chicken and pork are bursting with flavor and enliven any cuisine in which one chooses to use them.

Retirement Choices

The difficulty of choosing the right retirement or long-term living spot is finding the section of Mexico that is *just right* for you. This is where this book should be of help. You can choose a tropical climate to escape winter, or you might want a dry, pleasant summer season. Like cool evenings and warm days? Balmy to warm evenings? Many people select the best of all worlds by living by the beaches in the winter, then, when humidity and temperatures begin to rise, move to their favorite village high in the mountains.

The nice thing about making a search for the right place is that it's fun to do and you can do it simply by using your tourist card privileges. You can travel about, live a few weeks here or there and make comparisons. You can see what kind of North American neighbors you will have, and get their opinions on living there. One thing you'll find out: there is no one place that can suit everyone. Your needs and desires are usually so unique that only you can decide.

Mexico is truly a *foreign* country, and a country where you can have a great time just trying to select an ideal retirement location.

CHAPTER THREE

Two Mexicos

Many people find it hard to believe that living in Mexico can be economical. "Why, we paid $175 a day for our condominium in Cancún," said one indignant couple, "so, how could you possibly live there for $600 a month?" Admittedly, this was an extra-luxurious, three-bedroom condo with a balcony overlooking the beach. Yet most tourists report paying $80 a day and more for rooms.

Mexico is a real tourist mecca. You can escape the snow and ice of New York or Chicago on that three-week vacation, and many people love to do it in real style. The beaches are marvelous, restaurants offer great service, with white-jacketed waiters and a menu that is as good as any Sheraton or Hilton in the United States. For only three weeks, what difference does it make if you pay $70, $80, maybe $100 a day for a room? One Acapulco hotel charges $280 a day, but this includes your own private swimming pool and a car. Well, it's 20-below zero back home, and you've earned a little luxury in your life. Besides, a $80-a-day room in Mexico is a marvel compared to a $160 room in New York. But with prices like this, how can you possibly expect to live or travel in Mexico on $600 a month?

Two Realities

The answer is that Mexico is divided into two realities, one for tourists and one for residents. Tourists pay different rates, often for the same things. Tourists make their reservations with travel agents, who earn their living from 10 percent commissions. They aren't likely to even have the $25 rooms among their listings.

But most North Americans who live in Mexico would think it absurd to lay out that kind of money, not when the $25 room is more than adequate. They can't afford to pay $175 a day for a condo, not when $175 a *month* is considered moderately expensive. People who live in Mexico consider it ludicrous to go to a high-priced hotel restaurant and dine on Holiday Inn cuisine when so many marvelous local restaurants offer tasty local specialties at a fraction of the cost.

One of the most important changes we've observed in the nine years since the research for the first edition of *Choose Mexico* was done is the increased difference between the tourist and resident economies. It seems that Mexican entrepreneurs (and the international ones who run the fancy hotels and restaurants) have learned that tourists are willing to pay much higher prices than are common in Mexico.

Is the answer to inexpensive living to stay away from the luxury resorts, like Acapulco, Cancún or Puerto Vallarta? Not necessarily. Acapulco, for example, can be one of the *cheapest* places to live in Mexico! From its initial marketing as a beautiful place for beautiful people, the town has overbuilt hotels and apartments. As soon as one high-rise is completed and half-full, another is started. There are plenty of $25-a-day hotel rooms, and $200-a-month apartments. The bargains are to be found away from the beach, on the hillsides with gorgeous views of the Pacific. Twenty years ago, these were top-of-the-line accommodations, but in order to compete, they continually lowered their prices. So what if you have to walk five blocks to the beach when you save $80 a day! If you are going to be a resident, this is what you look for.

One thing to keep in mind about living expenses in Mexico is that foreign tourists make up but a tiny part of the population. The vast majority of the tourists are *Mexican*, wage-earners who can't possibly afford to spend like the foreigners. A $20 hotel room represents about two day's wages for most Mexican workers. Ninety percent of the people in a resort town work there. They average about $150-$300 a month in wages, so they can't afford to pay much for rent or groceries. Most of the housing market is aimed at them, and rents and prices are scaled accordingly. You are either a rich tourist or a resident.

In March of 1991, in Mazatlán, the authors looked at a nicely furnished, two-bedroom unit in a modern-looking building about six blocks from the beach. It had a balcony and lots of windows to permit sunshine to brighten things. It had a secure parking space and maid service for an extra amount. All in all, it was a very pleasant place that would have rented for at least $700 a month in a similar California beach town. The rent: $275 a month. I have friends living in St. Louis who pay more than that just to heat their homes in the winter.

How to Find Housing

As a potential resident or retiree, you must make this a do-it-yourself project. Might as well start out traveling like a resident from the beginning! Pick up one of the low-cost travel guides to Mexico at your bookstore or library, the "Mexico on a budget" kind. They tend to be accurate about inexpensive hotels and travel tips. Except for the Christmas holidays and Easter week, you will seldom have any problems booking the hotel of your choice.

Don't bother with a travel agent, because the kind of hotels that budget books recommend usually don't pay travel agent's commissions and aren't on their computers. In 40 years of traveling in Mexico, I've never had problems finding an inexpensive hotel. Cab drivers are helpful, but often they get a tip from some hotels for bringing guests, so naturally they want to take you to their special hotel. Take anything a cab driver tells you with a grain of salt. Don't be persuaded to deviate from your original choice, even though the cabby tells you the hotel is closed or that he knows one that is cheaper. See it for yourself first; the guidebooks are pretty accurate. Cab drivers are not.

Once you arrive and are safely entrenched in an economical hotel, you can start looking for an apartment or a house for rent. If you are in a place where there are a lot of North Americans, you'll usually find listings and announcements posted on a bulletin board in the favorite "gringo" supermarket. Sometimes you'll see "for rent" signs in windows, or advertised in the local English-language newspaper. But the best way is to ask other foreign residents. They always seem to know what is vacant or what is about to be vacated.

Often, your hotel will have an apartment or suite for rent. This is a great way to test the town for its potential without getting involved in longer-term rental agreements. (Few landlords are willing to rent for less than two or three months.) A hotel rents by the day, week or month, and often charges only a little more for an apartment than for an ordinary room. We've rented some nice ones for between $15 and $20 a day. Particularly common are hotel efficiencies in resort places like Acapulco and Puerto Vallarta.

Like most furnished apartments, hotel kitchens come equipped with dishes, silverware, pots and pans, five-gallon jugs of purified water and even dish towels. The bonus is that every day, a brace of efficient maids scour the tile floors, change the linen, bring in fresh water, exactly as in a hotel. In addition, they do your breakfast dishes and put them away in the cupboard! We usually leave a small tip every day, and it's greatly appreciated.

In some areas, like Guadalajara and Lake Chapala, many apartments are owned by North Americans. It seems that every time a gringo couple decides to retire in the mellow climate of Lake Chapala or Ajijic, they think about building a house. Next, it occurs to them to build a few rental units for supplementary income. The end result is a predictable over-supply. Rents are forced to a low level to keep the apartments rented. These landlords are invaluable sources of information about the area. The only drawback is that you will probably have to wash your own breakfast dishes and sweep out the place yourself, or hire a maid to come in to do it for you. In 1991 the going price was about $15 to have a woman come in two days a week to clean and do the laundry. Can you handle that?

Our recommendation to non-tourists is to take a hotel-apartment that rents by the day or week, even if it costs a little more than an ordinary hotel room, even if you have no intention of cooking many meals. There is nothing like starting the day off with breakfast on your patio or balcony, relaxing in pajamas while you plan the day's adventures—infinitely more fun than spending half the morning getting dressed and waiting for a slow waiter to bring a second cup of coffee.

For the finicky or those worried about "the tourists' disease" there are the satisfactions of preparing your own meals, using purified water and taking other hygienic precautions. Your food is as safe as if cooked in Omaha.

A few tips about apartment-hopping in Mexico:

— Invariably you won't find a can opener in the kitchen. Don't ask why, just bring or buy one.

— Be sure you have matches for lighting the stove and candles for candlelight dining on the balcony (and for frequent power outages in some areas).

— When freezing ice cubes for drinks, use bottled water, *not tap water*, which may or may not be drinkable. As an aside, we note that many tourists religiously avoid drinking tap water, then brush their teeth with it. And they wonder why they get the trots! Remember that when taking a shower, if you open your mouth to sing, you are going to get water in the mouth. You can safely hum to your heart's content, however. Bottled water or boiled water is the only kind that should enter your mouth in any form.

— It isn't necessary to avoid fresh fruits and salads. Just wash everything in a solution of bottled water and water purification pills, which can be purchased at any drug store for pennies per box. (They won't spoil the taste.)

The "Tourist Disease"

Why do they call it the "tourist disease?" Many people believe that only tourists are affected, and that local residents "build up an immunity." In fact, no one, including local people, builds up an immunity to the most serious of the disorders, amoebic dysentery. Residents avoid getting sick by observing some simple rules of hygiene. When they don't, they get sick just as do the tourists. We repeat this advice several times in *Choose Mexico* because we know of many people who have been scared off by an unhappy experience with *turista* on a Mexican vacation or have heard of others who suffered through their whole two-week visit. It doesn't have to be that way. Ask anyone who lives there.

Everyone has bacteria in his digestive system; they are necessary for good health. But a phenomenon common to anyone who travels from one place to another is encountering a new strain of bacteria. The resident bacteria begin to fight and finally, the stomach gets tired of all the fuss and decides to have a little diarrhea to end all the nonsense. This is a mild form of the "tourist disease," and nothing to worry about. It's the bad-guy amoebas you must worry about. But common sense can avoid problems. Most Americans who live in Mexico report that they seldom if ever have "tourist" problems.

As a potential resident, you must re-learn a few basic habits. These will distinguish you from the two-week tourist, and keep you from a lot of misery. Before long, these rules become automatic, and you won't even have to think about it.

Of course, don't drink the water in any form other than boiled or bottled. By the way, you don't have to boil it for hours and hours; this doesn't do a thing. Since no organism can survive at temperatures higher than 150 degrees Fahrenheit, just bringing it to a boil is sufficient. Some water systems are all right, but we recommend boiled or purified water anyway; make it part of your automatic habits. Always soak salad vegetables (lettuce, tomatoes, anything that isn't going to be cooked or peeled) in water and purification tablets for twenty minutes.

Finally, one of the most valuable pieces of advice this book can give you about avoiding *turista*: when selecting a restaurant, don't be impressed by the nicely-dressed waiters, the immaculate linen and sparkling silverware; check out the clientele. Notice if local people eat there. If local people don't patronize a place, there's one of three explanations: the food is overpriced; it is poorly prepared; or it isn't fit to eat.

Too often, a "tourist" restaurant is owned by absentee owners and operated by low-paid employees who really don't care if you get sick or not. They know you won't be back again anyway, and you eat in so many places you won't know where you got the "bug." But a family-operated restaurant, one that caters to local people, can't afford to have anyone get sick. Word gets around, and they are out of business. One of this book's authors lived in Mexico as a youth for many years and has traveled extensively throughout the country for the past 40 years. Only twice has he caught the curse. Both times he ignored his own advice and patronized a spiffy, tourist-only restaurant where no Mexicans ate!

Don't Drink the Water?

Why all this fuss about boiled or bottled water? Isn't *any* Mexican water fit to drink? If not, why not? The answer is that some water is probably okay, particularly that coming from desert areas where the water is pumped from deep wells, or that flowing from the high mountains where few people are around to pollute it. The problem is that Mexico has many priorities well ahead of the construction of modern sewage disposal plants. The costs would be astronomical and the money is simply not there. Even where there are facilities for modern disposal, expanding construction outpaces them. So, much of the sewage goes into septic tanks and eventually seeps into the ground. Where there is a high water table, such as you find at the coastal resorts, some sewage, with its amoebas and bacteria, finds its way into the water table. Wherever water is drawn from shallow wells you can have problems. A further complication in Mexico City is that the water and sewage pipes are often damaged by frequent earthquake activity, and they leak, not much, but enough to sometimes make you sick.

To become a healthy non-tourist in Mexico, you have to continually follow common-sense rules. Before long you will become so used to it that when you return to the United States you will hesitate before using tap water to brush your teeth.

Two Price Systems in Mexico?

You often hear people say, "There are two prices in Mexico, one for the Mexicans and one for the gringos." They believe, for example, that separate menus are handed to you depending on your nationality. This simply isn't true. Most prices are fixed by government decree, and the government is serious about enforcement. When you rent a room, for example, the ceiling price is supposed to be clearly displayed at the desk and in your room.

But, as we have observed earlier, there *are* two price systems—not for Mexicans and foreigners but for residents and tourists. You won't find different prices being charged to the two groups in the same restaurants and hotels; you'll find higher prices at the hotels into which tourists are booked by travel agents and the restaurants in those hotels. Residents, whether Mexican or foreign know of equally nice places that charge a fraction as much.

Restaurants and stores are anxious to have residents' repeat business, particularly the non-tourist places, and they aren't going to overcharge you very often and expect to ever see you return. However, that old game of bargaining goes on in Mexico. Some kinds of merchants seem obligated to quote an unrealistic price, and often feel cheated out of the fun if you go ahead and pay without a little arguing.

How do you know if you're paying the right price or the tourist price for anything? Don't all Mexicans expect you to bargain? Should you offer one-third the asking price? These questions are relative to the product being offered and the price asked. For example, if you are in a market, and the vendor wants the equivalent of a dime for a handful of onions, ask yourself: "What do I gain by arguing him down 20 percent?" A nickel means nothing to you, but plenty to the vendor. Actually, individual entrepreneurs face a lot of competition in the native markets, so they try to keep their prices attractive. They want to see you become a regular customer, and usually go out of their way to make you happy.

On the other hand, if you're buying something that costs a lot of money, then a 20 percent discount would be significant. If it's big money, sometimes it's worth bargaining hard, just as you would when buying an automobile or house back home.

Bargaining is an art form that you might enjoy, but accept the fact that you will never win. Just as you never really beat an automobile salesman at his game, you'll never quite get the last value in Mexico. It's fun to do, and no one gets hurt feelings. Yet hassling over pennies doesn't mark an American as an astute bargainer; it marks him as a cheapskate.

It's interesting to watch the tourists bargain. As soon as they settle down on the beach a swarm of eager vendors begins landing like flies on a lollipop. They'll offer jewelry, blankets, sweaters, you name it, and the bargaining begins in Spanish, English and sign language. Everyone has a glorious time, and in the end, the poor merchant reluctantly agrees to drop the price of the $40 necklace to only $10. The tourist is delighted at his prowess in saving $30, and the vendor looks discouraged that he allowed such a fine $1 necklace go for only $10. Like the automobile salesman back home, the beach salesmen are experts. But don't get the idea that everyone you meet is trying to scalp you. Most merchants you deal with in your everyday living situations are anxious to do business with you, and take pride in having a good relationship with *Norteamericanos*.

If you visit a store with price tags on all items, it's pretty sure that they mean business, unless you are talking big money. If you are thinking about a 100 dollar purchase or a 1,000 dollar deal, then maybe it's worth your while to bargain against the posted price. You may not be successful, but it's worth the try to shave off ten or 20 percent. But if the price is only two dollars, you're wasting your time haggling.

One complaint occasionally heard about *Choose Mexico* is that it is drawing more and more North Americans into the country. "They come down here, throw money around, pay big wages, leave big tips and ruin things for the rest of us!" is the way one woman put it.

It's true that when more foreigners move into a town or village, the demand for domestic help creates a boost in wages. It's also true that we tend to pay more than the going rate for lots of things. This means more money circulating in the community, and slightly higher prices all around. The final result is that Americans pay a few cents more for goods and services, and the Mexicans have more money in their pockets, more food on the table and better clothing for their children. Because Americans are known to pay higher wages, the local people are eager to work for them. Working for an American family is prestigious, and they will try very hard to be good employees and keep their jobs.

Our stock answer to complainers is: Mexico is not your private discovery. Mexico is not for the sole benefit of a few stingy gringos who want to keep the local economy depressed so they can save a few pennies. We are guests in that country, and as guests we should rejoice in any improvement in the living standard of our neighbors. If you have to pay $1 an hour for help instead of 75 cents an hour, just remember how much you would pay back home, and think of what that extra money will buy for a Mexican family.

There are two Mexicos, one for tourists and one for residents.
The happiest residents are those who consider themselves part of
the community, and by the same token, they are the best-liked by
their Mexican neighbors. The unhappiest residents are those who
try to change things and make Mexico into a bargain-basement
copy of the United States.

COOK THOMPSON — 1992 ... NATIONAL UNIVERSITY, MEXICO CITY

CHAPTER FOUR

Managing Your Money

W hat does $600 a month amount to in Mexican terms? It is several times the minimum wage for a Mexican who works six days a week. It is three times the salary earned by a school teacher who may have several children to support. In 1991 at the time of writing, school teachers throughout the republic were on strike for higher pay. Their goal was $400 a month, 50 percent below our $600 figure. While we feel that $600 to be the bare minimum for North Americans living in Mexico, it still provides a much higher standard of living than the vast majority of Mexicans enjoy and clearly a better way of life than possible in the United States or Canada on that same amount of money.

As we mentioned in the first chapter, when we wrote the first version of this book, pesos were selling at the rate of 150 to the dollar. By the time the second edition hit the presses, the peso to dollar ratio was 2,270. By early 1992 your dollar would buy you more than 3,000 pesos. However, that looks better than it is. Even though you receive 20 times as many pesos for your dollar, you can't buy 20 times as much goods and services. That old demon inflation marched side by side with exchange rates to even things out. Nevertheless, even though the dollar lost some of its clout in Mexico, its purchasing power holds up there far better than in most other countries of the world. Today's dollar still buys far more in Mexico than it does at home, and two or three times as much as in many European nations.

The original, wild inflationary spiral was finally contained through heroic efforts on the part of the Mexican government after six years of chaos. The official devaluation is now controlled and has leveled out over the past years to almost nothing. Barring some drastic change in policy, the dollar-to-peso ratio will probably not change significantly for some time to come. This may or may not be good news for Americans, because it means dollars won't buy nearly as much during the time of the inflation binge. On the other hand, the economy promises to remain stable. While it does, our dollars still have leverage. Not as much, but enough.

Horror Stories

The original devaluation was disastrous for anyone whose savings were in peso bank accounts. Those with dollar accounts were hurt even worse, because, when the government took over control of banks, dollar accounts were converted into pesos at the *official* rate, which was a fraction of the dollar's true value. The horror of this gambit is legendary. Less than a decade ago, someone with two million pesos in the bank ($100,000) could live quite comfortably on the interest. Today, that same two million pesos would be worth just $666.66! Today, the current interest on two million pesos is just under $14 a month. There's a lesson in this.

After the initial shock of devaluation, investors were helped by tremendous interest rates—over 150 percent for a time. Wouldn't it seem that interest rates of 150 percent should be a moneymaker? But the only reason the government-controlled banks offered that rate was to keep pace with inflation and to discourage money from fleeing the country. You see, by government decree, interest rates vary with the rate of inflation. Obviously, inflation has been slowing, because the interest rate is now about 24 percent and dropping.

We are pleased that we recommended so strongly in our first edition that retirees keep the bulk of their funds at home and arrange for a monthly transfer of only as much money as needed for living expenses. While acknowledging the lure of those astronomical interest rates, we cautioned that, while they were barely keeping up with or even lagging behind inflation, we thought that the temptation should be avoided. Our caution during those early years of the 1980's was vindicated. However, the growing stability of the peso has changed the picture somewhat. Proceed with caution.

Despite high interest rates, those hurt in the 1982 devaluations will never recoup their losses. Fortunately, many North Americans heeded the obvious warning signs and converted their peso accounts to U.S. money markets at just the right time. The warning signs were plentiful and obvious, yet many people remained tranquil in the face of impending disaster.

What are the warning signs? When the peso becomes dramatically over-valued against the dollar, watch out. When you can buy U.S. goods cheaper at home than you can in Mexico, you know the peso is in trouble. When local businessmen begin changing pesos for dollars to invest in U.S. real estate or when Mexicans start going to the United States for vacations because Mexico is too expensive. Then it's time to convert your pesos to dollar accounts in U.S. or Canadian banks! Those who paid attention made money; those who didn't, didn't.

Current Investing

The future? If we could predict the future, do you think we'd be writing books instead of counting our money? Again we emphasize, there are no guarantees. With this in mind, let's analyze how the peso has been faring lately against the dollar. Let's suppose you had put $1,000 dollars into a peso money-market fund in February 1989 and withdrew it two years later, in March 1991. The interest rate in February 1989 was 48.82 percent and the peso was selling at 2,316 to the dollar. Over the two-year period, interest varied between 54.68 percent and 24 percent, which it was in March, 1991. The 1991 dollar was worth 2,990 pesos, which means a loss of 22.5 percent in dollar value over two years. Yet because of high interest rates, the original $1,000 investment was worth $1,683 for the two-year investment. Not bad. These rates, by the way, are net returns, annualized, after Mexican taxes have been deducted. So, you can see that in the short run, dollar investments have done well. But between 1982 and 1988, it was a different story. How much you should entrust to savings accounts or any other Mexican investment vehicle depends both on your financial circumstances and on your courage.

Tourist Prices

Of course, if you confine yourself to resort hotels and restaurants catering to well-heeled tourists and shop in stores where prices are not displayed, it's possible to spend almost as much as you would in the United States, and more. The proprietors of these establishments are well aware of the prices you are accustomed to paying, and they are happy to make you feel at home. Residents know where to stay and how to shop. That's where this book comes in.

In today's economy, you will find imported goods expensive in Mexico. You needn't buy imports. Almost everything you need is manufactured in Mexico—with a few exceptions, such as Scotch whisky, which costs three or four times as much as ordinary booze. If you can't learn to substitute brandy, gin, or tequila, ask your visitors from the 'States to bring a few bottles to help you stock your cabinet. Do not abandon hope, however. New factories are rapidly being established in Mexico to manufacture everything from American cars to Japanese computers. Perhaps a Scotch distillery will be next.

As we state frequently in this book, tourists' expenses are one thing and residents' expenses another. If you go to Mexico for an exploratory visit, as we strongly recommend, expect to spend substantially more than $600 a month. A $20-a-night hotel will cost that much. You don't really start saving money until you rent a house or apartment and cook most of your meals at home. It's the same just about everywhere, but in Mexico it's less expensive than in the U.S. either way you go.

Leave Your Money Home

If this were a book for tourists, it would be easy to give such good advice as, "Come to Mexico as soon as you can, bring money and enjoy a wonderful vacation." For those planning to settle here, the situation is a bit more complicated. Do come down and enjoy Mexico, but prudence suggests that you leave the bulk of your funds in the United States. This advice was urgent when our first edition came off the press, right after the disastrous devaluation of 1982. However, with distance from the event, our caution is wearing thin. We see many North Americans making money on the high interest rates, and barring any unforeseen catastrophe, ought to continue to do well. It's important to note that most are still cautious, keeping one foot in the U.S. market and ready to pull out of Mexican investments at the first sign of danger.

Of course, you will open an account with a Mexican bank to pay your bills, and as many do, you can have your Social Security checks or any other pension or investment income sent to you monthly. In an emergency, you can get "cash advances" at most banks using a MasterCard or Visa card, but of course, you will pay a stiff premium for this, just as you do back home.

Long distance banking can be a headache as well as expensive for several reasons. You usually have to pay up to 1.5 percent service charges to your Mexican bank to accept your foreign check, and you must pay another 1.5 percent to convert your pesos into dollars. We're talking 3 percent per transaction just to use your own money! However, retirees here have discovered a couple of ways to get around this.

One way is to open a peso account with a reputable Mexican investment firm such as Allen W. Lloyd's. An account can be opened for less than $1,000, and current interest is paid on the investment. In 1990 this amounted to 42 percent although by mid-1991 it had dropped to about 20 percent annual interest. Once you have an account, you can cash personal checks from your U.S. or Canadian bank without any charge. Local residents typically drop into Lloyd's once a week for operating expenses.

We mention the Lloyd's company only because there are branches in the major retirement areas and because these branches specialize in dealing with English-speaking investors. One retiree we interviewed said, "I keep $5,000 in my account, and I'm very pleased with the interest. I was even more pleased when it was drawing 42 percent. However, I'd advise against keeping more in the account than you can afford to lose, just in case another deflation happens." Other residents are less cautious, keeping much more money in the accounts. One single man said, "I could damn near live on the interest until it dropped to 24 percent!"

(For more information: Operadora de Fondos, Lloyd, S.A., Ave. Marianno Otero 19154, Guadalajara, Jalisco, Mexico. Tel. 21-90-50.)

A second strategy is to open a "Friendship Senior Checking Account" with Los Angeles's California Commerce Bank (a subsidiary of BANAMEX in Mexico with 700 branch offices throughout the republic). As a chartered U.S. bank, California Commerce is insured up to $100,000 just as all other banks are. Their services are designed specifically for American senior citizens (55 years or older) who live in Mexico. BANAMEX will let you deposit or cash checks from its U.S. subsidiary without a service charge. With a checking account at BANAMEX you also receive a free credit card and an ATM banking card so you can draw cash from an automatic teller instead of having to stand in line to cash a check. Dollars on deposit in California Commerce's unique Friendship Senior Checking Program earns an extra one percent bonus over current U.S. rates for regular depositors, and there is no monthly service charge. To get the high current rate of Mexican interest you need to invest about five million pesos (around $1,600) although that isn't necessary to have a convenience account. Dollar accounts, at this time, are not permitted in Mexico, so your investments are automatically converted to pesos. But you can draw up to 200 real dollars at a time from BANAMEX without any service charge.

(For more information contact: California Commerce Bank, P.O. Box 30886 Terminal Annex, Los Angeles, CA 90030. (213) 624-5700 or BANAMEX (Banco Nacional de Mexico: International Dept., Isabel La Catolica 43-44, 06089 Mexico.)

Investing in Mexico—Risks and Rewards

How safe are Mexican banks? The fact is, your peso accounts are guaranteed by the Mexican government, and it can be confidently stated that no one has lost a peso over the years. Although this is true, you must remember that while you cannot lose the number of pesos in your account, the value of your pesos can drop dramatically. Thus although you lose no pesos, you could certainly lose dollar value. Since 1988, this hasn't happened but, as we've said before, there are no guarantees.

Over the years, periodic official devaluations have hurt investors who invested their money in pesos. The first one I remember was about 1948, when the peso was dropped from five per dollar to seven the day after my father switched several thousand dollars into his peso checking account. Then it went to eight, where it stayed for many years, then to 12 and finally to 20 just before the crash. That happened in 1982, a particularly painful drop, with the peso losing half its value overnight, then in half again within a month or so. $1,000 worth of pesos bought in January 1981 could be sold for about $7 in July 1991.

As you can see, the history of the peso over the past 45 years hasn't been precisely one of stability. So why do folks keep investing in peso accounts? Because of high interest rates that are very attractive in the short run and that offset the smaller losses in the long run. Hopefully, this disaster of the early 1980s will never happen again, or if it does, it will not be so drastic.

Mexican Stocks

Mexico's stock market is known as the *Bolsa*. It is similar in many ways to securities markets in America and Europe, but there are important differences. For one thing, the Bolsa is on a smaller scale. Not only are far fewer issues traded but the daily volume is a tiny fraction of that on the New York Stock Exchange. The market is so thin for most issues that liquidity can be a very serious problem. If Mexico's economy expands, there is probably much money to be made on the Bolsa. Some retirees who read the financial pages daily in Mexico, or who find a trusted financial adviser, may raise their standard of living to celestial heights and leave princely inheritances, but for the average person of moderate means we strongly counsel prudence and patience. There are too many ways to enjoy oneself in Mexico without either being a millionaire or making financial gain the focus of one's life.

Real Estate as an Investment

At the time of our first edition, there were real estate bargains available that would be unthinkable in the United States or Canada. Early readers of *Choose Mexico* rushed down to snap up these bargains. As you can imagine, when a flood of buyers, waving fistfuls of dollars hit the retirement areas, housing prices shot up. They doubled, then doubled again. However, since the prices were so low in the first place, even at these quadrupled prices, the homes are bargains nevertheless. A $40,000 house that once sold for $10,000 is well worth the new price, considering that a similar house in California would cost $250,000.

The truly interesting thing about the real estate market in the popular retirement areas is that rents have not gone up at the same rate as housing prices. A $20,000 house that used to rent for $200 a month, may now be worth $60,000 today, therefore it would seem that it should rent for $600 in proportion. Not so. Since the rental markets are controlled by supply and demand, the new owners would be lucky to get $300 a month rent on their $60,000 investment. For this reason, this writer feels that in some locations, the retirement real estate market is over-priced at this time. Of course, you must realize that this writer also predicted the collapse of the California real estate market back in 1972—and to date, the value of property he sold in 1972 is only worth eight times as much.

Warning: Do not rush down to Mexico, planning on joining the real estate boom. Housing prices can go down, just as quickly as they've gone up! Some things you ought to know before buying a home are discussed in Chapter Seven, but our principal caveat bears repeating here: know, or be advised by someone who knows, a lot about the area, the laws, the real estate market and construction. Above all, know yourself, before you seriously consider buying a house.

Some Budgets of Full-time Retirees

Fran and Judy Furton who live in a pleasant Guadalajara neighborhood in an unusually spacious (2,444 square foot) and attractive house they purchased several years ago have kept extremely detailed records of their living expenses for over a decade. Their monthly average for 1991 was just over $900. That includes, however, all expenses for operating two automobiles; a maid for four or five hours, five days a week; substantial expenditures for books, magazines and papers; and considerable dining in good restaurants both in Mexico and on their frequent trips to the U.S. That total included the cost of operating the

Leoni Manierson 1992

satellite television system on which they were watching a New York station when I dropped in, but did not include their weekly massages. They recently estimated that they could easily live on $800 a month in an equivalent (rented) house if they gave up one car, ate out less frequently, had the maid only once or twice a week and watched their long distance calls more carefully. As we hope we have established in earlier chapters, eliminating the second car and moving to a smaller house would get their budget down to our $600 level. The Furtons report that many people they know get by on much less.

This example is from Guadalajara, but costs are similar throughout Mexico—quite a bit higher in Mexico City or near the U.S. border and a little lower in smaller towns. Certainly there are more places where a $600 monthly budget would suffice than where it would not.

CHAPTER FIVE

Staying Healthy

Far too much of the discussion of whether Mexico is good for your health boils down to the question: Can you drink the water? The short answer to that question is "Yes, but not water from the tap." We'll cover that in detail a little further on, and hope we can persuade you that it is a relatively trivial concern. Far more important is the fact that the vigor and happiness of the typical U.S. retiree in Mexico points to the ways in which the country is indeed a very healthy place for older people.

There are both physical and emotional reasons for this. The climate in most places where retirees have chosen to live is healthier in several ways than in the communities they have come from. For one thing, it is dryer. The attractions of a low-humidity climate have been bringing people suffering from respiratory and rheumatic diseases to the American Southwest for generations. With the exception of its coastal areas, Mexico is blessed with a climate that is at least as dry. In addition, Mexico possesses something the U.S. Southwestern states do not. It has (again, in the communities favored by retirees) temperatures that are moderate year-round.

Water and Sanitation

Too many people avoid Mexico because they fear for their health. They have heard that no one escapes *turista* or "Montezuma's Revenge" and imagine a stay made miserable, if not dangerous, by gastrointestinal woes. Some Mexican water supplies are indeed contaminated, but clean, safe water is available everywhere, and the contaminated water can be purified easily, as can vegetables and fruits that have come into contact with that water. As we've noted in Chapter Three, every prudent Mexican and foreigner recognizes the importance of guarding against the hazards of impure water and untreated raw fruit and vegetables. The necessary steps are incorporated into his or her life, so that these precautions become as natural as washing one's hands before meals (which is also a very good idea in Mexico as elsewhere, since recent studies report that one's hands are likely to be the source of the bacteria that gets into one's mouth).

Water is safe after being boiled for a few minutes. Treating it with chlorine tablets or treating it with a reliable filtration device also takes care of bacteria or amoebic problems. If you have a maid, she will make sure you always have an ample supply of purified water both in the kitchen and in the bathroom so that you will not be tempted to brush your teeth or swallow a pill with tap water. Fruit and vegetables fresh from the market are stored separately from those that have been made safe by a brief soaking in purified water to which some chlorine tablets have been added (available inexpensively at any drug store).

Ice must be made with purified water and, like fruit and vegetables, should be consumed only in places where you can be confident that the necessary precautions have been taken. The law in Mexico is that ice cubes must be made from purified water. That requirement, however, does not extend to bulk ice. Almost always, restaurants and stores will use purified water for ice cubes since it is so inexpensive there is no reason not to. If a restaurant doesn't follow the law, cheating by using tainted water, its customers will soon know about it and will no longer patronize the place. Bad restaurants don't remain in business long. In the beginning, you'll have to rely on the knowledge of the local Americans about which restaurants to avoid; in time you'll develop your own sound instincts.

As an added protection against gastrointestinal illness, many travelers dose themselves heavily with antibiotics or consume huge quantities of Pepto Bismol (which is readily and inexpensively available in Mexican pharmacies.) However, they do lay themselves open to the side effects of these medications. We've found that taking the precautions we've listed here usually makes this kind of self-medication unnecessary.

Health is More

Good health, however, is more than avoiding unfriendly bugs. It involves your total physical and mental well-being and your whole outlook. If Mexico is the right place for you, you can be healthier there than you could be anywhere else. Almost everything that can make you happy will also make you healthy—the climate, the good food, the constant activity. These latter, in addition to the common-sense principles of sanitation discussed above, are the essential prescriptions for good health. If you have a chronic illness, your doctor will have some additional rules and perhaps some medications for you, but you should find them no more onerous in Mexico than in your home town.

Health Care

Americans living in most parts of Mexico report the availability of competent English-speaking doctors and dentists. The questionnaires we mailed to retired Americans when researching this book devoted special attention to the quality of medical and dental care, access to hospitals, and the availability of medications. We emphasized these areas because books written a decade or more ago treated health care as a problem—at least outside of the biggest cities. We are gratified to report however, that today, according to responses received from retirees in every part of the country, there are good doctors and dentists in most cities of any size. Quality hospitals are within easy traveling distance, and most of the commonly prescribed medications are stocked by Mexican pharmacies.

A few of our respondents stated that they might go to Mexico City or to the U.S. for an unusual or extremely serious illness, but most indicated that they thought they could find sophisticated facilities and personnel in the nearest big city. Since we know of people who, if they became ill in Miami or Los Angeles, would go to hospitals and doctors in New York, we are inclined to conclude that the needs catered to by the services that fly patients to the U.S. for treatment are more emotional than medical.

Doctors

Many doctors in the U.S. are Mexican-trained. As the number of qualified students seeking entrance to U.S. medical schools exceeded their capacity, many young Americans went abroad for their medical education. Mexico was one of the countries in which they found training facilities of top quality. In short, there is no more reason to be concerned about the qualification of a reputable Mexican doctor than there is about an American one.

Although not every town is blessed with a first-rate hospital, few are far from one. Few drugs require prescriptions in Mexico, and those that do can be filled at any pharmacy. If, however, you need some special or unusual medication, it would be wise to bring a supply with you on your initial visit and, if you find it is unavailable there, to confer with your physician when you return to the U.S. He can tell you what may be substituted for your medication. If there is no substitute available in Mexico, receiving a regular supply from the U.S., though a nuisance, should pose no problems. Incidentally, most prescription and over-the-counter drugs cost less than 20 percent of their U.S. price.

Medicare

As we've said, routine and emergency medical care of high quality is available many places in Mexico. Nevertheless, those retirees who are eligible for Medicare (which does not pay for care or treatment received in Mexico) or who have a trusted physician in the U.S. will wish to return there if they become seriously ill. If they're not well enough to travel by routine means, there is a commercial "air evacuation" service that provides emergency air transport north of the border. For a monthly fee, one can arrange to have this service available when needed. Air transport of casualties, which was first employed in Korea and came into its own in Vietnam, has been adopted in civilian medicine and without question has saved many lives. How appropriate this air service is (except to enjoy the financial benefits of Medicare) may be a moot point. If nothing else, it gives Americans in Mexico the emotional security of knowing that in the event of serious illness, within a few hours they can be under the care of American doctors in an American hospital.

Health Insurance

Of course, many Americans retiring in Mexico are too young to qualify for Medicare and rely on other health insurance to pay major medical expenses. Many U.S. insurance companies cover you wherever you travel or live. Certain carriers pay a slightly smaller percentage of the total when you are out of your home area, but since health care in Mexico is so inexpensive relative to U.S. costs, that won't be a problem. Most Blue Cross plans will pay for your hospital stays while in Mexico, but require that you lay out the money and wait for reimbursement. We advise that you check with your insurance broker to determine the extent of your coverage while in Mexico and to discuss any adjustments necessary to maximize your protection at minimum expense. In Guadalajara, the American Society offers low-cost health insurance to its members. Among the better plans offered in Mexico is through ClubMex (See Appendix for address).

Another option that has just recently become available to Americans in Mexico is coverage, at very low cost, by the national health system. Each year there is an open enrollment period when you can join. The cost is about $190 a year. There is a six-month waiting period, and enrollment is only open during the months of January-February and July-August. This plan covers medical, hospital, prescription drugs, even dental care and eye examinations. We believe this is something to investigate after you are there and have had the opportunity to learn about the quality of the hospitals and physicians in the community in which you decide to live.

Several folks we interviewed stated that although they had insurance coverage back home, they never used it. One man said, "I have a major medical plan that covers everything over $15,000. But when I went to the local hospital for emergency treatment, the bill came to less than $2,500! This covered several doctors for separate opinions, surgeons, anesthesiologist, hospital stay, laboratory work, X-rays, electrocardiograms, sonograms, prescription drugs and follow-up care for three months following surgery." He added, "A friend of mine paid more than $2,500 for just one night in a Las Vegas hospital!"

People with Handicaps

Many of our readers have inquired about the provisions Mexico makes for people with physical handicaps. From what we have observed and been told by people who face the problem, Mexico is still far behind the U.S. in dealing with air pollution, accessibility and the myriad other issues that we also neglected until fairly recently. On the positive side, the gentle climate does make getting around somewhat easier and the low pay scale enables people who need help to afford it more readily. Also, on recent visits we noted more curb cuts, particularly in the larger cities.

There are provisions for wheelchair access in most airports and in many railroad stations and bus terminals. Sources of detailed information include:

Mexican National Railways
Estacion Central de Buenavista
06358, Mexico, D.F. Mexico
Greyhound Lines, Director of Customer Relations
Greyhound Tower, 111 West Clarendon
Phoenix, AZ 85013

Each airline, domestic or foreign, can give you information on the arrangements it can make for wheelchairs or other assistance.

Climate and Health

Mexico's varied climates offer a choice of temperatures and humidities, but almost all, particularly those where North American's have established their homes, feature the lack of extremes that have earned the label "eternal spring." With one's energies freed from combating the winter winds and the humid summer swelter, flourishing health immediately feels attainable. Life in Mexico is outdoors year-round. Most houses have little or no provision for heating or air conditioning. If the weather becomes brisk, you simply put on a sweater. When warm, you stay indoors for a siesta during the hot part of the day. One doesn't breathe air stale with artificial heat or chill but rather air crisped by mountain altitudes, softened by warm oceans, or dried to crystalline clarity by empty deserts.

Diet

For the tourist traveling in Mexico and eating in restaurants, adhering to a special diet—perhaps one low in sodium, in sugar or in fats—could be difficult, though clearly not impossible. For someone who lives there and prepares his own food, or has it prepared by a servant, there is no special problem. As noted in Chapter One, one of the delights of living in Mexico is the abundance of fresh fruits, vegetables and poultry. In many places fresh fish is always available. Many diet convenience foods common in the U.S. aren't to be found in Mexico. Neither were artificially sweetened, carbonated beverages until recently and they're still not as available as in the U.S. Nevertheless, with reasonable inventiveness, almost any dietary prescription can be followed.

Mexican cuisine is discussed in greater detail elsewhere in this book, but we should add a brief reassurance here for those potential retirees who may feel intimidated by its notorious spiciness: you could live in Mexico for years without ever being forced to eat anything the least bit *picante*, even if all your dining were in restaurants. Any town is likely to have several restaurants where the food is "continental" rather than Mexican, and not all dishes in thoroughly Mexican restaurants are highly spiced. In the more elegant restaurants, the dishes are rather bland, with an emphasis on French sauces.

Lack of Stress

Volumes have been written on the role of stress in causing illness. It has been implicated as an aggravating factor in chronic conditions common in people past middle age. Visitors to Mexico, almost without exception, comment on the lack of stress and the relaxed atmosphere there. Perhaps it is the absence of many negative and unnecessary forms of stress that makes so many Americans consider Mexico a healthful place to live.

Mexico offers freedom from the nagging annoyances of unpleasant weather, unpleasant people, economic insecurity, relentless status-seeking and the nagging, confining fear of crime. Relaxing doesn't mean doing nothing, but rather a feeling that makes exercise and outdoor activities fun rather than a chore. Lethargy comes from inactivity, from boredom and fatigue. Perhaps it is the stimulation of the unfamiliar, the vibrancy of Mexican culture, its sights, sounds and smells. One encounters few bored and unhappy retirees there. Visitors to Mexico, almost without exception, comment on the relaxed and healthful atmosphere. It can be healthful for you, too, if you learn to live in it.

CHAPTER SIX

Your Legal Status

We are often asked, "Do I have to give up my citizenship if I retire permanently in Mexico?" Of course not. Very few North Americans would consider Mexican retirement if this were the case. Fortunately, there are a number of ways to become a legal resident of Mexico and none of them affects your citizenship in any way. The options open to you range all the way from using the tourist cards readily available to anyone wishing to visit Mexico to *Inmigrado* status which gives you all the rights of Mexican citizen except the right to vote.

The rules have been undergoing changes since the original publication of this book, and even more are possible. For example, it used to be that the income requirements were very low—with a minimum of $550 a month for a couple. That's been raised to as much as $2,200 monthly in some cases. Pressure is being applied to the government to liberalize this requirement. We hope the government will listen. Meanwhile, the vast majority of North Americans living in Mexico will continue to be officially "tourists."

We list below the three kinds of residence permits and a brief summary of the advantages and disadvantages of each status:

Tourist Card: (FM-T)

Advantages: No income requirement. No need for legal help to obtain. No cost to obtain.

Disadvantages: Must be renewed every six months by a trip to the border. Does not allow you to legally bring in household goods, appliances, etc.

Visitante Rentista (FM-3)

Advantages: Applications processed rapidly and routinely. Cheapest (when you figure in cost of trips to the border to renew tourist cards) and easiest way to reside in Mexico according to government.

Disadvantages: Income requirement of $1000 a month for the head of a family plus $500 per dependent. Good for five years, and must be renewed yearly with current proof of income. Does not allow you to import your household furnishings legally.

Inmigrante Rentista (FM-2)

Advantages: Gives many rights and exemptions (such as from auto user taxes) not available to tourists and FM-3 holders. Allows you to import household furnishings and car.

Disadvantages: Need to show monthly income of $1,700 plus $500 per dependent. Longer, more difficult process to obtain. The auto must be removed from Mexico after five years.

Inmigrado

Advantages: Possessor has all the rights of a Mexican citizen except the right to vote. Can work or operate business.

Disadvantages: Granted only after five years as Inmigrante Rentista. Same income requirement as FM3.

Tourist Card

The easiest (and by far the most affordable) way is to enter Mexico on a tourist card good for six months. You can usually apply for and receive a slight extension of the card, but most people simply return to the border once every six months and obtain a new card. Although there is no legal income minimum and no restriction on how many times a card may be taken, we reiterate our opinion that $600 a month is the minimum necessary for comfortable living. Many people enjoy a bus ride to El Paso or Tucson every half-year for a spree of shopping and renewing their cultural roots. We know folks who have lived in Mexico for decades and return every six months to Texas or Arizona for a shopping spree and a new tourist card.

Your exploratory visits to Mexico should always be made under a tourist card, which can be obtained free from all Mexican tourism or consular offices, upon presenting proof of U.S. citizenship. Such proof can be a birth certificate, voter's registration card, passport or notarized affidavit. Carry this proof with you, for sometimes it's necessary to produce this as well as the tourist card. If you're entering the country by air, the airline ticket office or travel agency can issue a card, but the airlines aren't authorized to issue one that's good for more than 90 days, whereas the consulate will give you a six-month stay if requested. If you wish, a multiple entry card can be issued but the process is somewhat more complicated. Your tourist card should be carried with you at all times while in Mexico. (We can't recall ever meeting an American who was penalized for forgetting to have his or her card handy, but we've read about it happening.) You will usually be asked for the card when changing money at the bank or if stopped for a traffic infraction.

Visitante Rentista (FM-3)

Another option is Visitante Rentista, or non-immigrant pensioner status. You will, like a tourist, be prohibited from owning a business or holding a job and will have to renew your permit every year for a period of five years. Then you have to leave the country, re-enter and start over. The income requirement is currently $1,000 a month and $500 a month for each dependent. You must be at least 55 to obtain this status.

There are six requirements:

1. A letter of request (prepared free of charge at Delagación de Servicios Migratorios Office), plus a letter in Spanish signed by two persons stating they know the applicants and verifying the applicants' address. (Also obtained from above office).

2. A valid passport, two copies of your tourist visa and a notarized copy of the passport.

3. Marriage and birth certificates (for spouse and dependents).

4. Marriage affidavit certifying that you and your spouse are living together.

5. Proof of income of $1,000 per month plus an additional $500 per dependent. (There is no requirement that you spend this

amount, only that you prove that you will continue to receive it.) Social Security or other pension income qualifies. You must prove that your last three pension checks were deposited in a Mexican bank account.

6. A letter from a doctor stating that you are in good health and free of communicable infectious diseases, including AIDS.

7. An application form containing a photograph of the applicant. The form is obtained from the Mexican immigration authorities and the whole process is, of course, something you undertake only after you have been in the country for a while.

Inmigrante Rentista (FM-2)

The most advantageous status obtainable immediately is that of retired immigrant. It offers the right to leave and re-enter Mexico as often as you wish. It also exempts you from import and export taxes on most household goods, on personal effects and on your automobile. You can bring them in or have them sent, and take them back to the U.S., without penalty. (Of course, as with any immigration status, you're exempt from Mexican income tax on your pension and other funds received from outside the country.) Under this status, you may not work or engage in any remunerative activity in Mexico. (In no case, however, do these provisions affect a writer, artist or photographer doing work in Mexico to be sold outside the country.) You may buy real estate for your residence as long as it isn't located within 62 miles of the border or 31 miles of the coast. Even in these "forbidden zones" it is now possible, under a new law, to obtain use of land for your residence. This involves long-term trust agreements, and a lawyer or bank in Mexico can furnish you with the details.

To obtain Inmigrante Rentista status you must file an assortment of documents ranging from passports, birth and marriage certificates, to a certificate of good conduct from your local police department in the United States. Most important,however, is proof of a fixed monthly income of at least $1,700 for an individual and an additional $500 for his or her spouse and for each dependent child over 15. You must provide evidence that this income will continue for at least five years.

You do not have to leave Mexico during the five-year "probationary" period, but you must renew your permit and pay an

Your Legal Status 73

annual fee. After you have been an Inmigrante Rentista for five years, you may apply for the status of permanent resident (Inmigrado), under which you will have all privileges except voting. None of this affects your American or Canadian citizenship.

The process of obtaining Inmigrante Rentista status is, like any dealings with Mexican bureaucracy, complicated and exasperating. If you are blessed with the patience of a saint, you can probably do it all yourself. If not, it may be worth the additional expense to retain a Mexican lawyer. Whereas this status is not difficult to obtain, if you are going to Mexico for a relaxation you may not want to spend your time in lines in government offices. Besides, in Mexico, even lawyer's fees are moderate.

Inmigrado

The most permanent type of residence is enjoyed by the Inmigrado, an immigrant who has all the rights of a Mexican citizen except voting rights. He or she may own a business, hold a job, practice a profession and, with certain restrictions, own property in his or her own name. This status is granted only after spending five years as an "Inmigrante Visitante," or FM-3 status. The income requirements must still be met as for the FM-2 status: $1,700 for an individual and $500 for dependents. Again, you don't have to spend that much, but you must prove that you have that much income and will have it for the five years during which you are qualifying to become an Inmigrado.

If you expect to own a business or to earn money in Mexico, this income requirement is probably not excessive. However, for most of us, the other options that do not have such stringent conditions are much more feasible. If you're going there to rest, retire, write a book, paint, or anything else that doesn't require you to earn income *in Mexico*, you needn't become a Inmigrado.

Which Status Do You Need?

The Mexican government asserts that either of the Inmigrante documents is much preferable to a tourist card, which requires you to leave the country once every six months. That's true, but the tourist card lets you experiment with living in the country before going to the expense and bother of seeking more permanent documents. Whichever you choose, the government of

Mexico will welcome American immigrants and tourists (and their dollars) warmly. There are no indications at all—economic, political or otherwise—that it will become more difficult to travel or move there.

Which status is right for you? You will probably have gone through one or more 180-day tourist cards before making any binding decisions, so you will undoubtedly have received the advice of many long-time residents and will have heard more arguments than we could possibly make for or against each possibility. Above all, we emphasize once again that the current unrealistically high income requirement for the permanent resident statuses need not be an insurmountable barrier to happy, affordable retirement there and that this requirement, like all the regulations we have listed above, is subject to change.

Living with Mexican Laws

Many Americans are concerned about the differences between the Mexican and the United States' legal systems. Some dread the possibility that they might end up in a dreary Mexican jail because of some misunderstanding. This fear evaporates in the Mexican sun, however. We have found no American resident there who expressed concern about the law. Of course, if your retirement plans include dealing illegal drugs, this reassurance does not apply.

Mexican law, like most European systems is one of codified statutes. This is often referred to as "Roman law" or the "Napoleonic Code." North American law, on the other hand, is based on English common law, in which each case may be considered unique and each decision may be based on prior decisions in other courts. Our system is beneficial for the legal profession because almost any position can be argued in court, and extenuating circumstances can be pleaded. The outcome of a civil or criminal case is often unpredictable.

As we stated earlier, in Mexico the system is not so complicated. Almost every possible violation or transgression is thoroughly codified or listed in law books, and extenuating circumstances play little role. Instead of long jury trials to determine punishment or damages, the magistrate simply looks up the law code that applies and that's it. Awards in damage suits are usually limited to the actual proven losses, so lawyers don't have a field day with punitive damages and payment for mental anguish. Also, criminals aren't routinely given probation or early release from jail to repeat their offenses over and over. Sentences are longer and parole is not as easily available as in the U.S. The law is that on the second conviction (even of relatively minor offenses), a criminal is judged to be a "habitual" criminal, and upon a third conviction, is sentenced to 20 years away from society. That doesn't mean nine months in the slammer and then parole; it means 20 years. Perhaps as a result, crime, particularly in smaller towns and cities, is much less frequent than in most places in the U.S. Juvenile gangs, as we know them, are unknown in Mexico; kids don't want to take a chance on 20 years in prison for petty foolishness.

Automobile Insurance

If you plan to drive your automobile in Mexico, it is essential that you purchase an insurance policy from a Mexican company. Theoretically, there is no difference in costs between policies, since the rates are set by the government. However, in practice this is not true. You can save a bundle by going through an RV travel club, or through one of the agents listed in the Appendix of this book. Buying insurance from one of the large agencies at the border can be very expensive. Mexican insurance is not required, but if you don't have it you are taking terrible chances. No U.S. insurance companies will cover you farther than 62 miles from the border, and many won't cover you at all. The problem is, Mexican authorities do not recognize any insurance other than legitimate Mexican companies. Also, when you rent a car in Mexico, make sure insurance is included; usually it is.

The reason we stress adequate car insurance is that in the event of an accident, Mexican law requires that your vehicle be held until damages are paid or until you guaranty proper payment. If there is bodily injury involved, they can detain you until the problem is resolved. Since courts usually grant damages for only the actual damages to the car and for a stipulated amount of damage for time off from work in case of an injury, you never have to worry about lawsuits. But if you don't have insurance, you could have a lot to worry about.

Mexican cops are not empowered to assign fault for the accident, so whether or not it was your fault, you'd better have the appropriate proof of insurance with you—always keep the policy with you when you drive. The good news is that the insurance companies are very good about helping you and making sure your auto is fixed. We've heard of them finding hotel accommodations for their clients while their auto is being repaired. So, drive as carefully as you do in the U.S. and stop worrying.

Bringing Your Car into Mexico

In January 1992 Mexican border officials started enforcing some new regulations designed to prevent tax dodging by Mexican nationals illegally importing American cars. They apply to anyone who drives more than 12 miles into the Mexican mainland (but not to any of Baja California).

The rules now require that you must present:

1. A copy of United States insurance policy effective for at least two months from the date of entry, or a surety bond from a Mexican company for the full (Blue Book) value of the vehicle.

2. A copy of the vehicle title. If you don't own the car you need an affidavit from the owner or lien-holder consenting to its being driven into Mexico. (If you've rented the car, you just need a copy of the rental agreement.)

3. Your driver's license.

4. Vehicle registration.

5. Proof of nationality.

6. A Mexican Tourist Card.

Mexican Labor Laws

In the main, Mexican labor laws are similar to those in the U.S. as they apply to the maximum work day and week and employment of minors. There are, however, some special provisions regarding vacations, bonuses and termination that are of particular relevance to the employment of domestics.

Workers with more than one year's service are entitled to an annual vacation of at least six workdays. This increases at the rate of two workdays a year for the next three years (to a total of 12 days vacation a year). In subsequent years, two workdays vacation are added for each five years of employment. Thus, if someone worked for you for 19 years, he or she would be entitled to a vacation of 18 workdays or three six-day weeks.

Workers are also entitled to an annual bonus equal to 15 days wages (paid before December 20) after one year of employment. Those who have not been employed for a full year get a bonus prorated for the time they have worked.

To avoid having an employee bring a case to the State Labor Board when his or her employment has been terminated, the employer needs to get the employee to sign a form in front of witnesses and then file it with the authorities. There are a number of grounds for which an employee can be dismissed for cause (including more than three absences from work without permission in a 28-day period).

In general, the labor laws do a good job of protecting workers without unduly burdening the employer who understands and abides by them. Check with your neighbors for the exact rules for hiring help. In one location, a contract is signed every week, guaranteeing employment of five days a week, eight hours a day—and stipulating that if the employee completes the work satisfactorily before the eight hours is up, he or she may go home. This way an employee can be hired for a four-hour day.

Police in Mexico

Police officers in the United States are generally thought of as highly trained and professional. Taking a bribe is considered sleazy in the extreme and we are horrified to hear of such a thing. Although few fall into the category of being highly-paid, with overtime and bonuses, most U.S. police officers earn $30,000 to $50,000 a year. American taxpayers consider this is a good investment; they feel they get what they pay for. But in Mexico, there is a great reluctance to pay public employees decent wages, sometimes not even living wages. The result is that many government employees, including police, feel they should be compensated by the public for any services they perform. Americans have difficulty accepting this local custom and speak harshly of "bribery and corruption." Local Mexicans choose a softer term, *la mordida* (the bite), and take a more tolerant attitude, considering payments as a tip, as one might give a waiter for his services.

In contrast with the adequately-paid and professional U.S. cop, police in Mexico come from the lower socio-economic classes, have little or no training and are pitifully underpaid. Many Mexican police earn the minimum wage, which can be as little as 13,000 pesos a day ($4.33). From this meager amount they must pay a "mordida" to their superiors for the privilege of holding the job.

Now, nobody could possibly expect a man to feed and clothe a family on that, not even in Mexico. Therefore, the cop is expected to supplement his salary by collecting "fines" (spelled *mordidas*). Officially, this is frowned on, but the officials who frown disapprovingly over this practice fully expect the collection of mordidas to continue, and they encourage it by refusing to pay a living wage. Furthermore some have their hands out for their share of the mordidas. Again, the cop feels that he is doing nothing wrong by collecting the fine from you, and he considers that he is doing you a favor by not issuing you a ticket and making you go to police headquarters to stand in line to pay your fine while another cop is removing your license plates because you've parked in a no-parking zone.

If you ask Mexican taxpayers why they don't pay police a living wage, you'll hear: "What? Spend my taxes to pay a cop to chase speeders? Let the foolish speeder pay the cop's wages, not me. If and when I get caught speeding, I'll pay. Not before!"

The author who has driven nearly 100,000 miles in Mexico over the years, affirms that he has never been stopped for an offense for which he was not guilty. Not that he hasn't paid more than his share of mordidas, but then, he admits to doing more than his share of speeding and selecting bizarre parking places. The other author says that, perhaps because he has not driven nearly so much, or perhaps because he speeds less, he has never been stopped, never paid a mordida and does not personally know anyone who has been hassled unfairly for a traffic offense.

North Americans universally detest the idea of giving bribes to cops, but the fact is, this is the system in Mexico, detest it or not. There is nothing we can do as individuals to change this system. Raising hell with the cop or accusing him of being a crook will do nothing but aggravate the situation—seriously aggravate it.

What to do if you're stopped? Remain cool, determine what the problem is, and then decide whether to pay or not to pay a mordida. If you feel you are innocent, insist on a ticket. This will mean a trip to the police station to pay a moderate fine, but it will deprive the cop of his earnings for that incident and helps discourage harassment of other foreigners. (As a matter of common practice, a cop won't bother stopping you unless he can convince you that you've done something wrong—or else he won't get his mordida.) If the cop refuses to give a ticket and still wants money, insist on a receipt (a *recibo*) for your fine. Also, do bargain; offer half of what he asks—but only if you are guilty.

This is not to say that all Mexican cops lack professionalism and pride, or that they cannot be honest, competent and conscientious. (Remember, they don't consider taking mordidas dishonest.) They can be very tough on real criminals and are usually extra careful about protecting foreigners. As a matter of government policy, police are far more tolerant of foreigners than with Mexican citizens when it comes to minor indiscretions. We've seen North Americans get away with offenses (such as public drunkenness) which would land an ordinary citizen in jail for three days. Treating tourists or foreign residents roughly or unfairly is a serious matter which can cause repercussions throughout a department. Should you have an unpleasant experience, you are morally obligated to report it by calling the Ministry of Tourism's 24-hour hotline in Mexico City at 5-250-0123.

In Mexico City, there are "tourist police" who speak English and whose job is to see that the tourists are assisted. They have a tendency for overkill, however, and will attack you with friendliness, practically insisting that you visit the places they think you should. They'll flag down a cab, push you inside and send you off to the tourist market before you know what's happening. (While this may seem very friendly, you must realize that the cab driver is usually the cop's brother-in-law, and they split the commissions the cabbie gets for delivering you to the tourist market.)

Not every Mexican cop will be patient with every faceless tourist, and if, like a few Americans, you think you can get away with treating a policeman like a flunky, you may be in for some unpleasant moments. They have as much pride as any Mexican, and will usually treat you with the respect you show them.

Mexicans are Serious about their Laws

Many laws in Mexico seem to be honored in their violation, which sometimes gives an American the wrong impression. For example, the largest piles of trash and garbage are invariably found stacked around signs that proclaim: Do not throw garbage here! Speed limit signs have no relation to the speed of the traffic. Stop signs are invisible, and stern prohibitions are simply a challenge. The foreigner residing in Mexico, however, would be wise to consider himself or herself a guest. Obeying laws should be no more an imposition than it would be in the U.S. If you park in a no-parking zone, you might find your license plates impounded. To get them back you have to go first to a bank where you get a receipt for the fine you must pay, and then to a central office where confiscated plates are held.

Some things are not taken lightly in Mexico, especially anything that has to do with business relationships. If you break a lease, you may find that the landlord has impounded your belongings and the judge agrees with him. The law might come down very heavily on you if you cheat someone out of money or refuse to pay a legitimate bill. As we've noted above, there are rules for dealing with employees such as a maid or a gardener, and you should find out what the local interpretation of the laws are. For example, you are expected to give full-time employees a bonus at Christmas by *law*, not by custom. Trying to get away with something on a real estate deal can be expensive, as many an American can attest who tried to circumvent the laws against buying *ejido* property and lost all his investment.

A North American who normally obeys the laws in his own country can expect no more trouble in Mexico than he would at home and probably less, since he is acting with the care of a guest in a foreign country. But those who think that the law applies to others, those with contempt for the customs of their host country, or those who feel that the law shouldn't apply to Americans as it does to Mexicans, are likely to be disabused of these attitudes in short order.

CHAPTER SEVEN

Locating Housing

For some reason or other, we North Americans think we have to own a house. Maybe it's something left over from the depression, a security blanket of sorts. Of course, during the past few years in the United States, home ownership has been a way of keeping ahead of inflation, and in many parts of the country, achieving great appreciation of value. We write the loan interest off our income before taxes, and overall we come out pretty well financially.

But things aren't necessarily the same in Mexico. For one thing, few homes are sold with bank loans (although the owners of new developments will sometimes finance) —you usually pay cash—so you have no interest payments to deduct from your income. Therefore, you have a large capital investment in a home, from capital that would have been bringing in dividend or interest income. Also, since you're retired, or perhaps living on savings, you probably won't have much income tax to pay or much income to deduct from in the first place.

But doesn't property ownership protect you from inflation? Not necessarily. Get rid of the notion that during times of inflation, property is *always* a hedge against falling purchasing power. When you are in a country where there is hyper-inflation, property doesn't rise in value with the economy, instead it *drops* in value! Why? Because in order to keep ahead of the inflation game, people need hard currency (usually dollars) in their hands to manipulate and invest in things that go up in value. Real estate value is set by how much rental income it might bring in if it were rented. But when inflation eats into tenants' income, it erodes their ability to pay good rents. Therefore, property becomes a lousy investment; people reason "Better sell and get some dollars!" But nobody wants to buy, so prices fall even faster.

This is what happened during the inflationary jump in the early 1980s. As the value of the peso plummeted, so did dollar values of real estate. In the last part of the 1980s, however, prices stabilized and began creeping up, in terms of dollar-to-peso ratio. In fact, in some places property has taken astounding jumps, primarily because of the demand by North Americans and the liberalized Mexican laws concerning buying property. Where we once might have cautioned against buying, we are forced to admit that many have made handsome profits through real estate buying and selling in Mexico. Only one caution need be made here: what happened before can happen again.

Having pointed out that property ownership is different in Mexico, we need to add that, despite the drawbacks, many North Americans find great joy in buying old colonial homes and restoring them. Others want to build their own places, doing their own designing and testing their artistic abilities as architects. Fortunately, with the low cost of labor and the availability of unusual building materials such as custom-made tiles and hand-formed bricks, the cost of redoing a home is certainly reasonable.

Legal Technicalities

Until quite recently, the matter of buying a house was very complicated and restrictive. There were basically two ways to buy property: either become a Mexican immigrant (with FM-2 status) or purchase your property through a bank trust and then lease the property back from the bank. This bank trust is known as a *fidecomiso*. The Mexican government's attitude was one of restricting foreign property ownership as much as possible.

These restrictive laws weren't necessarily discriminatory and unfair. Were it possible for rich foreigners to simply walk in, plunk down cash on the barrel head and take possession, Mexico would soon have become mostly foreign-owned. Citizens would have little chance to compete with affluent foreigners; property ownership for Mexicans could be a thing of the past.

Just consider what is happening in the United States vis-à-vis wealthy Japanese investors buying up not only factories, but homes, condos and golf courses. For an excellent example of foreign ownership, look at the Hawaiian island of Oahu, where million-dollar homes are rather ordinary. The trend toward foreign ownership of the United States is causing genuine concern among many citizens, resulting in a clamor for restrictions against foreign ownership.

Despite the Mexican government's efforts to restrict foreign ownership, the foreigners seem to have won. For the first time in several generations, all restrictions are off in most parts of Mexico. A tourist can now buy a home in Mexico as easily as he can in his home state or province. Because of this change in federal law, foreigners can hold an *escritura*, or fee-simple title deed, for the property in their own names. Fidecomisos used to be for 30 years and then had to be sold—no longer. They can be renewed at the end of the lease.

Exactly how these laws are going to work out for foreigners remains to be seen. The laws are too recent to be sure of their application. For example: we understand that if you buy a house as a tourist—with an escritura—you are not permitted to rent the house during your absence. But, when buying the old-fashioned way of going through a bank trust, you may rent your property. This isn't to say that tourists do not rent their properties in their absence, but it's possible that the government could crack down at some time in the future. There could be other restrictions that may come to light in the future. Under no circumstances let any money change hands before you have assurances that everything is in order; people have been hurt by real estate salesmen who say, "we'll take of the details *mañana*."

When considering property in the 1990s, our best advice is to consult with local retirees, real estate experts and a recommended lawyer to make sure what you are getting into. It is our understanding that the bank trusts are usually the most inexpensive way to go, and you still have the right to sell, rent or dispose of your property as if it were owned outright, and you can leave your property to heirs without the problem of Mexican probate.

The good news is that the onerous part of the bank trusts has been changed. Previously, a lease could be for just 30 years and it was *not* renewable. That is, if you bought a house with a 30-year lease and decided to sell after 10 years, a new buyer would only have the remaining 20 years of the lease. This meant that the longer you owned property, the less valuable it was for a new owner. But today, leases are indefinite and can be renewed forever (whatever forever means). Also, leased property can be changed over to private ownership upon payment of fees.

It's our understanding that even Inmigrados and Inmigrante Rentistas may not buy land within 100 kilometers of the border or fifty kilometers of the ocean unless they go through a bank. This is no problem, you simply have your attorney set up a bank trust. The big change is that at the end of 30 years, the owner no longer has to sell to a Mexican citizen; he can renew the trust.

A major caution still is that many desirable properties, often choice ocean-front parcels, belong to *ejidos* (community farms) that cannot be sold without government permission. That law *is* enforced. Many North Americans have discovered that they have lost their money to someone who does not own the property. It isn't always that the seller is cheating you intentionally. He may sincerely believe that the land his family has been farming for generations is his to sell. This is another good reason to have a good lawyer look over your deal.

Ejidos are communal agricultural projects the government started years ago as a way of redistributing land ownership. After the Revolution of 1910, much land was expropriated from for-eigners and ultra-rich landowners. Millions of acres which weren't being utilized were allocated to poor farmers. The land was to be owned and farmed in common, rather like a corpora-tion. The farmers, as long as they worked the land, continued to be part owners of the communal plots. But these lands can never be sold. *Never*, regardless of what some suede-shoe real estate salesman may tell you. Once a family moves away from the land, their plot reverts back to the ejido and the communal organiza-tion.

However, even this rule may be in the process of being changed. There is a process known as *regularizacion* which sup-posedly changes ejido lands into regular, fee-simple properties, but we know very little about this, and we are quite skeptical about the process.

Banks usually won't establish a trust or deal with a piece of property unless they are confident that all transactions are legal, so, between the bank and a competent lawyer, you should be safe. Read that last phrase over and memorize it before you go house-hunting: *a competent lawyer*!

When the peso was incredibly overvalued, before 1982, the housing market was overvalued as well. Four-bedroom homes that once sold for less than $30,000 went for over $200,000 at the 20-to-1 exchange rate. North Americans were priced out of the market. Then came the sudden devaluation, with the peso dropping from 20 for the dollar to 200. Housing dropped drastically. At first, a panic among residents found many frightened souls putting their places up for fast sale, which further depressed the prices. The $200,000 house dropped back to the $30,000 range again. So much for housing being a hedge against inflation.

Around the Lake Chapala area, the market in 1992 seems to be relatively steady. A pleasant two-bedroom, two-bath furnished home in Ajijic costs between $53,000 to $80,000 for 1,000 to 2,000 square feet on a nice-sized lot.

Utilities are $15 to $20 a month and real estate taxes less than $10 a year. Closing costs are about $1,200 dollars, which includes drawing up a trust deed (or fidecomiso) or a direct, fee-simple title (or escritura).

Real Estate Bargains

The kinds of housing that Americans typically buy are sometimes priced a little higher simply because sellers know we can and will pay more. But there are some great bargains to be found in Mexico today. This is particularly true if you go for something away from the usual gringo circuit. However, look carefully before you force your money on a seller of a $20,000 house. It can be, and probably is, very rustic inside and out according to our standards. The plumbing might be sluggish, inadequate, possibly non-existent, and the electrical wires strung around the walls and ceilings like spider webs. The inside walls will probably need plaster and the doors and window frames new wood. The whole place will be begging to be rebuilt. For many, this can be a project of love, for others, a nightmare.

Shopping for the right kinds of tile, looking for tropical woods for the doors, and working with a contractor to rebuild a house can be as much fun for some as it would be a chore for others. You must know yourself before undertaking something like this. The payoff, if you decide to go ahead, is that a dream home can be built through the investment of a little money and a lot of effort.

Do You Really Need to Buy?

Before you plunk down your savings on a house, you ought to question some of your basic beliefs about real estate, beliefs that may be valid at home, but not necessarily in Mexico. Property ownership in the U.S. has many advantages. One is the tax break on interest payments. Often it's cheaper to own a house than to rent when everything is considered, including the usual increase in value every year.

In Mexico, however, if you have to pay cash, you won't have interest to deduct from your income. Secondly, you probably can rent much cheaper than you can buy. For example, a house that sells for $50,000 (a really nice one) can usually be rented for about $300 to $350 a month. Is it wise to tie up $50,000 of your savings for a place you could have rented for only $300 a month? It may be worth it if you are thinking of the fun you are going to have fixing it up, or if you have a need to *own* your place. If you are selling a house in the U.S. and will have a capital gain larger than the $125,000 on which those over 55 can get a one-time tax forgiveness, you may want to check with your tax adviser on the renting vs. buying question.

If cost is your primary consideration, you can't beat renting. Even if you have to own something, *please* do yourself a favor and rent for a period of time to make sure you want to live there.

Fortunately for the renter, rentals are abundant in most areas. Prices for a small apartment or house can start at less than $200 a month. Many people we interviewed seem to think $250 is an ordinary rent. $300 a month and over can rent a wonderful place. You can pay much more, and if you want to rent a Mexican-style house you can pay far less. We met one man in Lake Chapala who indignantly denied that a person could live in Mexico on only $600 a month. It turned out that he read the first edition of *Choose Mexico* and immediately got on the telephone to rent a huge house for $650 a month, without ever having visited Lake Chapala previously. It was a nice place, but we're sure he could have rented something equally nice even in that relatively expensive community for much, much less. (By the way, this book never suggests that you can live *anywhere* in Mexico on $600 a month.)

Example from Personal Experience

To illustrate the rental market, here is our experience on our last trip to San Miguel de Allende. We found an almost new place, two large bedrooms upstairs and a bath, another bath downstairs with a large living room, a small dining room and a kitchen for $200 a month (on a one-month basis). Had we taken a lease, the rent would have been $150. Everything was furnished, including extra bed linens and tasteful wall hangings and folk statuary. The furniture was typical colonial-style, massive, dark wood, with bright fabrics. We had a lady come in two mornings a week to clean the house (my wife shamelessly saved the dirty dishes for her), and she did the laundry, including the bedding twice a week. She charged us $10 a week for all this and worked very diligently. This is a great way to study a town and see if you want to stay permanently or not.

Of course, if you wanted to, you could look into even cheaper housing. After all, to the local people who earn between $80 and $200 a month, rents like we were paying would be out of the question. We've seen houses renting for $35 a month or less. But be prepared for something quite rustic. Whereas an American landlord is expected to fix things when they break or wear out, Mexican custom makes maintenance the responsibility of the renter. Therefore, when the plumbing fails or the roof leaks, you are on your own. Nothing is done by the owner, and the condition keeps deteriorating until everything collapses. Then he sells it, buys another, and starts all over.

Finding a Rental

Looking for rental property can either be a frustrating experience or a pleasant adventure. Simply walking around town may give you some leads, as a *se renta* sign might be showing in a window here and there. Don't be put off by the outside appearance of a building. A rough adobe facade could conceal a beautiful patio with delightful apartments clustered about a flower-perfumed garden. Colonial buildings tend to look inward, rather than show themselves to the passerby.

Usually there is a bulletin board at one of the local *supermercados* (supermarkets) where apartments and house offerings are placed. Sometimes there are English language newspapers or weekly bulletins that contain such information. Where there is an English-language library, it can be an excellent source. However, most of the renting or buying is done by word of mouth. This is particularly true for Mexican landlords, for they seldom advertise in newspapers, and depend on friends and neighbors to let the word out that their house is for rent. Ask anyone with whom you have any contact, and eventually you will find something.

Some of the best bargains in rentals can often be found in house-sitting arrangements. Many Americans who own or lease property return to the U.S. for three or so months every year and want other Americans to watch their home while they are gone. They are also happy to derive a small income to help with the upkeep of the house. Keep your eyes and ears open, and you might even try placing your own ad in the local English language paper. These places are furnished of course, often include a maid and/or gardener. (The homeowners don't want to risk losing good help while they are gone, so they pay the wages while they are away.) To be a house-sitter, be prepared to furnish good references.

Cultural Differences

Mexican kitchens are almost always remarkably different from your kitchen back home. In the United States, the kitchen is an important part of the home. The kitchen will be delightfully roomy, with colorful curtains in the windows and a large kitchen table with comfortable chairs. Americans spend a lot of time in the kitchen; we usually eat all our meals there, at least breakfast and lunch. But most middle-class Mexican families wouldn't any more dine in the kitchen than we would take our meals in the garage. In middle-class Mexican homes, the kitchen is the domain of the maid, the cook and the gardener; the lady of the house seldom enters. The result is often a stark, utilitarian room with a minimum of conveniences and ugly plumbing fixtures. There may be a table and chairs, but only for the use of the servants.

In some of the more luxurious homes the house actually divides into two separate sections: one part for the owners, and the other consisting of the kitchen, servants' quarters and their bath, garage and patio. The servants have their own key, which will unlock their section of the house but not the owner's.

Neither the authors, nor most of the readers of this book are members of the United States' tiny upper class in which the presence of domestic servants is taken for granted. In fact, many of us are uncomfortable with the very idea of having people around the house who are paid to do things we could do for ourselves. Thus, there is an adjustment to be made to Mexican society in which domestic service is neither demeaning to those who perform it nor embarrassing to those for whom it is performed. The Mexican family whose income and status in the community would define their U.S. counterpart as lower middle class is almost certain to have some household help. If you live in Mexico on a monthly income of $600 or more, you will be perceived as someone who can afford a maid and may be expected to employ one. This does not mean, however, that you have no choice. If the whole idea of domestic service and the economic/class system it reflects is repugnant to you, no one can force you to participate in it.

We initially resisted the idea of employing a maid, but then compromised by hiring a woman to come in just in the mornings. She arrived each day (except Sunday, of course) just after breakfast, cleaned the kitchen, scrubbed the tile floors, and did the laundry, and maybe did some preparation for the noon meal. Gradually we became used to her, because she was so unobtrusive and careful to keep busy in some part of the house where we were not. Later we discovered that we liked having someone living in the maid's room who could always serve as a built-in house sitter when we were visiting in Acapulco or Mexico City.

Leases and Agreements

If you enter into a rental or lease agreement, you may find yourself signing an official-looking document complete with colorful government stamps. If it's a long-term lease, there will probably be an escalation clause that pegs the rent to the value of the dollar vs. peso. More than likely, the rental terms will be in dollars rather than pesos. An item to insist upon is a clause on subleasing rights. Many landlords, particularly Mexican, don't like the idea, but you should protect yourself against liability, in case you decide to take a long vacation to visit friends and family in the U.S., or you feel you've had enough of Mexico and need to get out from under the lease. Furthermore, should you obtain a very long-term lease, and you plan on putting money into the house to fix it up to your specifications, you need a way to recoup this money if you decide to move on.

A very important consideration in renting a house or apartment is the presence or absence of a telephone. It takes an inordinate amount of time to have a telephone installed in Mexico. The last we heard it was something like a year's wait! Thus, you can imagine that a house with a phone will demand a premium. It may seem like a small thing, but if you get involved with the English-speaking community's social life, a telephone can be a great way of keeping in touch.

Finally, be sure you have a complete understanding of the rental terms, and insist on a receipt each month as proof that you are living up to your end of the rental agreement or lease.

House-Hunting is Never Easy

We know of at least one retiree who returned from Mexico quite disgruntled because he couldn't find a suitable apartment the first week he was in Guadalajara. Just as in the United States or Canada, you can't expect a "dream house" to suddenly appear the moment you step off the airplane. You have to look, search, maybe even bargain to find your ideal place. If you have a hotel, or a hotel apartment, you needn't feel pressured to take the first thing that comes along. You'll have time to explore, compare housing, and might even have fun making decisions! Our advice is to take your time, and don't expect miracles.

CHAPTER EIGHT

The Market & The Kitchen

Long before the Spanish arrived, the open-air market was a prominent feature of Mexican life. A few tables shaded by awnings, farmers with something to sell and townspeople with money or items to trade was all that was needed for a *tianguis*. From Mexico City to the smallest villages, that tradition is still alive today and continues to be much more than just a commercial institution.

Outdoor markets are common throughout the world. Even in the United States where they seemed to be disappearing, they are staging a comeback in the form of farmers' markets in big cities and garage sales and flea markets just about everywhere.

In few places, however, are they as prominent or as important to the life of the community as in Mexico, where on one or more days of the week a whole neighborhood will be transformed into a sprawling marketplace and most of its inhabitants drawn into its transactions.

Fun and Savings

For the North American resident or visitor, these markets are an opportunity both to buy everything from produce to machine parts at substantial savings and to observe the inner workings of Mexico close up. One thing that fascinates me is the juxtaposition of items as traditional as tethered chickens and trussed-up (live) pigs with other articles as contemporary as transistor radios and cassette tapes.

In addition to these informal, weekly outdoor markets, every city and town has one or more permanent *mercados*, usually under public auspices. Usually they are housed in great tin-roofed sheds but spill out into the surrounding streets. They, too, are operated by a collection of entrepreneurs, each offering his or her own specialty, be it fruits or vegetables, meat, or even clothing and hardware. At first you might feel intimidated by this seemingly disorderly hive of vendors vigorously hawking their wares. They tend to cluster together according to the product being offered. Thus, for vegetables, you wander about the section where stand after stand of produce sellers display tomatoes, onions, avocados and potatoes in attractive arrangements. Wander a few steps away and you might find yourself in a profusion of clothes, or birds in cages, or perhaps stands where cassettes and records are sold, with these wares blaring at top volume.

Many Other Shops

Not everything in the mercado will appeal to you, at least until you are used to it. Those stalls where sides of beef hang in the open, dotted with flies, can be passed by in favor of meat markets with sanitation and refrigeration. Usually modern meat markets can be found in the mercados or at least nearby.

Melons and other fruits displayed are often cut and sliced: these are best enjoyed for their aesthetics; make sure the melon you buy is whole. You can slice it when you get home with the assurance that it hasn't been a parade ground for flies. Any fruit that can be peeled is perfectly safe to eat on the spot. With fruits and vegetables that need washing, better wait until you can purify them in your kitchen.

Before you begin to worry that you are going to have to do all your buying from street vendors, let me assure you that the supermercado has arrived in Mexico. Even smaller towns have miniature versions of the U.S. supermarket. Although you could do all your shopping there, you would not only miss one of the delights of Mexican living, but also severely limit your choices. Like its counterpart in the U.S., the supermercado is a convenient, usually economical place to buy packaged foods, domestic paper goods, laundry soap, beer and liquor. For fresh fruit and vegetables, meats and poultry, and baked goods, go to the mercado, or community market.

Fruit and Vegetables

Because most fruits and vegetables sold locally are grown in small family plots—without the aid of U.S. mass production techniques, and not force-fed with chemical fertilizers—they taste great. The oranges have seeds, but the variety is amazing and the juice sweet and refreshing. Avocados are an adventure, there being at least a hundred different kinds, each with a slightly different flavor and texture, making the bland U.S. varieties pale in comparison. Carrots are often small, but are so sweet and tasty you could make a meal on them alone. Asparagus, broccoli and swiss chard are so flavorful that you wonder if they're the same variety as we get up north. Indeed, they may not be. There is much agribusiness in Mexico, shipping its products to the north. Like its U.S. counterpart, it concentrates on a few varieties—generally those that will survive the long journey. In the mercado, however, you are buying from small farmers who grow whatever their fathers grew or grows best on their land. The emphasis is on flavor, not convenience or uniformity.

Meat

Cattle are seldom grain-fed in Mexico, which means it takes longer to raise them for market—six months to a year longer. This extra maturity accounts for the rich flavor of Mexican beef. Of course, range-fed beef is tougher and more stringy, which for some will counterbalance the tasty flavor. The meat can be aged in your refrigerator, and it can be cooked in ways to compensate for toughness. At better meat markets, you can purchase grain-fed beef if you prefer an extra-tender steak. Most good restaurants serve tender beef.

Pork is another story. Most of the pork in the markets does not come from pig farms where the animals are penned so tightly they can't move and fed garbage until they are artificially fat. In Mexico, pigs wander loose around farm houses and in small villages, sometimes as commonly as dogs. They exercise and run free until they are ready for market. The result is a lean, red-meat pork, sometimes with the consistency of steak. The flavor can be incredible. If you cook this pork until it is well-done, it is perfectly safe.

Outside of the mercado there are many other shops, bakeries and small markets. Some cater to foreign residents, and their prices reflect this. Yet, food prices are so low in Mexico and competition so vigorous, that it is difficult to be concerned that the dozen eggs that cost the equivalent of 80 cents in the market are selling for 85 cents in the shop where the proprietor speaks English.

Prices

What about prices of foods? Some books on Mexico, published when inflation was not a major factor, contain detailed tables showing comparative food prices for cities and towns across Mexico. The differences in food prices among cities were both predictable and trivial. Fresh produce and meats were slightly more expensive in resort towns like Acapulco and priced lowest in less popular towns like Oaxaca, but over all, they varied only a few percentage points. That seems still to be the case, and these differences become less significant because prices are significantly lower than in the U.S.

For example, these are some recent prices from Guadalajara supermercados:

T-Bone Steak	$2.58/pound
Veal Cutlets	$2.80/pound
Pork Chops	$2.42/pound
Catfish	$ .83/pound
Tomatoes	$ .35/pound
Carrots	$ .18/pound
Bananas	$ .27/pound
Papaya	$ .22/pound

Shopping Daily

One difference between food shopping in the U.S. and in Mexico, is the frequency with which one needs to shop. You can buy food so fresh in Mexico that it seems a shame to let it sit for several days in the refrigerator. In addition, going to the mercado is fun. People who normally shop once a week at the U.S. supermarkets quickly fall into the Mexican habit of shopping daily. They discover the fun of planning a menu around what looks best

in the market rather than what's available in the freezer or fridge. Shopping is an engaging form of social interaction and a fine way to practice Spanish. The standkeepers quickly recognize you and sometimes put something extra in your bag after you've paid, as a token of good will. You can bargain in most markets, but it is hardly worth it, because of the low prices.

You will quickly learn to identify those who take advantage of your relative wealth by jacking up their prices. Rather than bargain, simply avoid those stands and deal with friendly merchants who give you the right price and who show you they appreciate your patronage. Outside of a few convenience foods, most items that Americans are used to are available in Mexico. Food packaging, however, tends to be several years behind the U.S. Maybe this is because people prefer fresh foods to prepackaged mixes or frozen TV dinners. Bacon, for instance, often must be sliced to order rather than prepackaged in transparent material. Sometimes there are seemingly arbitrary little shortages that can be annoying if you allow them to be. We once searched for several weeks for oatmeal that was not pre-sweetened, although it had been available a month earlier and was again later. Some things are sold in different base quantities. For example, eggs can be bought by the dozen, but are much cheaper by the kilo; oranges, though available by the kilo, are cheaper when bought by number. When you shop every day, getting your purchases home is not a serious problem, even if you don't have a car. All over Mexico, Americans and Mexicans can be seen carrying groceries in locally produced straw bags. In some parts of the country, the bags have straps that go over your shoulders, in others, straps you hold in your hand. (If you get tired of walking, taxis are affordable.)

Wherever you are, the straw bag filled with groceries proclaims that you are not a tourist, but someone seriously living in Mexico. Lately, however, plastic shopping bags have been pushing aside the straw woven ones. Although they're cheaper and can be thrown away without regret, they will never be quite the same as the straw bags.

Mexican Cooking

Once you get those delicious meats, fruits and vegetables home, what you make them into will be up to you. There are Americans in Mexico whose menus seldom stray from those of their former neighbors still living in Dubuque or Toronto. (We think they're missing something.) On the other hand, if you want to experiment with the varied cuisines of Mexico, your kitchen is an excellent place to do so. You are in control and can make adaptations in seasoning to bring the dishes closer to your tastes.

Diana Kennedy's *The Cuisines of Mexico* is the standard English language cookbook for Americans who want to share what Mexico's many peoples have to offer. You can use this book as a source of recipes, as a guide to ordering in restaurants where menus aren't in English, or as a source of answers when your maid asks what you'd like for dinner that day. Don't expect your maid to be able to prepare all the dishes in the book. However, once your Spanish is good enough, or if you are skillful at teaching by example, you may have your maid cooking Mexican foods of which the neighbors have never heard.

A pleasant, though not essential, part of your preparation for retirement in Mexico might be studying Mexican cookbooks and trying some dishes. Even if the ingredients are not all readily available, you will find some recipes you can make with what is at hand.

As we've asserted several times in this book, Mexican cuisine is rich and varied and by no means limited to chiles, beans and tortillas. Nevertheless, were it not for the creative use of maize (corn) tortillas, beans and chiles, plus cheese, there would be many more people suffering from hunger and malnutrition in Mexico. These inexpensive ingredients formed the foundation of the pre-Cortés diet and are staples of Mexican cooking today. Meat, poultry and fish are used sparingly, almost as a seasoning. The result is comparable to much Asian cooking: delicious, inexpensive food that is actually more healthful than the standard American diet which emphasizes red meat.

Years ago, nutritionists wondered why Mexicans seem to thrive on a combination of foods that violate many basic nutritional values then held by most Americans. They discovered that the nutrients, particularly the proteins, in the daily Mexican fare fit together in an almost perfect balance. The U.S. scientific community now believes that fats, not carbohydrates, are the cause of America's endemic obesity and the resulting heart and circulatory problems. Also the Mexican custom is to eat the principal meal, *la comida*, in the middle of the day. Traditionally, this is a leisurely meal during the long siesta hours and might include a nap afterwards. They tend to limit the *cena* or evening meal to a light snack. If one wants an elaborate meal in the evening, the custom is to eat very late. In Mexico City, for example, many restaurants don't even open their doors until 9 o'clock, and are still serving meals at midnight. Enjoying the main meal during the siesta is ideal for the retiree. The maid will be there to prepare it, and you can make your own supper from the leftovers or enjoy the cena in a restaurant with friends. In addition, it is healthier and more comfortable, particularly as you grow older, to avoid heavy meals late in the day.

Household Help

Most Americans of moderate means have either no experience with servants, or perhaps that of having a cleaning woman once or twice a week. During the past 40 years, even in homes affluent enough to afford hired help, the trend has been to substitute "labor-saving" devices for human assistance. The middle-class homemaker spends more time in the kitchen and laundry or behind a vacuum cleaner than his or her counterpart of a generation ago. Not only has help become expensive, but in the U.S. it is a rare employer or employee who is fully comfortable with the roles and relationships involved in domestic service.

When Americans hear that domestic help is readily affordable in Mexico, they often wonder whether they would like to hire someone to cook, clean and do laundry. They visualize someone who is a servant because he or she is unable to find other employment, someone who deeply resents his or her situation and feels demeaned by having to take orders and work in someone else's kitchen.

In Mexico, as we've said, domestic service is considered an entirely acceptable occupation. Despite low wages, there are enough benefits to make domestic service desirable and satisfying for many. Some benefits are tangible, like the guarantee of one or more nutritious meals each day and the higher wages usually paid by foreign residents. Americans often treat their help better than local employers and are more egalitarian and generous in ways that sometimes aren't apparent. Other benefits include the status a domestic servant gains from close connection with the relatively affluent foreigners. In short, domestic service is not considered a last resort as it often is up north. When American residents speak of the loyalty and good nature of their servants, they are neither being naive or condescending. Servants can truly help increase your involvement with the country, as well as making life easier and more comfortable.

Often a person will work for more than one employer and will be happy to work for you two or three hours a day, doing the breakfast dishes, scrubbing the tile floors, and maybe doing laundry. For these chores, the maid will need no English and you no Spanish. The workers' energy and efficiency will amaze you. They evidently feel that since they are being paid by the hour, they must fill up each hour and will look for things to do. With one maid, we had to be careful not to lay out our clothes on the bed to wear after a shower, for when we were ready to put them on, chances were they would be hanging on the line, already washed. Anything that wasn't hanging up or in a dresser was fair game for the wash tub. If you wish anything complicated, the maid must be taught procedures that may be strange to her unless she has experience working for Americans. If you want a roast chicken for lunch, you must make clear how long you want it cooked, what kinds of seasoning, and what, if anything, to put inside. Even something as simple as making picnic sandwiches can be a mystery to someone for whom bread is a luxury, seldom if ever used in her house. If, on the other hand, you want to try *chile con queso* or *chiles rellenos* she will need no instruction. Unless you're willing to take time teaching and explaining, you're better off doing the complicated American cooking yourself and letting the maid help you with shopping and cleaning up the kitchen afterward.

Gardeners

The gardener, sometimes called a *mozo*, is usually more than simply a gardener. He not only cares for the flowers, but also is a repairman, a bartender and a watchman. He helps the maid, runs errands, and negotiates with local business people for you. If you're going away to Acapulco for a week, often the gardener may agree to stay in your house to watch things. Many gardeners have several clients, and it's easy to find one who only wants to come in for an hour or two a day to water plants and make sure everything is working properly.

Some of your best practice in Spanish can be with the servants, and they can be helpful to take shopping with you. They know the proper prices and won't let you pay too much. We once had a maid who enjoyed shopping with us, because she loved to bargain. First she would argue for several minutes on the price of a dozen tomatoes. When she had beaten the merchant down to the very rock bottom price, she would then argue about how many tomatoes should be in a dozen. She wouldn't give up until the merchant surrendered and put thirteen tomatoes in the bag. She always looked so smug at having won the game that one would have thought it was her money she had saved.

PYRAMID OF THE SUN - TEOTIHUACAN, MEXICO   León Monroad 1992

CHAPTER NINE

$\mathcal{N}$eed to $\mathcal{K}$now Spanish?

If you're going to fully enjoy Mexico, of course, you must learn to speak Spanish. That should be obvious. However, you won't starve if you don't know Spanish, and you won't lack for social connections because you are too lazy to learn more than a few phrases of the language. You'll survive. Many North Americans have lived there for years and learned just enough to ask where the bathroom is or order another round of drinks. Occasionally they enter the wrong bathroom, that's true, but rarely does a waiter misunderstand an order for more drinks. If you plan on hanging around with Americans for all your stay in Mexico, or if you insist on living in expensive hotels and condos, then it really doesn't matter whether you learn Spanish or not.

But, once you do learn to communicate, you suddenly find new doors open to you. Mexico becomes a totally different place. Instead of being limited to a small circle of English-speaking friends, you can venture out into the exciting world of Mexico. You can participate in everything that is going on around you instead of being puzzled by what is happening, mystified at what people are saying. You will find yourself being invited to visit homes and join in festivities that before were inaccessible. You will have fun dealing with merchants, servants and neighbors, and entering into much closer relationships with them. You will no longer fear hassling with bureaucrats or arguing with policemen and taxi drivers. You will be in a much better position to locate those $10 hotel rooms when traveling like a resident through posh resort towns. In short, when you learn Spanish, you truly become a resident of Mexico and ready to enjoy the country to the fullest.

But, isn't it difficult to learn a foreign language? Yes, it is. Let's not kid ourselves, language learning is not easy. You often hear someone say: "Oh, I won't bother studying the language now, I'll pick it up when I get there." Unless you are under ten years old, the chances of your "picking up" the language simply by being around Spanish speakers are less than zero. This is not because adults can't learn as fast, or faster than children; it's just that they seldom find the right kind of learning situation. Lately a radically new direction in language learning, called *Total Physical Response* (TPR), is being adopted by more and more teachers. By all means look for a program where the teachers use the TPR approach to Spanish classes. TPR was developed by Dr. Jim Asher of San Jose State University (Calif.). According to Dr. Asher, a person retains his learning experiences far longer if he is physically involved by *doing* something at the same time he is listening or speaking a foreign language. Asher claims that this is the way children learn, and that adults can learn just as fast as children if they learn the same way!

There is only one way for adults to learn a foreign language: hard work, practice, study, and more practice are the only keys to language learning. Work can be fun, of course, and hopefully, tension-free. Studying Spanish can not only be enjoyable, it can be a rewarding activity, particularly after you are settled in your new home.

We highly recommend that one of the first things you do upon arriving in Mexico is to find a language class, even if you already know some Spanish. Besides brushing up your language, you find this an excellent way to meet people, to enlarge your circle of friends. You are likely to find that your fellow students will organize into their own social group, with parties and sightseeing trips outside of class. Spanish classrooms are among the very best ways to meet your fellow retirees in the community and to start making friends.

"Castilian" Spanish

"I studied Spanish in high school," you hear some people say, "but it was *Castilian* Spanish, and here they speak *Mexican*

Spanish. I'd have to learn all over again." This lame excuse for not being able to understand the language has no validity at all. The Spanish spoken in Mexico is excellent, with a very neutral accent with few of the differences that often distinguish isolated accents in Spain or South America. The bulk of the original European settlers in Mexico came from Extremadura, in the west of Spain and they brought this accent with them. Indeed, linguists will tell you that there is *less* difference between the pronunciation of Spanish spoken in and around Madrid (so-called Castilian) and that spoken in Mexico than there is between the English spoken in Nashville and that spoken in Milwaukee. It takes an expert to tell whether a speaker comes from Madrid or from Mérida, so please don't use that excuse any longer!

Your high school or college Spanish often doesn't work too well in actual practice because you went about it learning from books. You learned to memorize grammar and to read and write printed words. The problem is that letters, words and grammar are *not* language. Language is *a system of sounds plus the meanings these sounds carry.* Letters and words just represent the sounds; grammar rules try to explain what is happening. You might be able to recognize all of the written words in the book, you may be able to parse verbs all day long and memorize all the grammatical rules ever discovered, but if you can't understand the sound system, then you *don't know the language.* It's as simple as that.

What happens is, first we learn to read and write Spanish words. Then, when we hear spoken sounds, we mentally convert these sounds into Spanish words. Next, we mentally translate these Spanish words into English words, and finally attach meanings to the translated words, all the while trying to remember whether the endings of the verbs were in the pluperfect or imperfect subjunctive tense. In the meanwhile, the speaker has used a half a yard of rapid-fire words you didn't have time to catch. In school, unless you were lucky enough to have native speakers for practice, you probably didn't learn to listen and think in the language.

It's interesting to watch an American (who learned Spanish from books) ask questions in Spanish. The grammar is impeccable, and the pronunciation not bad. The question is understood perfectly by the native speaker, but the North American's face assumes a blank stare when the reply comes shooting back at him. Next thing he knows he's made the wrong turn and is in the wrong bathroom again.

Then comes the excuse that "Mexicans talk too fast." Listen to the way *we* talk, and you will realize that we speak just as fast and run everything together just as Mexicans do. We don't pause at the end of each word either, although in your college Spanish class, the students probably did separate each word quite distinctly. Again, spoken language and written language are two different things.

Before you embark on your travels to Mexico, it's a good idea to look around for Spanish classes at home. Look for a good conversation class, taught by a native Spanish speaker if possible. Another excellent way of getting a head start is by buying a set of cassette tapes for home study. This is particularly true if you already have a background in Spanish, but lack the listening and thinking practice in the language.

Not just any tape will do, however, because some systems perpetuate the emphasis on grammar and learning individual words. Find a system that gives listening practice at the normal speed of a native speaker. Some learning systems are good only for putting the listener to sleep with verb conjugations and vocabulary lists.

One of the best systems available is put out by the U.S. Government. These tapes can be ordered from: National Audio-Visual Center, Customer Services PF, 8700 Edgeworth Drive, Capitol Heights, MD 20743-3701. Credit card orders can be done by phone: 800-638-1300. It consists of three sections, each the equivalent of one year of university Spanish. The first section has fifteen cassette tapes and will give you a real head start. These tapes are produced by the Foreign Service Institute of the State Department. They're available in an astounding number of languages and are used to train diplomats and military personnel who are going to overseas assignments. The emphasis is on listening and repeating and stringing phrases into sentences. Although there is a grammar section in each chapter, it's there for your convenience more than as an essential element of each lesson. You learn grammar the same way a child learns it, by listening and by intuitive analysis.

I'm particularly excited about their Programmatic courses. These begin at a very elementary stage of sound-and-meaning exercises, giving you the chance to learn what the sounds mean without thinking in terms of letters and words. If you have a background in Spanish from your high school days, you can probably work through these tapes without consulting the manual, and learning as a child does, by hearing sounds and intuitively connecting meaning from the context. I studied Brazilian Portuguese this way and was delighted with my progress.

It Ain't in the Dictionary!

Although Spanish is a remarkably uniform language around the world, there are certain differences from locality to locality and from country to country. This is true of English, as well, but we are not always aware of it. For example, there are many words in the United States that vary depending upon where in the country a speaker lives. A *frying pan* becomes a *skillet* or a *spider*, depending on where you were raised. A *davenport* becomes a *sofa* or a *couch*, or sometimes a *chesterfield*. A Spanish-speaker may become confused if he knows the word "sofa," and you throw "davenport" at him. So you see, this problem of lexical differences isn't restricted to Spanish. If you've ever been totally confused by an Aussie or a Scotsman, you'll understand what we're talking about.

So it isn't surprising that some words you will encounter in Mexico cannot be found in your dictionary, particularly not a dictionary printed in Madrid or Buenos Aires. The solution to this problem is to read as many newspapers and locally printed books as you can and to buy a dictionary printed in Mexico City. Keep a notebook in which you write down every new word you encounter. Try to find ten words every day to mark into your book, then review these words several times a day; you'll be amazed at how your vocabulary expands. And, try to memorize the sound and meanings rather than the actual spelling of the words.

Early settlers in Mexico found many unfamiliar foods and cultural items with no Spanish equivalents. They simply adapted the existing Indian words. For example, the Spaniards called the unfamiliar turkey a *pavo* because it reminded them of a *pavo real*, a peacock. But Mexicans prefer the Aztec word *guajalote*. If you listen carefully, that's exactly what turkeys go around saying: "*Guajalote! Guajalote!*" It doesn't mean much to us, since turkeys aren't very good at making conversation, but animal behaviorists have discovered that *guajalote* actually translates into "Wow, do I hate Thanksgiving!"

Many words are influenced by Mexico's proximity to the United States. For example: most dictionaries claim that the word for grapefruit is *toronja*. But you might confuse a waiter, because most Mexicans order *grepfrut*! Also, local usage over the years changes the vocabulary, giving different meanings to words that seem to be obvious. Instead of *autobús* for bus, as in many Spanish-speaking countries, the Mexicans often say *camión*, which also means truck. Puerto Ricans will say *gua gua* and South Americans will say *micro*, or *colectivo*, for bus. We've heard people say: "*parque el carro*" for "park the car."

As we pointed out earlier, many people never bother to learn Spanish. So don't panic if you think it will take you a while to become proficient. There are enough people around who can speak English, and who are eager to practice it, that you can get by quite nicely. This is particularly true if you are adept at pantomime and charades. The nice thing about learning Spanish in Mexico is that people are always delighted when they see that you are trying to learn. Unlike the French, who seem insulted if you mispronounce even a tiny nasal whine, the Mexicans are very supportive.

They will tell you: "You speak very well the Spanish," as they congratulate you for your efforts. Of course, if you really *did* "speak very well the Spanish," they wouldn't comment about it. You know when you're close to getting a good accent when people stop telling you how well you speak.

So the answer to the question, "Do I have to learn Spanish" is: no, you don't have to, but you will be happier when you do learn Spanish.

CHAPTER TEN

Getting Around Mexico

One big advantage to living in Mexico is your opportunity for travel. You have the entire country to choose from, with many interesting locations just a few miles from anywhere you decide to live. At your leisure, you can afford to visit little-known or out-of-the-way places that ordinary tourists seldom chance to see. You can lope on down to Acapulco for a weekend as casually as you might visit the local lake or seashore back home. All of those exotic beach towns you've read about are just a bus ride away: dream places like Mazatlán, Puerto Vallarta, Cancún, plus dozens of hidden beaches and fascinating villages no one ever heard of outside of Mexico. You'll probably discover your own personal hideaway.

Mountain gems such as Zacatecas, San Cristóbal de las Casas or Taxco beckon to you, while the cosmopolitan atmosphere of Mexico City invites shopping and elegant dining for a welcome change of pace. Fortunately, any trip you might choose will cost far less than traveling in the United States. Most people find they can take regular excursions and still stay within the boundaries of their basic $600 a month budget. With abundant hotel rooms under $20 a night, how can you miss?

Air fares are deliberately kept low by the government-owned airlines so that Mexican citizens can afford to fly. For example, the round-trip excursion fare from Mexico City to Acapulco is currently about $60. The round-trip fare between Mexico City and Tijuana on the U.S. border is about $300. Excellent discounts are available for seniors and students. Some terrific bargains can be found in airline travel and accommodations packages available within the country.

Bus Travel

Although air travel is definitely more affordable here than in the U.S., the mainstay of the travel system is the nation's vast network of buses.

Bus travel in the U.S., where one company has a virtual monopoly of interstate service, is neither particularly inexpensive nor enjoyable. Mexico is a different story. Many companies compete for your business, each one eager to take you anywhere you can possibly wish to go. You get the feeling that your business is important to them. The government is building new terminals as quickly as possible, where all lines meet at a central depot in each town. There's little waiting time because buses depart every few minutes, heading in all directions. Clean restaurants, shops and services are all operated in competition with one another. Yet, the cost of a ticket is almost free by comparison with our Greyhound. For example: a ticket from Mexico City to Acapulco (375 miles) is $13.50 on an "Executive" bus, equipped with an amazing bump-free suspension, a restroom, latest release films shown on closed circuit Sony TVs and a friendly stewardess who serves coffee, tea, soft drinks, hands out pillows and generally assists the passengers on the trip. The first class fare to Puebla (81 miles) is less than $5. By the way, all first class service in Mexico is by reserved seating.

The best part about buses in Mexico is that rural areas are not cut off as they are in the United States. I've traveled in some of the most remote areas in Mexico, in high mountain villages, in jungle country and desert terrain, but despite how far from civilization it seems, before long, a bus comes puttering along, dependably carrying passengers from one village to another.

Don't misunderstand; there are several levels of bus service in Mexico, and not all operate with newest equipment. Sometimes, particularly in the second-class bus stations, you'll find some facilities as bad or worse than we are used to in the United States. Officially, there are two types of service: first and second class. On many runs the only difference is that second class-buses are permitted to take on more passengers than they have seats, allowing people to stand in the aisle (this is normal on our U.S. buses). Additionally, second-class buses are slower; they make more stops. Also, on some of the lower-end second-class buses, the kind you find in backward, rural areas, passengers are permitted to carry produce and even chickens and piglets to market. This adds immensely to the adventure of bus riding in Mexico! However, these aren't the kind of buses you find in bus terminals.

Most North Americans choose the first-class service. However, if you'd like to see Mexico on a different level than other tourists and you speak some Spanish, second-class travel may be an adventure you'd enjoy. Second-class buses—usually older and always slower—turn off the pavement at every opportunity to bump their way over unpaved roads and visit any number of picturesque little villages. While the bus takes on passengers and disposes of cargo, you often have 15 or 20 minutes to wander about the square, to inspect the inevitable church or to order a bowl of steaming chicken *caldo*. If you were driving, it would never occur to you to detour off the busy highway. The other passengers take pride in pointing out landmarks as you go along; they seldom have the chance to talk with a real *Norteamericano*.

Regional Diversity

Because Mexican culture—cuisine, handicrafts, music and architecture—like the climate and scenery, is intensely regional, travel within the country offers the stimulation that other North Americans have to go abroad to find. Another advantage of traveling *and* living in Mexico is that when, in your travels, you come across the unusual piece of pottery or furniture you just can't resist, getting it home is easy without the shipping and customs problems of crossing international borders. Many retirees' homes look like mini museums, so carried away are their owners by the beauty, variety and inexpensiveness of the handicrafts they encounter on their trips around the country.

Mexican Railroads

For the adventurous, particularly those with a sense of humor, rail travel in Mexico is a must. Most of the equipment is old hand-me-downs from the U.S. rail system. The coaches are right out of the 1920s, with the luxurious decor of those days still more or less in place. You can reserve *camarines* (one-room Pullmans with individual toilet facilities) or luxurious drawing rooms with full bath and showers and lounging sofas. The first-class section has ordinary recliner chairs, and the dining cars (when available) serve surprisingly tasty meals.

At least on some key routes, service is currently being upgraded and the travel time cut. Fares on the special trains making these runs are somewhat higher but are still extremely affordable. The fare on *El Constitucionalista* from Mexico City to San Miguel de Allende is $40 round trip, including breakfasts.

There is now an excellent first-class train from Monterey to Mexico City with which you connect via luxury bus from Brownsville, Texas, where many travelers leave their automobiles. Reservations can be made through a travel agent in the U.S.

Trains often charge less than bus transportation for the same routes. They can also be much slower, particularly in the mountains. Still, they are not only fun for travel, but offer some advantages over buses. Besides being able to move about and stretch the legs, many residents like trains because they can schedule their long, grueling trips at night, so they can climb into a Pullman bed and wake up in the morning at their destination, refreshed, and not very damaged in the pocketbook.

Second Class

On Mexican trains, second class is exactly what its name suggests. Sometimes the coaches are equipped with wooden benches for seats, but always with terribly dirty restrooms. Despite this, many North Americans prefer to ride second class for the atmosphere. Passengers are Indians, soldiers, farmers and anyone else too poor to afford the luxury of reserved first-class seats. Guaranteed is a vendor's stand offering sandwiches, cold beer and soft drinks. This is where you expect to find an American or two, leaning against the improvised bar, practicing Spanish with the second-class passengers.

Automobile Travel

Chances are, where you live in the United States or Canada, living without an automobile is next to impossible. Our society has forsaken public transportation to the point where it's almost nonexistent in many places. We depend on our cars just as a cowboy depended on his horse back in the wild west days. Without an auto, even the simplest shopping errands are all but out of the question. Fortunately, Mexico hasn't "modernized" itself to the point of phasing out public transportation. As we stated earlier, buses are everywhere. Just stand still and before long, one will come along to take you where you want to go.

Because public transportation is so easy, many Americans elect not to have an auto in Mexico. They find that the upkeep and insurance quickly carries them over their $600 budget. Nevertheless there are times when an auto comes in handy. You might want to show visitors the sights, or drive to the next town to do some heavy shopping and not want to lug your packages back on a bus. Car rentals are readily available and relatively inexpensive for these special occasions. We recently rented an auto for $27 a day, which included insurance and unlimited mileage. By renting a car whenever you need to make a jaunt to Acapulco or to Guadalajara, you can enjoy motoring whenever you need to without the ongoing expense of maintaining an automobile.

Other Americanos are so automobile-dependent that they can't visualize life without their car. They either bring it with them, or buy one in Mexico.

The requirements for bringing cars into Mexico are constantly being revised. We've listed some of them in Chapter Six. At one time you couldn't keep a U.S. car there for more than six months. This has been changed several times and we suggest that you get the most recent regulations just before you make your move.

If you come in on a Tourist Card good for a six-month stay, make sure that you get an auto permit that matches its duration. Otherwise you will have to drive to the border after three months to get a new auto permit.

As we also note in Chapter Six, any current driver's license from the United States or Canada is valid in Mexico. You need no other. However, you *must* have Mexican automobile insurance, which can be bought at the border and renewed most places in Mexico. Buy Mexican insurance. This is about the most important advice you'll find in this book! The law doesn't mandate that you have insurance, but common sense does. Also, bring proof of your U.S. or Canadian insurance.

We've heard several horror stories about Americans who drive without insurance in Mexico. Even in the case of a non-injury accident, the police must, by law, arrest anyone who doesn't have insurance, at least until they can prove they are financially responsible. You can't blame them for this; an American citizen would be sorely tempted to abandon his wrecked auto and return to the U.S. if the damages would be worth more than his car.

On the other hand, we've heard many heartwarming stories of insured motorists who've been given excellent treatment by their insurance agents. Typically, the agent found them a place to stay and watched over the vehicle to supervise the repairs and make sure the work was done satisfactorily.

An injury accident, however, is considered more serious, and police may hold a driver for up to three days to make sure there is no criminal fault. Usually, it's pretty clear what happened, and criminal intent rarely enters into it. Since Mexico has a no-fault insurance philosophy, you don't have to worry about getting sued by the other driver; his beef is with his insurance company, not with you.

Another tip on insurance: report any accidents *as soon as possible!* If you wait until you return to the United States to make your report, there's a good chance you've lost your claim. You must report the accident where it happens. And, if you are driving a rental car, you must report within six hours of the accident, or the insurance company won't pay! Too often, drivers of rental cars simply leave the car where it was damaged, thinking it is the rental agency's problem and that the insurance will cover it. By the time the rental agency finds it, it may have been stripped or further damaged, so it's your liability if not reported within six hours.

Buying Insurance

Insurance rates in Mexico are set by the government, so there is very little difference between companies. For the average driver who crosses the border for a three-week vacation trip, the daily rate doesn't seem like a big chip off the budget. Yet there are ways to cut down on your costs if you plan on staying six months or more. If you plan on doing your living/traveling in Baja, or on the west coast mainland as far south as Mazatlán, you may save a lot of money by joining one of the travel clubs and getting group insurance through them. (See Appendix for more insurance information.)

A typical policy should cover: collision, upset and glass breakage, with $100 deductible; fire and "total theft" (no partial theft); and wind, hail, flood and earthquake with no deductible. The foregoing insurance is often omitted on older cars to keep the cost of insurance down. Costs of repairs in Mexico are very, very low, and some people feel it's worth the gamble to go without full coverage. Myself, I don't bother with full coverage on an older vehicle. It would have to be a very serious accident to cost more to fix up an old car than the cost of an extended, full-coverage policy. While you might gamble on collision, property and bodily injury insurance are *essential*, no matter what you are driving. Only a fool would drive in Mexico without liability insurance. On the other hand, try not to *over-insure*. Since insurance awards in Mexico are usually limited to actual damages, it isn't necessary to insure more than $25,000 for property damage and $30,000 per person bodily injury.

However, although these amounts are adequate under Mexican law, there's always the possibility of having an accident involving a U.S. citizen, with subsequent litigation in U.S. courts. Some people feel better with higher liability insurance. It's up to you.

Buying an Auto in Mexico

Many residents avoid the problem of importing an auto simply by buying one in Mexico. For our money, the most practical and economical car in Mexico is the good old Volkswagen "Bug." This reliable machine is still being manufactured in Mexico by the Volkswagen people. You can buy a brand new one for about half what one costs up north for the cheapest imported iron! Used cars in Mexico are proportionally priced. With VW's so popular, you'll find mechanics all over who are expert in VW repair.

The real surprise comes when you visit a Volkswagen dealership garage. They are super-efficient places, with employees immaculately dressed in German-style uniforms. No matter what they do to your car, they won't release it until the motor is steam-cleaned, the car washed and the upholstery wiped down with vinyl cleaner. No extra charge; it's a matter of policy with most VW garages! All prices are posted, and at a fraction of what U.S. prices would be in similar garages. (This may not be true when you get closer to the border.)

In our last edition, we stated that a brand new VW engine could be put into your vehicle for a very reasonable amount. Well, this amount has increased considerably, but the real problem is that some of the Mexican VW parts do not fit the American-built VWs. American-made VWs used German parts, while Mexican VWs use Brazilian and Mexican parts. So, if you are going to buy a VW for use in Mexico, we recommend that you buy a Mexican-made model. Mexico also manufactures Datsuns, Toyotas, Fords and Chevys.

One bit of advice: don't think about buying a new VW and bringing it back to the United States. It won't pass the rigid U.S. specifications for items like smog, safety glass, etc. You'll never get it registered in the United States or Canada.

Gas Station Smarts

When considering buying a car, or bringing one into Mexico for long stays, keep in mind that vehicles which use *regular* gasoline (*Nova*) have two advantages. First, the fuel is about thirty percent cheaper than no-lead, and second, Nova is always available no matter where you go in Mexico. Sometimes, (particularly in remote, rural areas) higher octane no-lead gasoline(*Magna-sin*) is scarce. So, if you have a no-lead engine, always fill your tank before taking any long drives in the country.

Important: regular gas comes from the blue pumps, no-lead from the silver pumps and diesel from red pumps. Watch which kind goes into your car! Filling your gas tank with diesel will cause no end of trouble. Often those working around *gasolineras* know very little about autos, other than how to pump gas into your tank. Don't let anyone tell you that the red pump is gasoline!

Beware of cute little tykes who come running to start pumping gas into your car before you have a chance to think. Some of these kids have a scam where they clown around and get your eyes off the pump so you don't know how much gasoline has been put in. They then quickly set the meter back to zero, then quote you an outrageous amount and pocket the difference. In addition, if a pump isn't brought back to zero before starting, you'll pay for fuel you haven't received.

Here is a little advice, which if followed, will prevent you from ever being taken at a gas station. Before you pull into the station, make a close estimate of how many liters you will need. (There are 3.64 liters to a gallon.) Then multiply the number of liters by the price, which is standard at all stations. Round this figure off to the nearest even amount, and try to have the exact change ready. Next, always get out of your car and watch the whole proceedings carefully. Check that the pump has been turned back to zero; don't let anyone distract you from this mission. Always have a calculator in your hand—this makes them think you know what you are doing (even if you don't). Then ask for the exact amount of pesos you want to spend, rather than the number of liters. "*Cuarenta mil pesos, por favor.*" (Or write it on paper: i.e. "40,000 pesos.") This way, you only have to watch the pesos meter on the pump. If you have exact change, or ask for an even amount, you cannot be shortchanged.

When a boy wants to clean your windshield (this service is never provided by gas stations) consider that he is doing it for tips. We always say yes, even if the windshield doesn't need it, because it's probably the boy's only way to earn a few pesos, and a dime or a quarter's worth of pesos isn't going to make a difference to us. It will to the boy. If a herd of kids come around, choose one of them, and wave the rest away, or you'll have a forest of hands seeking tips. Once, a little entrepreneur (about five years old) pounded all four of our tires with a chunk of wood, then seriously announced that he had checked the air in the tires and that they seemed to be full. We gave him the customary coin plus an old tennis ball for his services. His look of delight told us that he will be pounding on tourist's tires for some time to come.

Rules of the Road

As in all countries, there are special customs and rules for driving in Mexico. You need to know these in order to understand what's going on around you on the road. These customs vary from region to region. For example, in the northern desert, where you might expect lots of high-speed driving, you find that, perhaps because of the long desert distances and the miles that wear down the life of a car, some drivers like to travel at 35 miles an hour. Maybe this accounts for the plethora of old Chevys and other vintage cars still creeping along the highways. They aren't driven fast enough to wear out.

Slow driving may be interesting, but is also very dangerous for the American who whips along at 70 miles per hour while others cruise at 30. A good rule is to drive as if there were a 35-mile an hour car around every curve, and be prepared to slow down. On the other hand, in Mexico City, where congestion can be appalling, drivers go as fast as they can. Sixty miles an hour seems perfectly reasonable to a cab driver in the capital as long as there is space between lanes to do it, after all, he is getting paid by the trip, not the mile.

This author refuses to drive in Mexico City. I try to enter early Sunday morning when traffic is lightest, park the car and take buses or taxis for the rest of my stay. Anywhere else in Mexico is a piece of cake, but Mexico City turns many a macho driver into a trembling wimp.

Turn Signals and Right-of-Way

In the United States, our system of turn signals seems self-evident. When the left signal is blinking, it means: "Be careful, I'm going to turn left!" The right side indicator is equally obvious. However, in Mexico, a blinking indicator could mean any number of things, depending on what the driver *wishes* it to mean. Generally, a left signal doesn't mean a left turn at all! It means: "It's okay to pass if you want; I don't see anyone coming, but if I do, I'll pull over to let you get by safely." Yet, sometimes, it means he is actually planning on turning left! If there's any possible left turn ahead, better wait. A right turn light usually means a right turn, but not always. Sometimes the driver is saying, "don't pass," or he may just be blinking for the hell of it. You never know. A blinking of both lights seems to say: "Look out, I'm going to do something silly, so stay clear!"

This makes sense when you consider that the vehicle in front has the right-of-way. If the guy in front decides to make a left turn, right turn, swerve into the next lane, or suddenly stop and ask directions, you have to be prepared to avoid him, while the people in back of you give you the same courtesy. Well, usually, they do.

At first, this system of right-of-way can be puzzling for the tourist, especially in heavy city traffic, with people swerving from lane to lane in front of you. What you must realize is that *you* have the right-of-way over all those behind you. Therefore, instead of worrying about *all* the cars in the road, as you must in the United States, you can concentrate on trying to outguess the car in front of you. Whatever lane changes you make are all right because those behind are watching you very carefully. You'll find that when you cut in front of someone they will obligingly drop back and give you room, instead of honking their horn and waving fists as a Boston driver might. Actually, we consider it a fairly good system, and most drivers, once used to it, find it rather easy to get around in Mexico (except in Mexico City). The smaller the town, the lighter the traffic and the slower people drive. Remember, the guy in front is always right. If you're in front, that guy is you.

One exception to this rule is when someone is passing you; then you must concede the right of way—no matter if they are passing illegally—always be prepared to help them get around you safely. Even if they are breaking the law by passing on a hill or curve, you are equally guilty if you don't drop back and let them pass.

Highways and Byways

During the oil bonanza of a few years ago, Mexico embarked upon an ambitious road-building project. The emphasis was on constructing new highways to reach areas that were previously accessible only by dirt or gravel roads. So there are miles of fine highways that go to some great places, places where you can drive all day on new roads and seldom see another vehicle. But because of a lack of funds, many other highways, the busy ones, haven't been maintained so well. There are many hazards to be aware of.

American drivers aren't used to watching out for road hazards. They take it for granted that manhole covers will be in place, that a sign will warn if a bridge is out ahead. They assume that shoulders are safe to park on in an emergency, and that farmers will keep their livestock off a busy highway. But in Mexico, the motto is "Driver Beware!"

What does this mean for the novice driver in Mexico? Simply that you must slow down and drive cautiously, just like most of the Mexican drivers. So you take an extra 20 minutes for your trip because you drive 50 miles an hour instead of 70. You'll find that you'll see more, and arrive a lot more relaxed.

The most important motoring advice we can give is *never attempt to drive the highways at night!* There are several good reasons for this. One is that livestock roam freely throughout the country. It can be somewhat distracting to be driving along at 70 miles an hour on black asphalt and suddenly come across an almost invisible black bull sleeping on the road. Cattle love to sleep on the pavement at night because it holds the daytime heat and makes a cozy place to bed down for the evening. A 1,000-pound animal can neatly remove the wheels from your car if you hit it fast enough. Even worse is clipping a burro. This cute little animal also finds the warm asphalt a great place to stand and snooze. When a driver zooms around a curve and cuffs a burro with his bumper, he finds that the animal is just the right height to flip up in the air and glide across the hood at 50 miles an hour. Burros stop looking cute when 200 pounds of bone, hide and muscle come crashing through your windshield.

Another hazard of night driving is suddenly finding the lane blocked by a line of large rocks. "What the devil are rocks doing across the road?" you may well ask. I once heard one nervous American speculate that maybe "bandidos" had placed the rocks as a roadblock. No, no. They are actually left there by truckers.

Here's what happens: truckers prefer traveling at night because it's easier to drive in the almost non-existent traffic. When a truck breaks down (a frequent occurrence) the driver pulls over to the side of the road. Since shoulders are often inadequate, he parks on the pavement. But, he doesn't want to crawl under the truck to make repairs and take a chance on another vehicle not seeing him and crashing into the back of the truck. So, he first goes back a hundred yards and places rocks, as large as he can carry, to warn other trucks and motorists. If the oncoming vehicle doesn't see the truck, at least he won't go much past the barrier, not with some 50-pound boulders tangled in the front end.

Usually, when the repairs are through, the rocks are rolled off the pavement. But not always. A related problem occurs in the mountains at night. A truck stops for some reason going up a hill. To get started again is a hassle trying to work clutch, brake and accelerator at the same time. So the driver puts a rock behind each rear wheel to prevent the truck from rolling backward. Then, with the truck resting against the rocks, it's much easier to get going. He leaves the two rocks sitting in the road, waiting for you as you round a curve. You can imagine the damage. They are easy to see in the daylight, but not so at night.

A final hazard about night driving is that some drivers routinely turn their lights off when passing on a curve to see if anyone is coming. Guess what happens when the car coming the other way also has his lights out. Also, some older cars don't have working tail lights, and some don't even have working headlights and their drivers are content to drive along simply using the moonlight for illumination.

Do you now understand why you don't want to drive at night? I have to admit that I violate my warnings from time to time, should I have a schedule to meet and driving after dark is the only way to get there. I've never had an accident, but the tension levels tell me it just isn't worth it.

The speed limit is usually 100 kilometers (about sixty miles per hour) but is posted much lower in towns. Sometimes the posted limit is ridiculously low, and you'll notice that few people observe the signs unless a cop is in sight, which is rare. Without many cops around to enforce the rules, your chances are excellent for getting away with driving 50 kilometers an hour in a 30 kilometer zone. Yet why take the chance? Drive slowly and safely in Mexico, and you'll never get into trouble.

Traffic Tickets

If you are stopped for a violation such as speeding or failing to observe a stop sign, the cop will probably hint that you can save a lot of time if you pay the fine directly to him. That way he won't have to take your driver's license and license plates to insure that you'll show up at the police station tomorrow to pay the fine.

Now, don't get upset and accuse the cop of being a crook. The system is that a traffic cop collects the fine and keeps it as part of his salary. Many of them are paid around $80 a month, so they're expected to catch speeders to earn enough money to live on. It's sort of like working on commission. Even in Mexico, a person can't feed his family very well on $80 a month!

If you've actually violated the law, you have no complaints coming; just negotiate for the fine and pay it. He's really doing you a favor by not taking your license plates. You either pay him, or you waste a day and go to the police station tomorrow and pay. The fines shouldn't be over three or four dollars. Haggling over the amount is usual, and the money should be folded and passed surreptitiously. I keep a couple of dollars worth of pesos folded behind by drivers' license, and simply hand it over when I'm caught doing something wrong. The cop usually tells me how dangerous it is to be going the wrong way on a one way street, or whatever, then apologizes for stopping me, and that's that.

What's the safeguard against cops stopping you for something you didn't do? Simple: insist on taking the ticket. That way he's wasted his time by stopping you; he gets nothing if you pay at the police station. For that reason, a cop seldom hassles motorists unless he can convince them they've broken a law. So, if you're innocent, say so and don't even discuss paying a fine. It will be an inconvenience for you, but it will make it easier on the next driver. If you're guilty, just pay up; that's the system in Mexico. Until Mexican taxpayers agree to pay police decent salaries, as we do in the United States, the system of *mordidas* will continue. You don't have to like the system, but don't try to change it single-handedly, or you may make an enemy of the cop.

Help on the Road

Don't be discouraged about driving in Mexico. If you take normal precautions and understand what is happening around you, it is perfectly safe. (This writer has driven many thousands of miles in Mexico, with only two minor accidents.) What if your car breaks down on the road? Chances are the first car along will stop to help if you are out on the highway. You'll quickly find that mechanics are everywhere: men who've spent their lives keeping their old machines running with innovative, creative repairs.

If you sit long enough you ought to see a "Green Angel" coming to the rescue! What's a Green Angel? To promote tourism and to help motorists in general, the Mexican government has a fleet of repair trucks that cruise the highways, looking for cars in trouble. These "Green Angels" (painted green, of course) patrol the major routes and try to cover each highway at least once a day and often twice a day or more. The trucks are loaded with gasoline, oil, spare parts of all descriptions, plus two trained mechanics. Usually, one of them speaks English. If you are in trouble, it is their duty to stop and make the necessary repairs. You pay the cost of parts, gasoline, and oil, but the labor is courtesy of the government.

You might want to take note of this phone number; it's the 24-hour "hot line" for the Green Angels: *5-20-0123*. You can call from anywhere in the country (assuming you have access to a telephone) and the dispatcher will get in touch with a Green Angel by radio. If you stay by the side of the road with your car hood raised, someone will surely stop, and can phone for you at the next town, or notify the police who can call the hot line.

Also, during peak tourist times, the Mexican army is utilized for tourist assistance. As you drive, you'll see olive-drab jeeps and trucks with soldiers sitting alongside the road, or patrolling the countryside. They sometimes have signs announcing: "Asistencia Turistica." While it's doubtful they could repair a car, they have radios in their jeeps and can call a mechanic or the Green Angels quite quickly. These troops are generally used more on the least-traveled routes where the Green Angels don't patrol, but can sometimes be seen on major highways.

If you drive very much in Mexico, you will from time to time come across random customs inspections out on the highway. Officials, sometimes military, sometimes civilians, stop traffic and check for contraband. Mexico is trying to protect its fledgling electronics and appliance industries and they are on the lookout for people smuggling TVs, toasters, etc., from the United States. Other items they are interested in are drugs, guns and ammunition. Please, don't have any guns or ammo unless you have the proper permits, or you can really get into trouble!

Often, a tourist misunderstands and feels threatened by these inspections. This has given rise to stories of "bandidos" or shakedowns. We've heard of people nervously thrusting money into the inspectors' hands, thinking that's what they want. This would be funny if the rumors weren't so damaging to tourism. The inspectors aren't interested in tourists other than making sure they are really tourists and not loaded down with appliances or .30 caliber ammunition. They neither want nor expect anything other than your cooperation in letting them look in your trunk or under the hood. But if you are going to force money upon them, most will gratefully accept.

One-Way Streets

Perhaps a word or two about a few other traffic customs are in order here. The system of one-way streets puzzles some American drivers. Since the streets in most older towns were designed for horse traffic, they are often quite narrow and, by necessity, one-way. The direction is indicated *not* by a large sign on the street corner as you find back in Omaha, but by small arrows high up on the corners of the buildings. These signs also control traffic in a unique and common-sense manner. The arrows come in three colors: red, green, and black. If the arrow you can see on the building is green, that means you are on a major street and have the right-of-way over any car coming along the cross street. A red arrow means you must yield. Black means it's first-come first-served, but always remember that the first one there has the right-of-way. Actually, this works rather well and keeps traffic flowing along the narrow streets with a minimum of congestion or accidents. Of course, just because you have a green arrow doesn't necessarily mean you can charge ahead with confidence: always slow down and look both ways; you might run into a tourist who doesn't know the system.

Please don't let any of these cautions frighten you. Driving is an excellent way of seeing the country. You can amble along at your own pace and stop where you like to explore villages or have a picnic on a country lane. The pace of driving is slow in Mexico, but it matches the pace of living in the country. Above all, don't worry about getting off the road and into remote areas. Just as in the United States and Canada, the more rural the countryside, the more simple and friendly the people. Farmers and other Mexican villagers are every bit as hospitable as farmers in Tennessee or Iowa, maybe more so.

CHAPTER ELEVEN

Where Americans Live

Forty years ago, when this writer lived in Mexico (a mere teenager then), the vast majority of the North American residents lived in Mexico City. We called ourselves the *British-American colony* in those days, about 100,000 strong. Mexico City was about the size of today's Milwaukee. Smog was a word applied mostly to places like Los Angeles, and the skies were as blue as Minnesota's in springtime. On most days you could see the twin volcanoes of *Popo* and *Ixti* off in the distance, snow-covered and glistening in the sunlight. That is, unless some fluffy white clouds happened to be lazing along to obstruct your view.

Servants worked six and a half days a week for $10 a month, and a gallon of Bacardi rum cost about a dollar. Taxi drivers painted teeth on the hoods of their machines and charged forty cents to take you on a hair-raising ride anywhere in the city. Mexico City was *the* place to live. There were more Cadillac dealers than Chevrolet dealers. The rich grew richer by the day, so it seemed, and gringos with dollars lived as well as the richest of the rich. They owned huge, luxurious homes in places like *Las Lomas* and *El Pedregal*. Twenty thousand dollars would buy a mansion. If they rented, $100 a month was considered extravagant.

In those days, Acapulco was an unspoiled little town with empty beaches and a sprinkling of jet set celebrities who tried to keep the place their special secret. But Americans in Mexico City considered it *their* private discovery! For them, Acapulco was to be enjoyed by chauffeured limousine. Why not? A limousine and reliable driver (round-trip to Acapulco) cost little more than taking a taxi from downtown Chicago to the airport. The old Acapulco road was curvy and picturesque, and best handled by an experienced chauffeur.

In short, Mexico City of 40 years ago was a paradise for people with dollars at their disposal. A person with as little as $100 a month income could do quite well. Hundreds of veterans who attended Mexico City College on the "GI Bill" reported that they had a great time on far less than $100 a month. (Remember the "52-20" club?)

Needless to say, things have changed over the years! But, do you know of *anyplace* where time hasn't marched on?

Today, with its swollen population of 15 to 20 million (no one knows how many), Mexico City suffers from Los Angeles-style smog and Paris-style traffic jams. You can no longer see Popo or Ixti except on rare, unusually clear days. Taxi drivers no longer paint crocodile teeth on their hoods, but still take you on unforgettable rides about town for just a little money. Servants draw at least $100 a month, and expect to have all day Sunday off instead of just Sunday afternoons as it used to be. Of course, rental limousines are a thing of the past, but who needs them with a super-highway connecting Mexico City and Acapulco?

The biggest difference over the years in Mexico is that today proportionally fewer North Americans live in Mexico City than in other parts of the country. Instead of living in the city and escaping to their "weekend retreats" in places like Cuernavaca, Tequisquiapan or San Miguel de Allende, Americans have moved away from the hustle and bustle of the city and made the "weekend retreats" their permanent homes. This way, they can visit the excitement of Mexico City whenever boredom threatens.

This is not to say that living in the city can't be an enjoyable, satisfying experience. A large number of North Americans still prefer Mexico City, insisting that it is the best place to live. Certain people *need* the stimulation of a big city. They demand a multitude of cultural activities, fine restaurants and theaters, and the like. These people cannot conceive of living away from the conveniences of a metropolis. These are the same people you find happily living in Manhattan or downtown San Francisco.

If you are one of those who must live in a city, then Mexico City could be the answer to your retirement location. Excellent restaurants are legion, museums are fantastic, ballet and theater are always available. Once we bought tickets to see the opera *Aida* at the Bellas Artes opera house for less than $4. Two weeks earlier the same troupe was performing the same show in New York for over $50 a seat. (Once you've seen opera at Bellas Artes, other theaters seem dreary in comparison.)

But, you don't have to live in Mexico City to enjoy its attractions. No matter where you live in the country, Mexico is always available at the cost of a bus or train ride. Incidentally, when residents talk about visiting "Mexico" they almost always mean "Mexico City," just as we mean "New York City" when we say "New York."

Birds of a Feather

An interesting thing about North Americans who live in foreign countries is the way they tend to cluster together. Rarely will you find a single person or a family living in a town or a neighborhood all by themselves. It's as if they cannot exist without a social circle of English-speaking friends, if not neighbors, and they seem to be continually looking to expand their network of friends. This is a big advantage for newcomers because once they locate an enclave of fellow expatriates, they have instant friends and companions. So, while you are trying on various Mexican locations for size, you are advised to seek out the "gringo" communities and accept help and advice from your neighbors. Therefore, let's investigate where the North Americans live in Mexico and why.

Choose your Climate

There are four major categories of retirement communities, which correspond to Mexico's four climate zones. We find the *tierra caliente*, the tropical parts of Mexico; the *tierra templada*, the higher altitudes where the climate is temperate, rather like Los Angeles; the *tierra fría*, which is the high country where the days are pleasant and the nights briskly cool; and finally, *el desierto* or desert country.

Finding the climate that is best for you is easy in Mexico. There are hundreds of places that could match your requirements, but if you are like most North Americans, you will consider social life with other English-speaking people a high priority. Let's take a look at these climatic zones and which towns attract the most North Americans residents.

Living in the Tropics

An imaginary line known as the *tropic of Cancer* crosses Mexico just north of Mazatlán on the west coast, and north of Tampico on the Gulf of Mexico side. The tropic of Cancer officially marks the northern boundary of the "tropics." Some rather dramatic changes in scenery and climate occur as you cross this line, particularly on Mexico's west coast. North of it, the rainfall pattern seems to be dry summers and wet winters, but south, the rain falls in the summer time, while winters are dry. To the north, you'll find lots of deserts and dry-farming areas, but to the south, everything looks greener, and vegetation is lush, just as you would expect from the tropics.

This is where the so-called *Costa de Oro* begins, running from Mazatlán south to Puerto Angel. A large number of North Americans choose to vacation, winter and retire here. Yes, this is in the tropics, but the temperatures are quite manageable. The reason the coastal towns don't swelter in the summer is because of the nearby ocean's stabilizing influence, plus the fact that with summer being the rainy season, there is often a light cloud cover that diminishes the sun's glare.

Acapulco, the Jet Set Pride

The first place on the Pacific coast to be developed as a resort, and eventually a retirement mecca was Acapulco. A magical tropical jewel, Acapulco sits on a lovely bay that is lined with some of the prettiest beaches in the world. Shaded by graceful palm trees and blessed with mild tropical breezes, Acapulco quickly became a hangout for the Hollywood crowd, the beautiful people and the jet setters.

For the North Americans living in Mexico City, it was almost unthinkable not to own or lease a weekend place in Acapulco. However, over the years, population pressures and competition from other resorts along the coast have stolen some of the glamorous shine away from Acapulco. It's no longer a small town; there may be as many as a million people living there today. But the beaches and natural beauty remain the same as in the pristine days of the 1940s and 1950s. The surf still sparkles in the tropical sunlight and the night air is as balmy and tropical as ever. Some things never change, thank goodness.

Many people automatically cross out Acapulco as a retirement possibility. They assume this city would naturally be super-expensive. But they are wrong. As we point out later in the book, places like Acapulco can be among the best bargains of all. Real estate and rentals can be found about as cheaply as anywhere in the republic! We'll discuss this later.

Puerto Vallarta, another of the glamorous beach towns, certainly attracts its share of American residents. Entering the resort marathon much later than Acapulco, P.V. (as residents refer to it) made lightning strides forward, fast becoming one of the major vacation meccas.

Fortunately, the growth isn't ruining the town itself. Because Puerto Vallarta strings along the beach, with steep hills just a few blocks away from the ocean, the growth has to take place laterally, up and down the beach, rather than going inland. For this reason, the town center manages to maintain a village-like atmosphere despite the growth.

Is it expensive? Of course, it can be. But we received a letter from a reader the other day who reports that he found a beautiful apartment up on a hillside, with a view of the town and the ocean for $155 a month.

All along the coast, from Boca de Tomatlán on up to San Blas to the north, you'll find beach villages where housing is inexpensive and English-speaking residents find their retirement havens. These are for tropic-lovers who want to get away from the hustle and bustle of tourist centers.

A bit farther north, and even closer to the border, is Mazatlán, where the foreign population grows daily. Perhaps a bit touristy, Mazatlán nevertheless has a growing retirement community.

Zihuatanejo, Barra de Navidad, Puerto Escondido, and other towns along the south coast also are attracting their share of tourists and retirees because of the combination of warm weather, gorgeous beaches and small-town atmosphere.

Too often we equate the tropics with ungodly heat during the summers. This all depends upon your point of view. For example,

Acapulco summers aren't as hot as those in Miami, Florida. June highs in Miami, for example average 88 degrees, yet only 84 degrees in Acapulco. Mazatlán highs average 81 degrees compared to 101 in Phoenix for June. Yet, tourism is way off during the summer months in tropical areas!

Gulf Coast

On the east coast of Mexico, there are some exceptionally lovely places, but relatively few Americans settle there because of the hot, humid summers. The winters, on the other hand, are delightful times to visit the Gulf Coast, because it is warm and green. Farther south, on the Yucatán peninsula, there are more Americans living year round, but mostly in the resort areas on the Caribbean coast in spots such as Cancún. Some delightful towns, however, have no foreign communities simply because of the harsh summers. If you like hot weather (as do the authors) you could find some great bargains on the east coast/Yucatán areas and have the challenging opportunity of making your way in a totally Spanish-Indian culture. Alternatively, you might elect to spend your winters there and the summers in the highlands or on the Pacific Coast.

Snowbirds in Paradise

The Pacific's Gold Coast and the Caribbean beach areas draw a lot of "snowbirds" who come just for the winter. They find a warm place to light until the ice and snow up north goes away. When spring makes the U.S. more inviting they disappear, and before long are replaced by a wave of "academics" who work at school or other jobs in the winter and are free in the summer. To those accustomed to hot and humid U.S. summers, even the Gulf Coast summers are okay.

But for those seeking perfect weather, the higher altitudes of the *tierra templada* makes living even easier. The point is, some places have an exceptionally fluid population, so it's new neighbors every few months. Other places are more permanent.

Temperatures south of the tropic of Cancer are pretty much governed by the altitude. Once above 3,000 feet, you find yourself in a temperate zone. Here the climate is steady, with pleasant temperatures year-round. The temperate areas can be divided into two general categories: between 3,000 and 4,500 feet, and between 4,500 and 7,000 (above which the colder *tierra fría* zone takes over).

The difference between these zones is that the higher elevations have slightly cooler summers, and winters can sometimes be chilly enough to wear a sweater every evening, and occasionally even during the day. From time to time you catch a chilly wind—the *nortenos* blowing down from Canada—which can send the temperatures into the mid-forties for a day or two. In these places you will usually find fireplaces in the hotel rooms and rental apartments, and a cheery fire on a brisk evening feels great. This nippy season is short-lived and usually by mid-day you'll be in your shirt sleeves.

Oaxaca, Guadalajara, Cuernavaca, San Miguel de Allende and Morelia are examples of the temperate climates that attract foreign residents. Guadalajara has a huge English-speaking community, as does nearby Lake Chapala with its small towns strung out along the lake shore. There are many active social organizations in the Guadalajara area, and newcomers should quickly find a network of friends. The climate is one of the best in Mexico. The year-round temperature averages there are generally as follows: January: High - 75; Low - 48; Mean - 61. April: High - 89; Low - 57; Mean - 73. July: High - 85; Low - 60; Mean - 72. October: High - 82; Low - 58; Mean - 70. This translates into cool nights, particularly in winter, and comfortably warm days most of the year. The only really hot days usually come in May and June and even then the temperature seldom gets above the low nineties. These are pretty much the temperatures you can expect throughout the temperate zone.

Higher Altitudes

Once you are much over 7,000 feet, the air becomes brisk and cool, particularly in the evenings. Actually, some popular places such as San Miguel de Allende are on the verge of being in the *tierra fría*. You commonly find fireplaces in the homes and see woodcutters driving burros through town with firewood for sale. The air in the high altitudes is thin and has little humidity (a great cure for some allergies). People who enjoy climates like San Francisco and Seattle feel at home in the temperatures of the tierra fría and those who enjoy mile-high Denver (without the snow) will not be bothered by the altitude.

Research by the National Institute of Cardiology in Mexico City shows that elevations under 10,000 feet won't affect a healthy heart, but if you have any heart problems to begin with, the thin air could keep you from adapting as quickly. Consult your physician before deciding to live at an altitude over 5,000 or 6,000 feet.

When you go above 8,000 feet, you run into some rather cold winters and some very cool evenings. In Mexico, few Americans choose to live that high.

Living in the Desert

If you like desert, you'll find much of Mexico to like. All of Baja and most of the northern states in the country are pure desert. People who enjoy Palm Springs or Phoenix retirement will find the Mexican desert cities and towns have some of the same benefits. Another plus for desert retirement is that it is closer to the United States. Someone living in Ensenada, for example, has only about a six-hour drive to Los Angeles on excellent highways. If a retiree gets lonesome for a "culture fix," it can be easily managed. On the other hand, if you choose to live in Cancún, driving north to visit the grandkids wouldn't be a spur of the moment kind of trip.

There are many inexpensive places to live in the desert and, as you might imagine, land there is very cheap. Sometimes the water in desert towns is of a better quality than in other places in Mexico, since it comes from deeper wells. The drawbacks of desert living are the same in Mexico as in Arizona. It can be very hot in the summer, and occasionally freezing in the winter. Food prices and wages in the north of Mexico are higher than in the south, mostly because of the nearness to the U.S. border. But they are balanced by lower housing costs. Compared to prices in similar communities north of the border, it is still a bargain. You can live within a $600 a month budget as easily here as anywhere else in Mexico. Try that in Arizona!

The towns in the desert country tend to be small, clean and unsophisticated. Few people have servants, partly because labor costs are higher and partly because you don't need a gardener to take care of a cactus garden. Air conditioning is popular, just as it is on the other side of the border, and many houses are built of the natural air conditioning material—adobe. With two-foot thick walls, an adobe house keeps cool in the summer and warm in the winter.

Choosing your Neighbors

With so many climates to select from, few people will have trouble finding something they like. However, it might be a mistake to choose a location on the basis of climate alone. You must make a detailed analysis of the needs of each individual in your family and determine how they would be met by the community you are considering.

If your town or village is so far from an urban center that it is impractical to visit a supermarket or hardware store from time to time, will you be able to put up with it? Often the selection of foods will be limited. In some villages, you purchase meat on the basis of what animal was just butchered. This week you may be able to buy all the beef you want, but no pork. Next week it will be the opposite. Some smaller towns have one movie house, and it may only operate on weekends. Is there anyone in your family who could survive on a diet of Mexican westerns?

If you have difficulty learning the language, you could find yourself feeling lonely if there aren't at least a few English-speaking neighbors around. Some people won't mind that. A few may actually find it an advantage, since it will force them to learn Spanish faster. We know Americans in Mexico who go out of their way to avoid speaking English, and who will walk across the street to avoid meeting a tourist. Certainly, people like this will have a much wider latitude than most in the choice of retirement places.

But for most of us, living in communities where there are few English-speaking neighbors can pose a serious problem. It is the rare American of retirement age who will not seek out the company of his compatriots, even if he enjoys cordial relationships with his Mexican neighbors. Unfortunately, not *all* gringos who decide to reside in Mexico are interesting, fascinating people. Frankly, just as there are bores in your home town in the United States, there are also bores who also choose to live in Mexico. So, if your friendships are to involve any selectivity, there must be an adequate number of Americans around. When the number falls below a certain level, you may find yourself spending evening after evening with people with whom you have nothing in common but language.

The lack of a large English-speaking community leaves many attractive places in Mexico bargain spots for those who don't need continual English social reinforcement. We encourage our readers to develop their Spanish skills and then examine themselves and decide whether they could live somewhere outside of the English-speaking enclaves. Our experience, however, is that most people do best in a community where there are dual opportunities to socialize. The ideal is an active English-speaking community to allay your homesickness and receptive Spanish-speaking neighbors, among whom you can develop another circle of friends.

CHAPTER TWELVE

Guadalajara/Lake Chapala

N o part of Mexico attracts more North American retirees than Guadalajara and the nearby little towns of Lake Chapala and Ajijic. Current estimates of its U.S. and Canadian expatriate population range between 25,000 and 30,000. There are more than 80 religious, civic, philanthropic, social and special-interest organizations serving this huge and diverse collection of individuals who have found Mexico's second city irresistible. Clearly, part of the appeal for some people is that there are so many other North Americans there, making for a very easy transition into living in a foreign country. There are a number of other equally valid reasons, however, including the area's prime climate, cultural riches and attractive setting. It is also convenient to get to and from the U.S., and its major airport makes it a transportation hub for much of the country. Prices here, although fairly typical for Mexico as a whole, are significantly lower than in Mexico City and somewhat lower, at least for housing, than in many of Mexico's other popular retirement meccas.

What Makes it Special

Guadalajara is a governmental hub, with local processing of immigration papers. Its two medical schools, excellent hospitals, 24-hour emergency pharmacies, and other medical care services are also factors. The climate, American residents brag, is the finest in the world. There is an average of one cloudy day per month and the average temperature ranges from 61 in January to 77 in May, so perhaps there is something to their claim (which is also

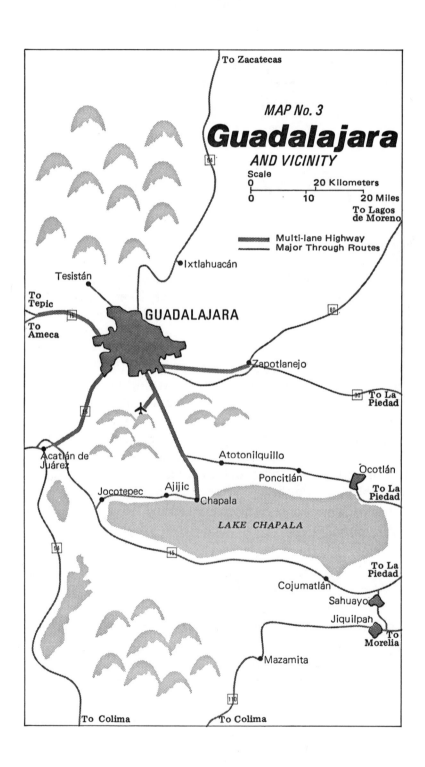

made by other Mexican cities). One thing Guadalajara undeniably has is proximity to Pacific beach resorts (about 150 miles), where one can escape those "frigid" 61-degree temperatures in January.

The center of much retiree life in Guadalajara is the American Society of Jalisco known to its several thousand members as "AmSoc." Its attractive headquarters building in the pleasant Chapalita section of Guadalajara is a hive of activity with bridge games, meetings to plan the members frequent (and very economical) outings all over Mexico, community service projects and just plain companionship spilling out of the meeting rooms and library into the lobby and dining area. The society offers low-cost medical insurance to its members and in other ways too numerous to count helps them to feel secure and at home in their adopted community. Unless you are quite familiar with Mexico and have already picked out another community to live in, Guadalajara is probably the place to start your search for the ideal retirement site. It may or may not end up as the place you decide to live in, but given its convenient location and good transportation to most parts of Mexico and the unequalled support it gives to newcomers, going there first can make the process easier and less intimidating. We have done our best to make this book comprehensive, but we know from our experience with the first edition that it is impossible to answer all the questions people will have and, what is more important, to convey the full savor of retirement life in Mexico. Guadalajara is full of people who are generous with their time and derive satisfaction from helping other retirees to learn the ropes. Most of them are so happy in Guadalajara that they will give short shrift to the other retirement sites around the country, but you can make up your own mind about that.

One reason that we would recommend Guadalajara as an excellent place to start your quest for a place to live in Mexico is the help offered by two American couples living there to new and prospective residents. Len and Nellie Friedman (through the American-Canadian Club) and Fran and Judy Furton (through Retiring in Guadalajara) are wonderful sources of information on just about everything you might want to know about getting comfortably settled in that part of Mexico. Their names, addresses and telephone numbers are in the section on "Resources."

There's Always Something Doing

One of the reasons for Guadalajara's appeal is the plethora of recreational and cultural activities available there. There are at least four golf courses, many tennis courts and swimming pools for the athletically inclined, plenty of movie theaters with films in English, frequent concerts and, with the great number of social organizations serving the retiree population, no end of parties, trips and other organized activities. There are at least two libraries with books in English and many bookstores and newsstands with U.S. publications. Cable and satellite television have revolutionized home entertainment and videotapes of American films seem to circulate freely in the retiree community.

Most American cities of the same size or even larger might envy Guadalajara its cultural richness and diversity. There is hardly a day in the week when there isn't a concert, a new art exhibition or some other event at the Institute Cultural Cabañas, the Degollado Theater or one of the city's many other museums and concert halls. A typical weekly issue of the Colony Reporter lists twenty or more such activities. The fare is thoroughly international and, like everything else in Guadalajara, the price is right.

Museums

Much of Guadalajara's cultural life is centered in the city's numerous museums. Perhaps the best known was made from the studio of Clemente Orozco after the artist's death; clearly the residents of Guadalajara are proud of this famous native son, whose murals embellish many public places. In addition, many other museums display the work of great artists of Mexico and the world. It is not without reason that Guadalajara has been described as "Mexico's Florence."

Shopping

Shopping isn't the authors' favorite leisure activity, but we can't deny that it seems to be a popular one in Guadalajara. Every time we turn around, there seems to be a new and fancier shopping mall somewhere in the city or its environs. They are much too similar to those in the U.S. for our taste, but the prices are lower (which isn't to say you can't go through a bundle of money in an afternoon). We doubt that anyone has ever counted the restaurants in Guadalajara, but we have no doubt that, if you went to a different one every night, you'd have your work cut out for you for several years, and before you reached the end, you'd have to start over so that you could try all the new ones that had opened while you were at it.

If all of that sounds exhausting, there's no reason why you can't do as we do and spend a lot of time sitting in one of the many beautiful parks and plazas scattered around the city enjoying the sunshine, the sights, sounds and, yes, the smells of Mexico. One of our favorite little parks is decorated with the busts of Mexicans whose heroic stature was earned in such unmilitary pursuits as poetry, philanthropy, education and music.

Churches and Synagogues:

Like every city and town in predominantly Catholic Mexico, Guadalajara is dotted with churches, most of them Roman Catholic. Mexico, however, for more than a century has enjoyed freedom of religion and many denominations are also represented here. The following list of some religious groups and the times of their services was compiled by Len Friedman who, as mentioned elsewhere in this chapter, is a great source of help to Guadalajara newcomers.

CHURCH	LOCATION	SERVICES AT	
Baptist	Colomos 218	Sun.	9:45 a.m.
Catholic	Tepayac & Zumarraga	Sun.	11:30 a.m.
Episcopal	Aztecas & Chichimecas	Sun.	8:45 a.m.
Jewish	Arias 651	Fri.	8:30 p.m.
(Beth Shalom)		Sat.	8:30 a.m.
Lutheran	1084 Av Los Pinos	Sun.	10::20 a.m.
Unitarian Fellowship		Phone	47-99-24.

Lake Chapala & Ajijic

A short drive from Guadalajara brings you to the shores of Lake Chapala and the town of the same name. Together with the nearby villages of Chula Vista, Jocotepec and Ajijic, this is perhaps the closest you come in Mexico to a North American enclave. The amenities are numerous—golf courses, good restaurants and a social life that may at times seem more than enough of a good thing. The area has been the subject of several recent books, videotapes and magazine articles. *Time* wrote: "Americans who settle near Lake Chapala find the sweet life." Prices, particularly for real estate, tend to reflect this popularity, yet we have met residents who claim that comfortable living is still possible at the $600 a month level. Perhaps one reason is that, for a while, building on speculation became so rampant as to provide a buyers' market for housing. Satellite antennas dot the horizon, supplementing the videotapes and cable television services. Clearly the links to the U.S. are numerous and strong.

The water in the lake is low, making it more of a scenic than recreational attraction at this time, but programs are afoot that promise to increase both its level and its purity. In 1990 and 1991 nature pitched in with record rainfalls. As a result, the water now extends seven feet further up the shore. Optimists believe that Lake Chapala is on its way back; pessimists still have their doubts.

Ajijic, once the stronghold of both Mexican and foreign artists, is now a fashionable residential community filled with upscale restaurants and boutiques. It has been described as "laid-back but not boring." We have heard of rental units at $250 per month, but this sounds a little low to us and, if Ajijic interests you, we suggest you check in person.

CHAPTER THIRTEEN

Colonial Cities

San Miguel de Allende

When we returned recently to San Miguel de Allende we were pleased to see that it was still a delightful place for retirement. We had been concerned that our book might have persuaded more North Americans to move there than it could comfortably absorb. We did hear of many who were inspired by our book to go there, but we did not feel that there were enough to change the character of this town which continues to enjoy a healthy mix of foreign and Mexican residents (something like 2,500 of the former in a community of somehere around 50,000 of the latter).

We were also worried that the relentless march of "modernization" might have destroyed San Miguel's colonial charm. That fear, too, proved to be unfounded. We did find the town somewhat more crowded, particularly during the summer months when "snowbirds" stream in from Texas and other nearby states. There are a number of new restaurants and shops to choose from—we thought there were enough already. We found as well that a few of the fanciest establishments had raised their prices, perhaps realizing that tourists, their principal clientele, neither know nor care what they should be paying. Most of all there is a feeling of greater prosperity. Perhaps, in the long run, that will make this unique place less affordable, but for now, at least, it has spoiled nothing and is good for the people of San Miguel and that, after all, is what is most important.

Other important new additions include a well-equipped modern hospital operated by a private nonprofit association. Its staff includes six specialists and one general practitioner. Less

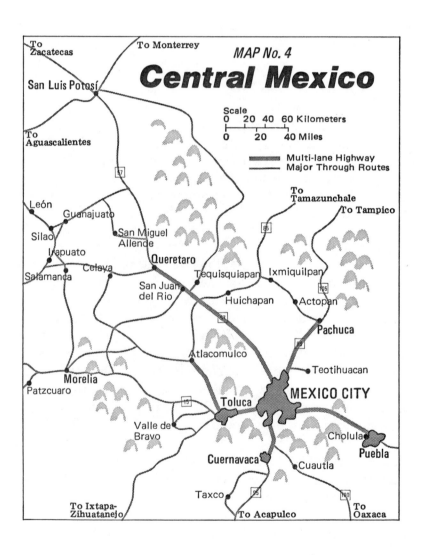

MAP No. 4
Central Mexico

Scale
0   20   40   60 Kilometers
0   20   40 Miles

▬▬▬ Multi-lane Highway
——— Major Through Routes

To Zacatecas

To Monterrey

San Luis Potosí

To Aguascalientes

León

Guanajuato

Silao

Irapuato

Salamanca

Celaya

San Miguel Allende

Querétaro

San Juan del Rio

Tequisquiapan

Huichapan

To Tamazunchale

To Tampico

Ixmiquilpan

Actopan

Pachuca

Atlacomulco

Morelia

Patzcuaro

Teotihuacan

Toluca

MEXICO CITY

Valle de Bravo

Cholula

Puebla

Cuernavaca

Cuautla

Taxco

To Ixtapa-Zihuatanejo

To Acapulco

To Oaxaca

vital, perhaps, but still a big plus is the new bus terminal. We heard of one couple who looked out the bus window at the old depot and decided to travel on. If they had stayed, they might have enjoyed the chamber music festival that has become an annual event.

Home of the Arts

There are few places in Mexico where North Americans have been as happy as in San Miguel de Allende. A colonial city just under four hours' drive or bus ride from Mexico City, it draws both visitors and residents from all over the world. What many of them share is an interest in the arts. They are attracted both by the handsomeness of the town and its natural setting, and by its several excellent art schools.

The 6,300-foot altitude produces a climate that is comfortable year-round, if you don't mind winter evenings chilly enough for a wood fire and summer afternoons warm enough to make swimming pool owners especially popular. San Miguel owes much of its attractiveness to three events in its history. The first was the depletion of the silver mines in Guanajuato, which rendered San Miguel obsolete as a way station en route to Mexico City and left it a backwater. Its fine colonial architecture was not demolished, consequently, to make way for the progress that afflicted many other Mexican towns.

The second was the arrival in 1938 of an American, Sterling Dickinson, who founded the art school that became the world-renowned Instituto Allende, which continues to draw outstanding artists and craftspeople from all over Mexico, the United States, Europe and Asia. A second school, affiliated with Bellas Artes, Mexico City's Palace of Fine Arts, also welcomes foreign students, but it places more emphasis on the education of younger local artists. In addition to these larger institutions, there are several smaller schools and artists' studios offering training in everything from painting and photography to weaving, stained glass, music and dance.

The third event contributing to San Miguel's unique flavor was the promulgation by the Mexican Government of a law designating the entire town as a national monument. Any development or construction that would change San Miguel's character or appearance must have express permission. Some grumble about the narrow streets, paved with what must be the world's sharpest and most irregular cobblestones. These same people lament the government's stubborn refusal to allow the erection of gleaming aluminum and glass facades on the homes and shops facing onto the streets. But Los Angeles, Houston and parts of Mexico City are always there to welcome anyone who cannot do without these symbols of progress. About one out of every 20 residents of San Miguel is an American or other foreigner. That ratio is sufficient to support an active English-speaking social and cultural life, but not large enough to make San Miguel a little bit of the U.S. in Mexico. There is no American enclave where foreigners are concentrated or huddled, and when North Americans there say that what they like best about Mexico is the people, they mean their Mexican neighbors, not just servants and shopkeepers, as well as their compatriots.

Recreational Opportunities

Particularly for a town of its size, San Miguel has remarkably diverse opportunities for recreation, ranging from golf, tennis and riding, to classes in yoga and dance, lecture series, amateur string quartets, bird watching with the Audubon Society, a duplicate bridge club, amateur theatrical groups, an American Legion post and a garden club.

Spanish is taught at the Instituto Allende, the Academia Hispano Americana and the smaller and more informal Inter/Idiomas at Mesones 15. Depending on the school, these programs range from a couple of hours a day to more than forty hours a week. There are students of all ages and, among other benefits, classes, whether in language or the arts, provide excellent opportunities for meeting people.

If the concerts, dance and theater in San Miguel and at nearby Guanajuato do not satisfy your cravings for culture, Mexico City is three and a half hours away by auto or bus, and a little more by train. Some residents wish that it were a little closer, forgetting that the distance is just about right to save San Miguel from being overrun by day trippers and other tourists (especially because there is no airport in the town or nearby).

Within a ten- or-fifteen minute drive (about $3.00 by taxi) there are several hot spring resorts open to the public where you can swim or just soak contentedly in the naturally heated water. We are not aware of any claims of curative powers, but we can testify to their calming effect on the spirit.

Good Restaurants

Because San Miguel is a magnet for North Americans and other foreigners, it is amply endowed with good restaurants with cuisines and ambiance that range from vegetarian health to continental elegance. Italian, French, Argentinean and Spanish food are all represented, as is even the hamburger, but we are happy to report that the golden arches have not yet appeared. Specialty food stores feature items as exotic as Dutch and Danish cheeses, German sausages, Arab pita bread and the international bagel. Although these delicacies may not be as economical as tortillas and frijoles, they are quite reasonable by U.S. standards.

San Miguel has so many supermarkets, drugstores, meat and vegetable markets, as well as a large indoor municipal market with its surrounding outdoor stalls, that each North American resident you consult is likely to give different advice about which is the most reliable and most economical. Actually, quality, selections and prices tend to be similar. When you have been in San Miguel a while and acquire Mexican friends, they can tell you the best places to buy such national specialties as *carnitas, chicharones* and *molé.*

A Most Unusual Library

San Miguel's unique public library (Biblioteca) serves a wide variety of functions. Its outstanding collection of English-language books, including many current best sellers, has recently been supplemented by an ample selection of classical and popular music on tape. Cassettes and books can be borrowed free after payment of a nominal membership fee. (We're not sure whether the library has videotapes yet, but they are available elsewhere in town.) Many small or middle-sized towns in the U.S. do not have these literary or musical resources. The library is in a restored colonial mansion whose handsome inner court serves not only as a pleasant spot to sit and read, but also as a place to meet friends.

Concerts and lectures are often given there in the evening. Once a week, Conversaciones con Amigos gathers there to provide all interested English speakers learning Spanish and Spanish speakers learning English a chance to practice with each other. Another weekly meeting is held in the courtyard of one of the town's several language schools.

In addition to the solace and stimulation the library provides to North Americans, it is also the base for an ambitious program of reading instruction and academic scholarships for under-privileged local children.

The Biblioteca and its philanthropic activities are supported financially by weekly House and Garden Tours that allow both tourists and curious residents to see how the most affluent live. Helping with these tours is one of the many ways that retirees in San Miguel can become involved in repaying the community's hospitality. Those we questioned stressed the number and variety of opportunities for public service, such as helping with the school for the handicapped, working with the local humane society, contributing to Atención, the weekly English language newspaper, and participating in the cooperative burial society. Work on behalf of the community and its demonstration of genuine concern for the people of San Miguel is one of the reasons for the excellent relationships most North Americans there enjoy with their Mexican neighbors.

Housing, Food and Transportation

Because San Miguel attracts the wealthy as well as the talented from all over the world, it is entirely possible to find a house that sells for $500,000 or rents for $2,000 a month. For-tunately for the rest of us, however, residents report that you can still find two-bedroom apartments with rents beginning at about $175 unfurnished. Two hundred dollars a month is a good rental to figure on for a conveniently located and attractively furnished apartment. A house is likely to rent for a little more, perhaps $300.

The monthly salary of a maid who works eight hours a day, six days a week, is uniformly reported at between $85 and $120 a month. Gardeners (who often serve as general handymen) are paid about 75 cents an hour. Few couples report spending more than $150 a month for all their meals including those in restaurants, some of which can only be described as posh. It is easy to spend $20 for a meal in the town's most luxurious eating places, but $9 is more typical for a charming, moderate restaurant, and there are plenty of places you would not hesitate to eat in where a full meal can be under $4. Much entertainment and recreation is free, and a bus trip to Mexico City, more than 160 miles away, costs about three dollars. San Miguel, therefore, easily qualifies as a town where a comfortable life is possible within the $600 a month figure of our subtitle. It is odd that it is considered one of Mexico's more expensive locations, outside of the seaside vacation playgrounds.

Several retirees in other Mexican communities have made the point that, if you have no interest in community service, writing, painting, sculpture, weaving or photography, and are not sufficiently affluent to be considered a patron of the arts, you could feel a little out of place in San Miguel. They may be right, but this town does have so much to offer that you might want to see for yourself.

Guanajuato

Many people consider Guanajuato Mexico's most beautiful and romantic town. Certainly its architectural splendor, physical setting and pervasively European look and feel place it in the running for that title. Its location on the slopes of a canyon makes for narrow streets and numerous stairways. Rather than a single central plaza or *zócalo*, like most Mexican towns, it has a number of small parks, each with its own special character.

The University of Guanajuato, with a 250-year history and a modern campus, is considered one of Mexico's best. The Juarez Theater displays nineteenth-century opulence inside and out, but annually plays host to the Cervantes Festival which showcases the international cultural treasures of the twentieth century.

For reasons we do not fully understand, Guanajuato, unlike nearby San Miguel de Allende, does not have many foreign retirees. You hear little or no English in its streets and shops. Perhaps that will change if the number of foreigners in San Miguel continues to grow and people who want a more Mexican setting begin to look elsewhere.

Taxco

Like San Miguel de Allende, Taxco owes much of its current fame and popularity with foreigners to an American. In the case of this colonial gem nestled in the mountains three and a half hours southwest of Mexico City, it was William Spratling, an Alabama-born architect and college professor. He came to Taxco in 1929 and, by 1931, had started the process of resurrecting its long dormant silver industry. In the eighteenth century, its wealth was based on the silver mines that had been worked since the time of Cortés. Today it is based on the almost two hundred shops or "one man factories" where silver is hand crafted into jewelry and flatware. Many of the best silversmiths began as Spratling's apprentices, and many of the well-known Americans who have homes there were his friends.

Towns that attract the wealthy of all nations as shoppers and as visitors won't have Mexico's biggest bargains. Taxco, however, is still surprisingly affordable. It's a bit less crowded and the pace of living less frenetic than in its neighbor, Cuernavaca, and though further from Mexico City, it is closer to the Pacific. We feel that anyone seriously considering settling in Cuernavaca should also look at Taxco.

Morelia

Ask a Mexican which is his country's most beautiful state and, unless pride in his birthplace triumphs over objectivity, he or she is likely to answer Michoacán. The green, rolling landscape reminds the traveler alternatively of New England's Berkshire Hills or of a painting of peaceful rural China. Michoacán stretches from the Pacific coast almost to Mexico City. Near its northeastern corner is the capital, Morelia.

The city's colonial flavor has been maintained by ordinances that strictly control the styles of new construction. Its cathedral is one of the country's most imposing, its university ancient and excellent. Morelia supports an active cultural life: music, drama, and dance thrive there as do the visual arts. A very recent addition to this scene is the spectacular Palacio del Arte which boasts 5,000 seats and is featuring internationally famous artists. Despite all these attractions, Morelia has been slow to catch on as a retirement site. Perhaps the relatively small band of American retirees there have done a better job of keeping the charms of their adopted home secret than some of their counterparts elsewhere. The foreign colony is, however, large enough to support an active social life, and settling there today hardly qualifies you as a pioneer.

Easy outings from Morelia include Pátzcuaro and Uruapan. The latter, justly renowned for its lacquered boxes and trays, also attracts special attention for the nearby volcano Paricutin, which in 1943, suddenly erupted in a cornfield and spilled molten lava over the surrounding villages and countryside. Pátzcuaro owes its reputation to the loveliness of its colonial buildings and of Lake Pátzcuaro. The lake is dotted with islands, including one covered by the Tarascan Indian village of Janitzio. The island is topped by a gigantic statue of José Morelos, one of Mexico's greatest heroes and a native of the locality. The lake is also the home of the *pescado blanco*, a delicious white fish caught by the Indians in their delicate "butterfly" nets and featured on the menus of the neighborhood's numerous restaurants.

Tequisquiapan

The small and attractive town of Tequisquiapan, although somewhat off the beaten track, is only a few hours' drive from Mexico City and, as one of its retired residents reported, "a day's drive to the world's most beautiful beaches!" After falling out of favor for a number of years, it is beginning to regain its popularity with Americans retirees. In the 1970s there were more than fifty in "Tequis." Then that number shrank almost to the vanishing point. Not too long ago a knowledgeable Lake Chapala resident referred to Tequis as a "delightful surprise." It is not, however, a surprise to many wealthy residents of Mexico City for whom it continues to be a popular weekend retreat. This well may be a time to act quickly, if it interests you.

A major problem with a place like Tequisquiapan is the lack of cultural and social stimulation. People who have spent most of their lives building a career and/or nurturing a family, and who have had little time for concerts, theater, and art galleries frequently discover them after retirement. It is not just those who have been "arty" all their lives who enjoy the lively cultural attractions of San Miguel or Guadalajara. This is at least equally true of the need for companionship. When you have a job or live in a neighborhood where you have grown up or spent much of your adult life, you may take friendships (or acquaintanceships) for granted. When you move to an unfamiliar place, particularly a small town where few people speak your language, their absence can make the evenings long and lonely.

Growth and development also helped to destroy the popularity of "Tequis" with American retirees. The construction of factories nearby and the influx of industrial workers has put a strain on the community, transforming it from a picturesque village with cobblestone streets into a small town whose cobblestones are buried under pavement. The people are still friendly, and the climate is still the same, however, and Tequisquiapan might fit your needs.

Querétero

Much of what we have said about Tequisquiapan is also true of Querétero. It, too is extremely attractive, filled with authentically restored colonial buildings and graced by tree-lined streets. It is also the Mexican address of numerous multinational companies and, as such, far from poor. Its prices are, accordingly, somewhat higher than communities where big spenders from abroad are less in evidence. We are reluctant to write off such towns as retirement possibilities, although we know very well that most of our readers will be more comfortable in places like Guadalajara or San Miguel. At the very least, they may be places to take another look at after you have been in Mexico several years, have some command of Spanish and are ready to leave the bulk of your fellow expatriates behind.

Puebla

What the colonial city of Puebla has is beautifully preserved sixteenth- through eighteenth-century buildings, a handsome Zócalo, a regional cuisine famous throughout the country, a landscape featuring snow-covered volcanoes (and an atmosphere clear enough to see them), lower prices than in many other large

Cesar Menconi 1992   CORTEZ PALACE, CUERNAVACA.

Mexican cities and reasonable proximity to the capital. What it does not have is a large expatriate population (if you exclude the Germans employed at the huge Volkswagen plant on the outskirts).

Puebla was the site of the nineteenth century victory of Mexican troops against a much larger French force that is celebrated each year on Cinco de Mayo, the fifth of May. It is also the home of *molé poblano*, the extremely complex sauce compounded of chocolate and ground pumpkin seeds, together with numerous different chiles and other spices. It is served over turkey or sometimes chicken and, for this writer at least, is furiously addictive.

Nearby in the town of Cholua is the University of the Americas, which offers courses in both Spanish and English and has an outstanding archaeology program. Cholua, too, is an extremely attractive location with its tremendous collection of churches erected on the site of Aztec temples and is reputed to include one for every day of the year.

Few Retirees

Why then, has Puebla failed to attract a larger group of retirees? One explanation offered by a knowledgeable Mexican friend is that the locals are so proud of being "Poblanos" that they are not eager to make friends with other Mexicans, let alone foreigners. That could account for the fact that there are not many retirees in Puebla now, but it need not be an insurmountable obstacle to its future as a retirement site. We could see no sign that the attitude of the locals was anything more negative than indifference—certainly there was no visible hostility. There is a small group of Americans there, a couple of golf courses and tennis clubs and, as everywhere in Mexico, many of the movies shown are in English.

We continue to believe that, as more prospective retirees in Mexico visit this community, more will decide that it is the place for them, and its chief drawback for many people—the lack of a large enough group of fellow expatriates—will disappear.

CHAPTER FOURTEEN

Mexico City and Vicinity

Mexico City

In the earlier editions of *Choose Mexico* we said that we couldn't recommend Mexico City as a retirement spot. After many subsequent visits there we still can't, but do feel that our readers should know what an exciting and cosmopolitan city it is. We wouldn't want to live there, but certainly would wish to visit it frequently.

Some of the effects of the 1985 earthquake are still visible, especially in the downtown area, but generally the city has recovered very well. One positive change has been the development of several modern and spacious parks or plazas where old buildings once stood. It was interesting to note the almost total lack of damage to the historic buildings that date back to the Colonial days.

New Construction

Also new since the first edition are a spectacular museum adjacent to the Aztec ruins near the Zócalo (uncovered during the building of the subway) and a fine collection of seventeenth-through nineteenth-century paintings and furniture in the Franz Meyer collection, housed in a part of the recently restored Church of St. John del Dios complex on the north side of the Alameda (Mexico City's Central Park).

High culture in the form of concert, opera and dance performances are as plentiful and affordable as ever at Bellas Artes (Palace of Fine Arts) and elsewhere. The best seats in the house for a symphony concert are still a tremendous bargain—far less than the cheapest seats in United States or Canadian concert hall. The famous Ballet Folklórico, which is a prime tourist attraction, is substantially more expensive—although still reasonable—demonstrating once more the dual price situation in Mexico. There are prices for residents, whether Mexican or foreign, and prices for tourists—also whether Mexicans or foreigners.

Truly a Big City

Mexico City is the country's capital and largest city, and it has many American residents. The city is enormous, with a population generally estimated at 20 million, but the proportion of foreign residents to total population is low and few of those foreigners are retirees. Why choose Mexico City over other, less crowded cities? Perhaps for the same personal preferences that make some people love New York or London.

Mexico City is definitely exciting. There is always plenty to do. The opera house is one of the most beautiful in the world, some great opera companies and symphony orchestras play there, and seats as we've noted, cost a fraction of what they would in the U.S. Its parks are wonderful, particularly Chapultepec which contains almost every form of recreation the residents of a great city could desire. Mexico City has outstanding museums and art exhibits, and abounds in excellent restaurants and smart shops. If the usual Mexican bargains are not enough for you, we even found a Price Club there on our most recent visit.

For the most part, it is an elegant city, with modern buildings and wide boulevards. Although the poor barrios on the outskirts of town have decrepit housing and even mud streets, you probably won't be settling there.

The climate is temperate, with cool summers and only slightly cooler winters. Though some find its mile-high altitude a problem, we have never been uncomfortable there.

Housing in Mexico City is expensive but there are still some attractive neighborhoods that are *relatively* affordable. It is important to find a home or apartment that has off-street parking and is not far from public transportation. This last is important. You'll probably not want to drive much in Mexico City. Perhaps the town's biggest drawback is its suicidal drivers and incredible traffic jams. Many smart residents use taxis, buses and the excellent subway system, renting a car for weekend jaunts to Acapulco, which is only a five-hour drive away.

Perhaps the biggest problem with Mexico City is smog. The residential areas where you might want to live aren't as bad as the industrial areas in the north of the city. Despite its reputation, the smog, at least in many parts of the city, is no worse than in Los Angeles (we're not sure whether that is much of a compliment), and we've seen days on end when a breeze clears the air and it's lovely. On a recent visit, the beautiful, snow-capped volcanoes were clearly visible from all over the city. However, there are also days when the level of lead, sulfur and other pollutants in the air make it dangerous to breathe.

The government is beginning to come to grips with the problem of air pollution, even restricting the days on which your car can be driven in the city. Nevertheless, it is unlikely that, given the magnitude of this problem and Mexico's many others, progress is likely to be very rapid.

Current Prices

The extremely clean, convenient and friendly hotel where we paid $7 for a room with color television, modern bathroom and view of the city in 1983 was $11 in 1988 and now is about $22. There are still restaurants where you can get an excellent four or five course meal for about $5.

Taxis, particularly the regular (non-tourist) ones are still extremely affordable, perhaps because public transportation offers such a good alternative.

Public Transportation

Mexico City's subway system (the Metro) is one of the wonders of the modern world. Its stations are filled with authentic Aztec relics, its cars are clean and modern and its routes have been extended so that you can use it to get almost anywhere in the city. Yet the fare is still only a few cents. Based on our experience as subway riders in New York, San Francisco, Washington, London, Madrid and elsewhere, we believe Mexico City is way out front. (It is best, however, to avoid using the subway during rush hours, since it does have to move the city's millions of inhabitants to and from work.)

Other Amenities

One thing Mexico City has that doesn't seem common yet elsewhere in Mexico is radio news in English. The FM station, Radio VIP, 88.1 on the dial, broadcasts CBS news programs on the hour plus many other English-language features during the day. Classical music stations abound and popular music stations seem to feature U.S. material. The latter is true throughout Mexico, perhaps all over the world, so if the top forty is your thing, just switch on your radio.

Once again, you don't have to live in Mexico City to enjoy its many attractions. Bus transportation to and from there from almost anywhere in the country is so inexpensive that you can make frequent visits without putting a dent in your budget. One example that startled us on a recent visit was a fare of about six dollars from Mexico City to Acapulco, about 260 miles. Other fares are comparable—a couple of dollars to Cuernavaca and less than five dollars to Puebla. In making an exploratory visit to Mexico, we strongly urge you to see its capital, but probably only after you've had a chance to look at some communities that are more suited to retirement living.

Valle de Bravo

Anyone who enjoys the active life—water sports including swimming and sailing, tennis and golf—and will have retirement income several times the $600 a month level should take a look at the weekend, vacation and retirement retreat favored by those knowledgeable Mexicans who can afford it and by a small group of U.S. and Canadian retirees. Valle de Bravo is a couple of hours drive from Mexico City on the side of a mountain west of Toluca. It is renowned for its climate which somehow manages to be significantly warmer than Mexico City in winter and cooler in summer. What is more, there is considerably more sunshine and the air is crystal clear. Despite the influx of boutiques and upscale restaurants, it still enjoys much of the serene beauty that must have characterized this country town before the construction of the huge lake that has made it so popular with sports enthusiasts.

The luxuriantly wooded hills filled with streams and waterfalls that surround the lake would not be out of place in New England or the Upper Midwest.

Rentals tend to be expensive and hard to come by, but much land is still available and building costs are low. With apologies to those of our readers whose lives, like ours, tend to be sedentary or whose budgets are too limited to consider such a trendy site, we thought we ought to let the more athletic retirees and prospective retirees know that such a place exists.

There are several excellent hotels in Valle de Bravo, some of them offering moderately priced weekend packages, so you can see it for yourself. Even if you don't or can't choose it as a retirement site, it's a wonderful place for vacations.

Cuernavaca

Moctezuma knew it. So did Cortés, Emperor Maximilian, Empress Carlotta, silver baron José Borda and most of Mexico's retired presidents. Numerous Mexican and foreign millionaires know it, too. Cuernavaca is a special city. Its location, only about an hour's drive from Mexico City, and its altitude, about two thousand feet lower, explain why so many of the capital's affluent residents make it their destination on winter days when temperatures in the capital are about a dozen degrees lower than Cuernavaca's year-round low seventies.

The wealth that has poured into this lovely valley is readily visible in its palaces, churches, mansions and gardens. Sit in the handsome town square (which sprawls from the main street up the hill to Cortés's palace that is today an outstanding historical and archaeological museum) and you will know that you are in a prosperous city.

A "High-Rent District"

One of the implications of this affluence is that Cuernavaca is probably one of the relatively few places in Mexico (outside of some Caribbean and Pacific resorts) where $600 a month would not allow you to live comfortably. $800 is probably a more reasonable figure for this "high-rent district." Part of the problem is the pressure to "keep up with the Joneses." Prices in its more elegant restaurants approach those in the U.S. Yet we enjoyed delicious food in some more modest spots for as little as $4.00 for a meal that included soup, pasta, main course, dessert and coffee. A simple breakfast in an outdoor cafe, however, was almost the same price. To live truly economically there, you would have to avoid the places frequented by wealthy Mexicans, tourists and most other foreigners.

But, oh those elegant restaurants. It's hard to imagine a more beautiful setting than the courtyard at Las Mañanitas. Filled with trees, flowers and sculpture, it makes you reluctant to go back to the more modest eating places where you know that the people at the next table are neither movie stars or ambassadors.

Retirees Thrive

Yet there is a thriving colony of retirees there and by no means are they all wealthy. *The Directory of Foreign Residents of the State of Morelos,* recently published under the auspices of the Navy League of the United States (and modelled after a directory published in San Miguel de Allende), lists about 400 individuals and families. I was assured that the next edition will include many more. There are several pages of associations and clubs ranging from Alcoholics Anonymous and the American Legion to a home for orphaned children supported largely by U.S. contributions and volunteers.

Also in the directory, together with numerous banks, beauty salons, delicatessens and so on, are a number of veterinarians, a video club and a washing machine repair service. The physicians and dentists fill several pages.

July Fourth brings a big bi-national celebration of the U.S. Independence Day and Mexican-American friendship with the trooping of the colors of the two countries, the singing of their national anthems and a feast that includes both hot dogs and *cochinito pibil.* All in all, Cuernavaca is clearly a community where you can enjoy many of the comforts of home in surroundings considerably more pleasant.

CHAPTER FIFTEEN

The Pacific Coast

W hen you hear people talking about the great time they had on their Mexico vacation, chances are they visited Mexico's west coast. Termed the "Gold Coast" by tourist agencies and travel writers, this section of Mexico draws by far the most tourists every year. There are a couple of good reasons.

First of all, because of the heavy influx of tourists, accommodations are plentiful, certainly more than adequate. But more important is the climate. The entire western part of both the North American and South American continents experience some fortuitous climatic conditions because of the enormous mass of ocean that controls climate and determines rainfall. The Pacific Ocean, with its deep, constantly evenly tempered waters, maintains a rather steady, year-round temperature on the coastal plains, winter and summer. This means you don't suffer excessive summer heat, and winter "northers" that blow down from Alaska are greatly moderated by the time they reach Mexico's Gold Coast.

Often you hear people saying: "I don't want to visit that part of Mexico. It's too tourist-plagued. I want to go somewhere more authentic!"

Think about this for a moment. Why do so many tourists travel there in the first place? Simply because the west coast is a wonderful place to visit! Not only is the weather good year-round, but it is beautifully tropical. Winter days are typically in the 70s and summer highs are in the mid-80s. Slender coconut palms embellish curving beaches, swaying with constant, warm, westerly breezes, making this almost a cliché of tropical beauty.

However, not *all* of Mexico's west coast is touristy and tropical. North of Mazatlán, north of the tropic of Cancer, the country tends to be more desert-like. This is because the coast here doesn't face the Pacific, but instead, faces the Gulf of California (or Sea of Cortés, however you please). The Baja Peninsula cuts off the Pacific's free-flowing breezes. Then, since the Sea of Cortés is enclosed, and not very deep, it soaks up the sun's heat and radiates it landward during the summer. Moisture-laden air holds its charge of water over the warm sea and hot mainland, waiting until the east coast to turn into rain.

Let's start our investigation in the north, and work our way south.

Northwest Mexico's Mainland

Several readers have asked about retirement places closer to the border than Mazatlán on the west coast. We wish we could locate an idyllic place for you, but it isn't all that easy. From the border south to Hermosillo, there are few places that Americans might want to live. This is desert country without the desert attractions we expect in places like Palm Springs or Phoenix. Many places are on a subsistence economy, with very basic living conditions.

The first nice-looking place is Hermosillo, about a 3½ hour drive south of Nogales. Hermosillo is modern and prosperous, with several comfortable-looking sections which might be suitable for North American residents. However, Hermosillo's prosperity comes from agriculture; it's the center of a very rich farming country. As far as we know, there are very few gringos living there, except for those who are there on business, working with agriculture.

Bahía Kino and San Carlos Bay

There is one place near Hermosillo that does attract retirees and long-term residents. That place is Bahía Kino, or Kino Bay. Here is where the affluent from Hermosillo come to build their weekend houses, and some of them are plush, indeed. We discuss this location in our chapter on recreational vehicle retirement, for it's a popular place for wintering in an RV.

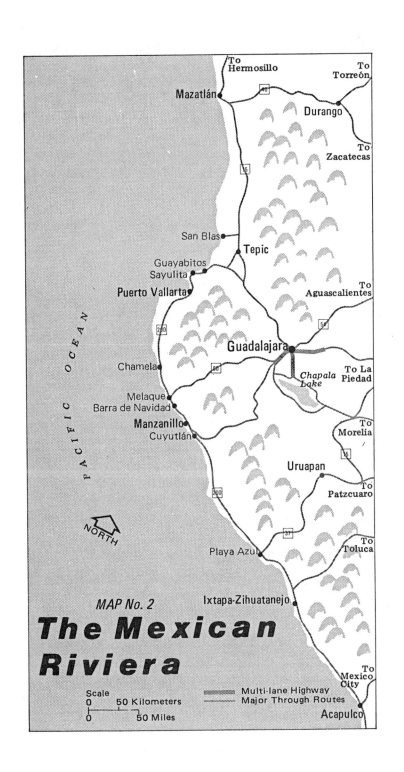

To
Hermosillo

To
Torreón

Mazatlán

40

Durango

To
Zacatecas

15

San Blas

Tepic

Guayabitos
Sayulita

Puerto Vallarta

To
Aguascalientes

PACIFIC OCEAN

200

54

Guadalajara

Chamela

80

To La
Piedad

Chapala
Lake

Melaque
Barra de Navidad

To
Morelia

Manzanillo
Cuyutlán

Uruapan

15

NORTH

To
Patzcuaro

200

37

To
Toluca

Playa Azul

MAP No. 2

Ixtapa-Zihuatanejo

The Mexican
Riviera

To
Mexico
City

Scale
0   50 Kilometers

Multi-lane Highway
Major Through Routes

0   50 Miles

Acapulco

Rentals aren't too easy to come by here if you're not dragging an RV with you. But several North Americans have constructed homes here, and we understand that some live here pretty much year-round, despite the hot summers.

Farther south, in Guaymas, you'll find another agricultural town. The downtown main street looks like a similar desert town in Arizona or California, with farm machinery outlets and hardware stores with farm implements the featured businesses. Guaymas is a place that's suffered from growing pains and hasn't suffered gracefully.

The big attraction here is north of town a few kilometers, at Bahía de San Carlos, or San Carlos Bay, as most RV fans call it. In addition to the Trailer Village, there's a San Carlos Residential Development Co., where you can buy a place or have one built to your specifications. Some very attractive cottages are springing up along the beaches and marinas. The majority of the retirees here are in RVs, but this is likely to change as more and more Arizona people move into retirement here.

Alamos, a Ghost Town Revived

South of Guaymas are two more agricultural cities, Ciudad Obregón and Navajoa. Neither has much to recommend it for retirement living. However, there is a little-known spot that we can highly recommend, just about 35 miles from Navajoa: Alamos. One of Mexico's oldest silver mining communities, it started operations in the 1500s, over four centuries ago! By the late 1700s, very prosperous, Alamos attained a population of over 40,000 and many substantial buildings. But like many mining operations, it came to an end during a series of catastrophes, ending with the "Great Depression" of the 30s. (What was so "great" about it, anyway?) At any rate, Alamos became a ghost town. Today, nobody seems to be quite sure where the original mine workings were.

Then, somewhere back in the 1950s the town was "discovered" by some North Americans. They began buying up old homes and mansions, then restoring them. They were so successful that the Mexican government declared the town to be a national monument like San Miguel de Allende and Taxco. Modern buildings are prohibited, and remodeling has to be done to preserve the original appearance. There are Moorish arches and covered walkways (*portales*), intricately fashioned wrought iron work, graceful fountains and elegant mansions (once homes of silver barons).

The English-speaking community is very active in Alamos, and engages in several worthwhile community projects, which makes the retirees well-liked by the local people. We understand that they regularly conduct house tours so that tourists and other residents can see some of the marvels they've done in restoring the mansions of two centuries ago.

Alamos isn't very large compared to some of the other gringo colonies, but it could grow. We estimate the total population to be less than 5,000. Many people live there year around, but many just retire there in the winter. A remarkable hotel, the Casa de los Tesoros—claimed by some to be one of Mexico's finest—is located here. Several inexpensive hotels are found on or near the main plaza. For the RV fans, there are three parks here.

Mazatlán

Mazatlán has long been popular as a place of retirement for Americans, particularly those from the western states. It's the first place south of the border that is genuinely in the tropics. As such, it attracts many full-time and part-time retirees who might not be interested in less-developed locations closer to the border.

In addition to its miles of sunny beaches, Mazatlán also boasts superb sports fishing and has a busy commercial port. It deservedly calls itself the shrimp capital of the world. Shrimpers from the warm waters of the Sea of Cortés routinely unload cargoes of unbelievably enormous prawns. Sometimes as large as lobsters, these delicious crustaceans are unfortunately destined for Japan (where price is no object) and U.S. residents seldom get a chance to sample them. However, you can often buy some if you meet the incoming boats and do some bargaining. They are magnificent sauteed with butter, minced garlic and a pinch of chili powder!

Many condominiums (at least one with its own golf course) with full amenities cater almost exclusively to North Americans. On the north part of town there is a neighborhood of rather nice homes, apartments and developments which are attracting a large American community. One should have no problem finding a social group to fit one's tastes.

Because there are so many tourists throwing dollars around, be prepared for higher prices and wages in Mazatlán. These prices aren't high enough to push Mazatlán out of our $600 category, but you could be strained somewhat. Some things, like taxis, seem way out of line, but, as a resident you would most likely have your own auto or use the public transportation system. The bus system, however is quite crowded, and seems unusually inadequate for Mexico. Perhaps we've only observed it at rush hours, however.

Because so many people speak English around here, it's an easy place to break into the culture and practice Spanish, knowing that you can always lapse back into English. At least on the strip of hotels, restaurants and shops along the lengthy beachfront, you can get by very well with a minuscule Spanish vocabulary.

For the older and/or less adventurous retiree, Mazatlán's lack of foreignness may be a major plus. It's a very comfortable, tourist-oriented place where you won't feel at all out-of-place. Residents report that there are many good English-speaking doctors and dentists and that the hospitals are excellent. Altogether, it might be a particularly good place for a three month or six month experiment in Mexican living. What better place to spend a winter, especially if you do not have to watch costs too closely.

San Blas

For those looking for a tropical village (small town, actually) that is "unspoiled" and truly Mexican, there is San Blas. Reputedly a pirate hangout during the days of the Manila Galleons, the town tries to maintain a "buccaneer" motif. Actually, the town was founded as a naval base to chase the pirates away, and also to outfit expeditions for the colonization of the west coast, as far north as Alaska. Yes, Alaska. The city of Valdez, Alaska, was named for the Spanish captain who sailed out of San Blas to plant a royal colony there. Enough history.

For tropical villages, San Blas is a jewel. It's a subdued place of a few thousand inhabitants, where often you'll see a momma pig herding her litter of piglets along the sandy streets. (Most all of the streets are unpaved.) The local people live in thatched-roof houses, and some of the buildings along the square date back to the time when the king's sailors used San Blas's main street for shore leave.

Rents and food are as inexpensive as anywhere in Mexico and there are several year-round English-speaking households. A resident told us the last time we were there that he had his choice of half a dozen houses, all for under $200 a month. Summers are hot and exceptionally humid, the kind of weather that makes you understand the value of afternoon siestas. Another problem is the "no-see-ums" that come out during certain times of the year. They've never been able to battle the little critters successfully. For this reason, you can have the town to yourself during the summers, provided you're liberally supplied with insect repellent.

There are three RV parks in the area. The one in San Blas itself practically closes down in the summer. According to the manager, it really fills up for the winter with gringos escaping the ice and snow up north. However, there are several beautiful places for RVs and possibly for house rentals between San Blas and Santa Cruz, about 13 miles to the south. The road follows the ocean through some nice little villages where we've noticed quite a few U.S. and Canadian license plates on cars parked in private homes and on RVs backed up against the beach.

Puerto Vallarta

For years Puerto Vallarta was a sleepy village, cut off from the rest of Mexico. The only road in was unpaved, and visitors had to come by mule, boat or the DC3s that used the dirt landing strip. When a paved road broke through the tropical forest from Tepic, Puerto Vallarta found itself in the modern world of tourism. Located on a long, narrow strip of land between the mountains and the sea, "PV," as its North American devotees call it, is only a few blocks wide in many places. For this reason, it hasn't grown very metropolitan and, although it expands further north and south every year, much of the town retains its village atmosphere. Cobblestone streets and old buildings add to its charm. The large developments, with high-rise condos and luxury hotels are going up outside of town. This is where the bulk of the tourists go, to hotels where they pay top dollar and where it costs several dollars to take a taxi into town.

The secret to retirement in Puerto Vallarta is to look for an apartment in the older section. There are plenty of them, and if you find a suitable one in the summertime, you can lease it for the year and keep it reasonably in the wintertime. Some of the more reasonable places are typically found on the tops hills behind town, offering gorgeous views of the town below and the ocean in the distance (about eight blocks to the beach).

You can pay more, a lot more, if you wish. A development north of town, Nuevo Vallarta, is one of the fanciest places we've ever seen. Some of the houses, set back on enormous lots, look as if they would cost several millions of dollars if they were in some posh U.S. spot. Then, they may cost that much here, too; it's a breathtaking place, but not something for a couple looking for $600-a-month retirement.

There are many full-time American residents of Puerto Vallarta. However, as in most of the tropical resorts, the population of retirees is very fluid. Many come here just for a few months and then either return home, or move on to another Mexican location. Our impression is that there isn't much in the way of retiree organizations, and the ambiance lacks the instant friendliness of other popular retirement places. "But the weather and the beaches make up for that," said one lady who has had a place there for 15 years.

As you might guess, tourism has pushed prices up considerably. Wages for local people are also higher, because there are many competing jobs available in the tourist industry. You can still make it on a $600 budget here, but it will mean less dining out and putting up with a huge floating population of gringo tourists.

Condominiums?

Condominiums are going up very quickly, both regular and time-share. Our view of time-sharing is that it should have absolutely no place in anybody's retirement plans! But the idea of regular condos had some interesting possibilities. We investigated one place in Puerto Vallarta, and we know there are similar developments in Acapulco and probably Mazatlán and other west coast locations. We're not vouching for these condos, nor or we encouraging anyone to invest, but the plan goes something like this:

The units are going up on a very desirable stretch of beach, or in a high-demand tourist area. Prices of the ones we looked at ranged from $75,000 to $150,000 for two-bedroom units. The salespeople are suggesting that you buy these units on a pre-retirement plan. All units are completely furnished and are operated as a hotel for people who don't live there full time. According to the developers, they can rent the apartments for $75 per day in the low season and $125 a day during high season. Management would withhold a fee, and deposit the rest of the money to your account. Ostensibly, this rent could pay for your condominium by the time you actually decide to retire.

On paper, this sounds like a great idea, but developers have a way of making things sound a lot better than they are. So beware! It all hinges upon the ability of management to keep the rentals full, and to fulfill all their promises.

Around the Area

There are some very attractive alternatives to Puerto Vallarta, within an easy drive. South of town, all the way to a small village called Boca de Tomatlán, you'll see many private homes built to take advantage of the ocean view. They look expensive. Boca de Tomatlán is especially pretty. A picturesque river empties into the Pacific here, cutting through a tropical canyon and crossing a shifting sandbar. The sides of the canyon have many sites for building small retirement homes, and there are several already available for rent.

In the first edition, we guessed that this would be the next boom area for retirement, but we were mistaken. At last count, there was but one North American family with a house there. Movie director John Houston had a place on the coast, around the mouth of the river. Before his death, he was a familiar figure in Boca de Tomatlán, where he would arrive by boat and snack on fresh-water lobsters.

North of Puerto Vallarta, on up to San Blas, there are several delightful communities on the beach. The people are friendly, the villages small, and each has a few Americans living there. A particularly inviting village is San Francisco, about an hour north of Puerto Vallarta. It is growing quickly, but prices of homes are still at bargain levels.

Manzanillo

Unlike many of Mexico's Pacific coast resorts, Manzanillo is an active commercial port as well as a sun-drenched playground. This is reflected in a harbor and downtown that are less charming than some, but also in prices that are noticeably lower. The downtown is strictly commercial without elegant restaurants or tourist goods, and most of the city seems rather ordinary to us. The foreign residents and retirees live along the coast north of Manzanillo. This is where the resorts, condos and luxury residential communities can be found.

Manzanillo is clearly a magnet for sports fishermen, billing itself as "the sailfish capital of the world." (Seems like we've heard this claim in other Mexican resorts!) All in all, the atmosphere here is more informal and relaxed than Acapulco or Puerto Vallarta. North to Barra de Navidad, you'll find numerous little villages on the ocean, and a scattering of North American retirees.

Like most of the west coast, average monthly temperatures here are in the upper 70s and low 80s year-round. There are some steamy days in July through September, which are the rainy as well as the hot months. (Miami, in comparison, is hotter in the summer, colder in the winter, and far more difficult to escape from when the heat becomes uncomfortable.)

Ixtapa-Zihuatanejo

Driving six hours south of Manzanillo, on a fairly new highway, you'll see some rather interesting country that heretofore wasn't available to travelers. Then you arrive Zihuatanejo, a little more than halfway to Acapulco. You travel through quaint villages and past rustic coconut plantations with copra drying along the roadsides. When you arrive at Zihuatanejo, you find yourself looking at a town just like Acapulco was 30 years ago.

Zihuatanejo is changing rapidly, however, from the sleepy little village it was a few decades ago. Hotels are springing up and business is booming. Fortunately, the glamorous resort of nearby Ixtapa draws off enough of the tourist trade to keep Zihuatanejo's prices within reach and its traffic relatively unjammed. Retiring there may give you the best of both—quiet and economy at home and the glamour of Ixtapa just a short drive away. Small mountains ring the town and the best building sites are up in the hills with spectacular views of the bay.

When bar-hopping in Zihuatanejo, you'll often find yacht captains and crews killing time between sailings. The harbor is very popular with yachts cruising between California and Acapulco, and the waterside bars never lack new faces. By the way, we always thought that retirement on a sailboat would be the ultimate. Many people do this, of course, and you'll find them in Mexican ports. But, the yachting people we've met report that getting to Mexico is a snap, but getting back north is tough, due to currents and prevailing winds. The wealthy sail their boats south, then pay someone to make the slow trek back to California.

Rentals are reportedly difficult to find nowadays in "Zihua" because apartment building hasn't kept up with the increasing demand. Where building has kept pace, however, is about 15 miles away at Ixtapa. This a luxurious beach resort that has all of the sophistication of Acapulco but on a smaller scale. The condos that are going up there look like mostly time-share arrangements, but regular apartments probably will be available before long. We did little research here because it looks like it's way out of range for most readers of this book.

Ixtapa is exciting to visit, a vacation paradise for tourists, but you probably could not afford to live there and might not want to if you could. Less than five miles away lies Zihuatanejo where you can afford to live, and from which you can make trips to Ixtapa whenever you feel like playing tourist. You may not want to leave Zihuatanejo often, however, since it has its own charms, including some picturesque and relatively uncrowded beaches.

Acapulco

One commonly thinks of Acapulco as a glamorous, expensive jet set resort. It is, of course. So, who would think about retirement in Acapulco, with its $150 a day hotels and elegant restaurants? Impossible? Not at all. In fact, Acapulco could well be one of the *least* expensive of your retirement choices! The reason is an accident of history.

Acapulco was isolated from the world until the late 1920s, when the first road was built that allowed anything but mules to make the trip. Suddenly, the beauty of the beaches and the idyllic climate were exposed to the world, and the rush was on. Hotels sprouted from nowhere, apartments and homes went up with top speed.

From the very beginning, Acapulco overbuilt its facilities. Competition between hotels and rental units has always been fierce, with price cutting the rule. The result has been a bonanza for a tourist or retiree who doesn't require the very latest of hotel or apartment accommodations.

Another important factor is the geographical setting of Acapulco. The bay is ringed with some very steep hills. Years ago, when most people drove their autos from Mexico City and when taxis and limousines were everywhere, it was stylish to build on the hillsides for the terrific views. But today, tourist preferences have changed: people fly in and insist on hotels right on the beach. Multi-story hotels and condos line the beach like elegant monuments to tourism.

This shift from the hills down to the beaches rendered those apartments and hotels that used to be the luxury places up on the hills passé. Consequently, rents drop in order to attract tenants. For less than in Guadalajara, San Miguel de Allende or Ensenada, you can rent a spacious apartment overlooking the bay with a view that is unequaled in the world! Of, course, you're not on the beach, and you can expect to climb a long way uphill to go home.

Throughout Acapulco there is a two-tiered rental system: there are the $150 a day rooms for the two-week tourist who buys through travel agents, and there are the $18 a day rooms for the tourist or retiree who doesn't demand a swimming pool and is satisfied with a ceiling fan rather than an air conditioner. To repeat: $18 a day can secure a clean, comfortable room in Acapulco. Two hundred dollars a month can move you into an acceptable apartment, although some blocks from the beach.

Luxury hotels that 30 years ago were reserved for the Hollywood crowd today go for $25 to $40 a day. Several of the more luxurious places either closed down from lack of business, or are being converted into condos and rental apartments.

Costs for living expenses other than housing are not bad either. Food in the markets is as inexpensive as anywhere in Mexico, because most people living in Acapulco are, obviously, not tourists or retirees, but ordinary working people who can't afford to pay more than ordinary prices for food, clothing and living expenses. Restaurants have a two-tiered system, too. Only a small proportion of the residents are foreign tourists who can afford expensive meals. Most tourists are Mexicans to whom a $10 meal is a luxury item; to the Mexicans who live and work in Acapulco, even $10 is outrageous. Therefore, if you stay away from the beachfront tourist traps, you can eat fantastically well for embarrassingly small amounts.

Transportation is great on city buses, and taxis aren't too bad if you learn to bargain for the correct fare. Acapulco is one place where an auto comes in handy. Even though traffic is heavy, you will find that with a car you can go up into the hills and find the bargain apartments. (It can be a nuisance to have to find a taxi every time you want to go up or down the hill.)

Servants are more expensive than elsewhere, and may not be as loyal. This is because of the competition for help with the hotels and tourist businesses. You may find a great cook, only to have him or her discovered by a hotel restaurant and recruited away. Most North Americans aren't used to having servants, so this shouldn't be any barrier to living in Acapulco.

If you are looking for a place in the tropics, even if only for the winter months, don't overlook Acapulco because you have been told by people who have been there only as tourists that the prices are high.

Puerto Escondido

With the completion of a paved road south from Acapulco, the *Costa Chica*, Mexico's southwestern corner, is now accessible. The drive south goes through some fascinating places, many of which could make outstanding retirement spots for those who don't need English-speaking neighbors. In one area, the people are descendants of black slaves who have lived in isolation and preserved some of their old customs. Another stretch of highway takes you through the only place in Mexico we know of where the women go topless. The Indian women wear a beautifully woven skirt of cochineal-dyed material and used to go around with nothing on top. With the opening of the highway and the concomitant introduction of Western customs, however, the younger women have taken to wearing slacks and blouses, leaving the traditional dress customs to the older women.

Originally "discovered" by the surfing and backpacking student sets are the towns of Puerto Escondido and Puerto Angel. The beaches are breathtaking, and development is proceeding slowly. Puerto Escondido has grown and the road along the beach is lined with small hotels and restaurants. Happily, they include some of the most pleasant and affordable on the Pacific coast. There are only a few apartments and houses for rent but, just north of the town, several elegant subdivisions are being laid out.

We found Puerto Escondido one of the most beautiful and welcoming beach communities on Mexico's west coast. We also found that it is attracting many residents of the United States and Canada who want a place to enjoy total relaxation in the sun for a few months in winter. Hotel and restaurant prices are still low enough to make this possible, even on a modest budget. We did, however, find it difficult to think of this area—or,indeed, any village on the beach as a place to establish one's year-round retirement home. When Mexico offers so many places where (because of their altitudes) summer temperatures are moderate, why settle on the hot coastal plane? Also, whereas the part-time residents we questioned assured us that they were never bored there, we wondered how stimulating they would find it, if they did not have homes elsewhere to return for the rest of the year.

Puerto Angel

Less than an hour to the south is Puerto Angel, which is a paradise for anyone who wants to "get away from it all." Not long ago, there were only a couple of main streets in Puerto Angel and, remarkably, few tourist businesses. There didn't used to be a single curio shop, or even a place that sold postcards. It is still a very quiet and restful place.

But FONATUR, the Mexican tourist development agency, decided that the area just to the south would be a great place to make into another Acapulco or Cancún. Already, in 1991, nearby

Huatulco has an international airport, several large hotels have been built and others are under construction.

It is hard to predict how rapidly this development will take place under current world economic conditions. Many of the roads are in, but street signs are scarce and the area has a very unfinished quality. Eventually some of Huatulco's international resort atmosphere is likely to spill over to Puerto Angel. Meanwhile, it may be just the tropical paradise you are looking for, at least for your next vacation.

Farther South to Guatemala

We aren't aware of any towns along the ocean to the south of Puerto Angel where many North Americans live, except those who are in business of some sort. Salina Cruz and Tehuantepec are interesting places, but not really the kind of places which might attract a foreign community. Tapachula, the most south-easterly town in Mexico, on the border with Guatemala, is interesting as one of the cleanest towns we've seen anywhere in Mexico. Several workers spend full time doing nothing but sweeping the sidewalks and streets and picking up trash. But as far as we know, there are no North Americans living there. Should there be, as with any other place we might neglect, we invite your corrections for our *next edition*.

CHAPTER SIXTEEN

Baja California

Baja California—a legend of mystery and romance for many who live on the west coast—is a long peninsula that juts south of California for almost a thousand miles. Baja is a world all its own. It's a virtual wonderland of desert scenery, secluded beaches, lost Jesuit missions, rugged mountains and deep canyons. Separated from the mainland by the blue, blue waters of the Sea of Cortés, the peninsula has been isolated so long that it evolved its own flora and fauna, distinct from anywhere else in the world. Zoologists and botanists pilgrimage here to enjoy themselves.

Baja's economy is also isolated from the mainland, and in some ways, has evolved its own economic character. Only one highway and one railroad come directly from Mexico, so all Mexican goods and merchandise must travel either that way, or by boat from Mexico. Naturally, much commerce comes by truck from the United States. Therefore, prices and wages are higher than on the mainland and some Mexican consumer goods aren't always found in stores. Despite this, Baja California is still Mexico. Prices are still bargains, at least in some places. Baja Californians are the same friendly people as you'll find on the mainland.

For many people living in the western United States, Baja California is the only part of Mexico they know. This is particularly true for Californians. They fondly recall long stretches of beach where enormous Pismo clams are there for the taking, moonlit grunion runs, camping, fishing, soaking up sunshine while drinking Tecate beer flavored with lemon and salt; these have long been major attractions here.

Generations of teenagers from California towns like Pasadena, Fresno or Sacramento tested their first adult adventures in Hussong's Saloon in Ensenada, a grungy, clapboard bar that boasts that it has changed nothing in the last 100 years but the sawdust on the floor. As a sort of rite of passage from juvenile to young adult, the teenagers order tequila cocktails or Carta Blanca beer, confident that no one would refuse them because of stateside technicalities like not being 21 years old. It's not all youngsters, though; you'll find a marvelous assortment of compatriots hanging over the bar or leaning elbows on the rickety tables. You'll meet yachtsmen stopping off on their way to Acapulco, stylishly-dressed Yuppies, shabby-looking 4-wheelers exchanging adventure tales of the back trails, RV enthusiasts, local Mexicans anxious to practice English (plus plenty of people our age so we don't feel out of place).

New Ground Rules

But Baja is more than simply a place for tourists to let off steam. More and more it has become a mecca for retirement, particularly for people from the west coast. In recognition of this movement, and to encourage it, the Mexican government made some special rules for North Americans who want to buy property here for long-term or retirement living. In some ways the rules have been relaxed, but there are certain strings attached, as we will see later on.

The biggest reason for retiring in Baja California is simple convenience. For someone living in Los Angeles or San Bernardino, having a home in Ensenada means being able to drive north to visit the grandchildren any weekend they choose. It means that friends they used to work with are much more likely to come down for a weekend visit than if they had a similar house in Puerto Vallarta or Lake Chapala.

One retired couple we interviewed owns a paint store in Bakersfield. Their daughter and son-in-law are learning to manage the operation, giving the couple some time to themselves for the first time in years. So, they started an early retirement program by buying a place in San Antonio Shores, about a 45-minute drive south of Tijuana. "We return home once a month." Elaine said, "We stay a week there, making sure the business is

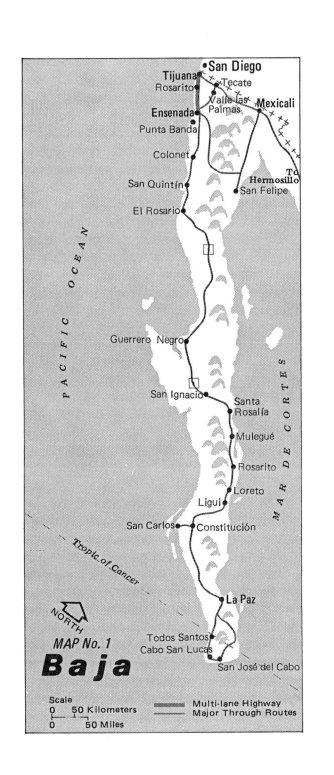

San Diego

Tijuana
Rosarito
Tecate
Valle las
Palmas
Mexicali
Ensenada
Punta Banda

Colonet

To
Hermosillo
San Quintín
San Felipe

El Rosario

PACIFIC OCEAN

Guerrero Negro

San Ignacio
Santa
Rosalía

MAR DE CORTES

Mulegué

Rosarito

Loreto
Ligui
San Carlos
Constitución

Tropic of Cancer

La Paz

NORTH

MAP No. 1
Baja

Todos Santos
Cabo San Lucas

San José del Cabo

Scale
0   50 Kilometers
0   50 Miles

▬▬▬ Multi-lane Highway
───── Major Through Routes

going well. We spend some time spoiling our granddaughter. Then we hurry back to Mexico for the rest of the month."

Since most of the northern Baja California retirement spots are within a few hours of the border, it's no problem to run on up to San Diego or Calexico for shopping. "You'd be surprised how often I find I need a special tool, or some nuts and bolts that I can't find here," said one man who is building a home in Ensenada. "In two hours I'm in San Diego. I visit the hardware store while the wife stocks up on hard-to-find grocery items. Then back home after a milkshake-and-hamburger fix at some fast-food place."

Because it's convenient and close, Baja offers a way to sample Mexico's graciousness and economical living without investing excessive time or money in the adventure. Here is an excellent place for pre-retirement planning to see whether you actually like Mexico and its people. It's also a place to move into the culture gradually, yet be close to Hollywood and Disneyland, if that somehow makes you feel more secure. Many local people here love to improve their English skills by practicing with you, so you won't have trouble making acquaintance with your neighbors. And, because there are so many gringos living here, you can quickly build a circle of English-speaking friends.

As we pointed out earlier, because Baja is isolated from the mainland, you'll find prices and wages higher and Yankee influence much stronger. Yet for the novice, these things aren't apparent, because prices and wages are so much less than back home that they seem downright ridiculous. In Ensenada, for example, a maid will come in to clean your house and do your laundry for $6.50 to $8.00 a day; a gardener-handyman will tend to your home for $10.00 to $14.00 a day, and a skilled carpenter or building tradesman will help you build a house for $25 to $40 a day. Maybe your Mexican neighbors can hire help a little cheaper, but anyone who would complain about paying these wages (or even more, after all, you are comparatively wealthy) shouldn't even bother with Mexico. A seafood dinner in one of the best restaurants in town costs around $12.00, and fresh vegetables in the market are about half what they would cost in Los Angeles.

Building a House

Seems like people who want to retire in Baja always dream of building their own house. *Los Angeles Times* columnist Jack Smith entertained the readers of his column by relating the often hilarious experiences he had while building his place near Ensenada. He later wrote a charming book about his encounters with his Mexican contractor, Mr. Gómez, and the multiple obstacles he had to overcome to become his own architect, builder and designer.

Building a home anywhere in Mexico is a unique experience, since one seldom has to bother with building codes and fussy inspectors. You make up your blueprints as you go along. This is evident in the many imaginative and innovative styles of homes you'll see in Baja. Sometimes they verge upon the exciting, the exotic, and sometimes the weird, but that's Baja for you.

Hold on now, building a house anywhere in Mexico isn't all that simple! Particularly not when it comes to owning the land where you want to build. At one time, property ownership suffered an extremely uncertain status in Baja. Promoters and fast-talking salesmen were selling every piece of property in sight, whether they owned it or not. Gullible Americans flocked to Baja and commenced building everything from weekend shacks to luxurious mansions. But Mexican law clearly states that a foreigner cannot own property within 50 kilometers of the ocean or 100 kilometers from the border. Alas, the day of reckoning arrived, along with huge, ominous government bulldozers. Many, many illegally-built homes were scooped into oblivion, much to the dismay of the "owners."

The resulting outcry sounded from Washington, D.C. to Mexico City. Pressured by the Ministry of Tourism and by local residents who *want* to see American retirement dollars invested in Baja, the government relented and changed the laws. They made it possible for North Americans to sign 30-year leases on the land and construct whatever they feel they are big enough to handle. This law is similar to 30-year leases elsewhere in Mexico (away from the ocean). As anywhere in Mexico, check with a recommended lawyer before plunking your money down. This advice is especially valid in Baja. The potential pitfalls of real estate deals are discussed in more detail in our chapter on housing.

The Free Zone

The northern part of Baja is known as the *zona libre* or the *free zone*. The government deliberately makes this area quite relaxed as far as immigration and customs are concerned. It isn't necessary to have tourist papers or an automobile permit to enter. You can enter the country at the border without even saying "hello" to the Mexican customs and immigration people. Don't misunderstand: this doesn't give you full rights of residency or any legal status at all. By law, your stay is limited to 72 hours, even though the law is seldom enforced, not unless you are a troublemaker. For one thing, there is no way to prove when you actually crossed the border.

But, if you are going to buy, rent or lease anything, you'd better pay attention to the law. Understand, you don't have to be a legal resident to have a house or trailer in the free zone. Many Californians have weekend places here and seldom stay long enough to bother with tourist papers or visas. If you plan on staying for a while, we recommend that you follow the entirely reasonable rules of the Mexican government. There are several ways to do this, all of which are covered in the chapter on legal matters. Getting a tourist card is simple, yours for the asking. Sure, there are people who ignore the rules and who are seldom if ever hassled, but we feel that if you are a guest in a country, the very least you can do is to comply with the rules. Again, let us remind you to be sure and check with a locally recommended lawyer before laying out any money for property.

Driving in Baja

What can we say? Driving here is no different from other parts of Mexico: don't drive at night, have insurance, drive carefully. The roads are average for Mexico, which says a lot for Baja, because until a few years ago, most roads were dirt, liberally spotted with two-foot-deep potholes filled with powder dust. Some of us maintain that it was better that way, but then, you other people didn't have four-wheel drives, and probably didn't enjoy riding around with a red bandana over your face to cut the dust.

In a travel article by Shirley Miller, entitled "Baja Alone" (from *Mexico West Newsletter*, June, 1988), she describes her trip driving alone from California to the tip of Baja and back. She reports, "Well, all I can say is that a woman alone driving the Baja highway from Tijuana to Cabo San Lucas is safer than she would be driving into downtown Los Angeles. Nary a problem with gasoline, my trusty 1980 Chevy pickup, the roads, or anything else, for that matter." Her only caution is that one should bring plenty of cassette tapes for the tape deck, because radio reception on the car radio fades rapidly away from civilization.

For those of you who travel in the states of Baja California or Sur, or Sonora or Culiacán, here is a tip that can save you many times over the price of this book. By joining one of the travel clubs listed here, you can buy your auto insurance at a fraction of what it might cost you elsewhere. We are aware of two clubs (there may be more) with a combined membership of about 6,000. One is: Mexico West Travel Club, P.O. Box 1646, Bonita, CA 92002, (619) 585-3033. The other is Vagabundos del Mar, P.O. Box 824, Isleton, CA 95641, (707) 374-5511. You can purchase full coverage on an average vehicle for as little as $150 a year! (See Appendix for more details.)

These clubs also send out newsletters about trends and events in Baja and have membership meetings in California (for those of you close enough to attend). If you are interested in fishing, these clubs are particularly valuable sources of information as well as a place to find fishing buddies.

Rosarito Beach and South

It's here in the *zona libre* where many Californians choose to make their homes. Starting at Rosarito Beach and going on south to Punta Banda, you'll find condos, bungalows, trailers, mobile homes, RVs and about any kind of accommodations you can imagine. The first place south of Tijuana where Californians tend to rent or lease is Rosarito Beach, which is within a commute distance to San Diego. The town abounds in small two-bedroom houses, crowded together and fenced, much like bedroom community suburbs across the border, but with a taco flavor. North and south of town are some more popular places to live, with sometimes more elaborate housing. Rosarito Beach is for those who need to be within easy driving distance to San Diego. It's Mexico, of course, but less Mexico-like than the rest of Baja.

The retirees here have formed a club they call the *United Society of Baja California*, and there's a monthly newspaper that has news plus listings of rentals and sales available in the Rosarito Beach area.

As you go farther south, there are several attractive clusters of gringo communities perched along the ocean cliffs. Most are weekend homes, but many are lived in full-time.

They've done some rather interesting and creative things with mobile homes here. They'll haul a large home down from San Diego, set it up where it gets the best view of the ocean, then proceed to build a masonry shell around it, complete with archways, tile inlays and sometimes even a tile roof. When finished it looks very Mexican, very picturesque, with little or no clue as to its origin. The advantage of this arrangement is that you have instant plumbing, bathrooms, electricity and built-in appliances—all working and easily repaired by buying parts in San Diego or Los Angeles.

Readers of Jack Smith's adventures with Mexican plumbing and electrical connections will understand how important these things can be. Smith managed without running water for many long months while his contractor, Mr. Gómez, struggled with the plumbing. Finally, the long-promised *mañana* came. Mr. Gómez proudly turned on the water connections. The main problem turned out to be that the kitchen and bathroom sinks had no hot water. Neither did the shower or the bathtub. But the toilet had plenty of steaming hot water.

Since there are few if any building standards or contractor license requirements, Mexican electrical wiring often looks as dubious as the plumbing, as if the electrician couldn't have been serious about the whole thing. Yet, it always seems to work. Well, maybe not *always*. Building a house anywhere in Mexico isn't something to be undertaken by the impatient, the fussy, or by those who possess anything less than an enormous sense of humor.

Between Rosarito and Ensenada are a dozen communities where Americans rent or lease. Some are quite stylish, with homes that border on the luxurious. Other communities are rather *cum-*

ccari men 1992

shaw, with slap-jack construction, more on the order of fishing camps. In fact, that's exactly what some places are. The better developments have security guards and limited access to outsiders. By the time you arrive in Ensenada, you are seeing some rather impressive homes and neighborhoods.

Ensenada

Ensenada is the metropolis of west-coast Baja. With 170,000 inhabitants, it's grown from a sleepy little fishing and tourist town of 40 years ago to a bustling little city. Fishing and tourism are still big industries, but the momentum of business has grown impressively. According to an informed source, there are around 15,000 Americans living here, many of them on a full-time basis.

When asked why they chose Ensenada as a retirement location, almost all respondents included the weather as a major consideration. "It has an ideal, Mediterranean kind of climate," points out one retiree. "It never gets over 85 degrees, and almost never under 50 degrees. And with a low humidity, it just seems like spring all year around." Another resident said, "I live in the most expensive neighborhood in Ensenada, and I don't have air conditioning, nor do I know anyone who does." Few houses have heating systems, either, since the ocean keeps winter weather from dropping to extremes. For all but the most luxurious homes, an electric heater or a fireplace suffices for even the coldest January days.

Owning a Business

As in other parts of Mexico, owning or operating a business is not easy for an American, but there are ways of doing it. Most people find a Mexican partner whom they trust, and give him 51 percent of the business. We've seen some very successful operations going that way. We imagine there can also be negative experiences, but that's life. Another way to legally own a business is by marrying a Mexican citizen. This can be either a drastic way to enter business, or a pleasant way, depending upon the circumstances. In John Dixon's case it turns out to be the latter, because his wife Cha Cha is very attractive and quite pleasant. John and Cha Cha operate a restaurant in Ensenada (called Cha Cha Burgers) and John is the president of the *Amigos de Ensenada* club, which makes him the unofficial mayor of Ensenada for the gringos. Although this is basically an American club, several Mexicans and Mexican businessmen belong.

The American businessmen in Ensenada are quite active in the local chamber of commerce. They've undertaken some rather innovative projects which have benefited the entire community, with positive consequences for the Americans living there. For example, they sponsor Christmas pageants, Easter parades, a wine festival, children's choirs and musical ensembles, plus library and charity events to assist the poor and needy. At first, some of these activities seemed strange to the local businessmen, who usually concern themselves with purely commercial affairs. But they've discovered that these special events generate local business and spending. Now they join in enthusiastically.

The local people recognize that the American residents are behind these events, particularly when the whole retiree community joins in to make things a success. As a result, American residents are viewed in a much more favorable light than if they were withdrawn and snobbish. An excellent English-language newspaper *Ensenada News & Views* is helpful in keeping the resident community informed and active in local affairs.

In Ensenada you'll find several motels that have small apartments for rent by the month. This is an excellent way of trying out the area and seeing whether this might be a retirement place. The town itself is full of rentals, at rock-bottom prices, provided you don't have to have English-speaking neighbors. One man we interviewed, a widower from Tacoma, reports that he pays less than $80 a month for a rather large place. He says the neighbors are very friendly and keep an eye on his house while he is away.

South of town are several beachfront resorts where rooms, houses and apartments can be rented, often with a view. All have RV facilities, and the largest one, Estero Beach, has a regular mobile home village, with many permanently located places. *RV Travel In Mexico* (see Appendix) is a good source of information on this subject.

Another 10 miles or so south of Estero Beach is Punta Banda. The American residents here have organized a club called *Sociedad de Amigos de Punta Banda*. The organization has about 300 members, and the total number of residents there is around 800 at any given time. The advantage of living in this part of Baja is that it can be a year-round thing, rather than having to flee furnace-like temperatures on the Sea of Cortés side.

Most of the residences at Punta Banda own travel trailers or motor homes, many of which have evolved in an interesting way. All along the coast you'll see this evolution of a camping trailer into something quite different. It usually begins with something like a 20-foot travel trailer. The first year, the owners build a nice flagstone patio and put up a picket fence. Since a 20-footer is a little cramped, the next year they build on a living room so they can spread out a little, and perhaps a storage room. Then, as the grandkids start coming to visit, they add on a bedroom or two. By this time, the old travel trailer is beginning to fall apart, so they pull it out and replace it with a kitchen. In its final stages, the compound rambles all over the place and has no relationship to the original conception of an RV lot.

A few miles south of Punta Banda the *zona libre* ends. From here on you need tourist papers. (Make sure you get your papers stamped here, because the next place to do it is in La Paz.) This is where the *real* Baja starts, according to the 4-wheel-drive enthusiasts and the true desert lovers. Long stretches of rolling and often rugged hills, sparsely covered with majestic-looking cardon cactus (similar to the saguaro cactus on the mainland), squat barrel cactus and strange, one-of-a-kind plants. This is the only place on earth where you'll see things like the weird looking cirio trees, often called *bojuum* trees (growing like upside-down carrots) or thick-trunked elephant trees (which bleed red, blood-like sap when punctured with a knife). Smoke trees, salt pines and cactus of all description add to the inventory of desert wonders. There are some small communities along the way, but with few, if any, North Americans living there. Some interesting places, like the wine-growing valleys around Santo Tomás and San Vincente, might be suitable for gringos who can get by without speaking English every day. As far as we can tell, there aren't too many living there now.

San Felipe

On the Sea of Cortés side of the peninsula, still in the *zona libre* part of Baja, is the town of San Felipe. Here you'll find miles of sandy beaches washed with warm gulf waters, a scenic setting beneath the towering peaks of the Sierra San Pedro Martir. When we first started going there 30 years ago, the town consisted of two bars, a gas station, a motel, a couple of RV parks and a row of disintegrating shrimp boats that had been beached by some storm of yesteryear. Probably fewer than 500 people lived there year round. The streets were littered with broken beer bottles and trash.

The town has changed a lot over the last 30 years. For one thing, when you first come into town, you are greeted by a tasteful set of arches with desert landscaping. The main streets are now clean and paved, where before all were of sandy dirt. Today, San Felipe has *nine* bars, ten RV parks, eight motels (some rather elegant) and a whole array of restaurants. The town even boasts three banks!

Well-patronized RV and camping parks line the beach north and south of the town's center. Some of them have constructed clever, two-story shelters over the patios, which serve as shelters for the picnic tables. The second floor presents a shaded view of the Sea of Cortés where some people pitch tents. It's a great place to wake up in the morning and look out over the sea, shimmering and blue-green, with fishing and shrimping boats crisscrossing in the early haze.

The town looks a lot more prosperous than before, and is remarkably clean. One of the drawbacks to San Felipe before was the bikers and dune buggy enthusiasts who used to drink beer and race their unmuffled engines up and down the town's two main streets. Apparently the police have cut down on the "party town" image somewhat. Conspicuous signs posted along the *malecón* (the beach-front promenade) announce that public beer drinking will result in arrest.

Between 14,000 and 15,000 full-time residents live here with an additional 3,000 Americans and Canadians who have living arrangements of some kind or another. At times, there are as many as 5,000 gringos in the area. A few heat-proof northerners stick it out all year, but not many. The problem here, unlike the Pacific side, is the ungodly hot summers. The sun literally bakes the town, making Death Valley look like a springtime resort in comparison. We're talking 110-120 degrees, and at that rate, you needn't mention low humidity; it's just plain hot!

The town empties out about the last of May and people begin returning around the last of September. But pleasant fall, winter and spring make up for the fierce summer weather by providing gloriously sunny days, perfect for enjoying the outdoors. You can be pretty sure it won't rain on your picnic here, because sometimes a year can go by without a drop. But when it does rain, as anywhere in Baja, the desert suddenly bursts into a symphony of lush green and brilliant flowers. This is an emotional experience that makes waiting worthwhile.

Arizona Alternative

Why San Felipe? This is basically a place for the retiree who uses his travel trailer or motor home for retirement. Those who customarily winter in Tucson or Yuma have discovered that by driving 120 miles south of the border on a good paved road, they can do a Mexico winter retirement instead. The bonus over Yuma or Phoenix is a vista of mountains and the lovely Sea of Cortés. By the way, fishing is fantastic here, with huge sea bass and enormous red snappers gnashing at your bait. In Yuma you can catch little catfish, and in Phoenix, you can't even catch poison ivy.

Of course, this is an RV culture—not very Mexican—because most all your neighbors will be from the United States or Canada. But many prefer it this way. They don't have to adjust to another culture, and don't feel pressured to learn a new language. Nevertheless, they are in a foreign country, and the opportunity to pick up some Spanish and make Mexican friends is there if they care to participate.

Like their RV retirees in the U.S., the Americans here waste no time in forming social organizations the minute they move into their winter quarters. They form clubs and elect officers just as they do in the States. Among the groups is a chapter of Alcoholics Anonymous and an organization called *Las Amigas*, which is a ladies club meeting every Friday for lunch. Although not very "Mexican" for the most part, San Felipe is becoming popular in its own way as a Mexico retirement center.

With all these *gringos* hanging around town and spending dollars, you are quite right to assume that prices are considerably higher than on the other side of Baja. In fact, many prices aren't very much lower than in the United states. Restaurant meals, for example, are pretty much as you would pay in Yuma. To park a motorhome or trailer in one of the nicer spots can cost $15 a day for a couple. Monthly rates are around $240 in the better places, with negotiable lower costs for longer stays. However, north of town you find the parking fees quite cheap as the accommodations become more and more rustic. Some people come here and "boondock," that is, use the self-contained facilities in their rigs and camp in the desert. There's a lot of desert here!

Houses and Condos

Many North Americans buy lots (lease, actually) either in town or south of town in developments and build their winter homes. Some rather impressive—and expensive—homes are going up in a development a few kilometers south for up to $150,000. Rentals are impossible to find; expect to buy or else bring your RV.

Labor is much higher here than in Ensenada because of the booming economy. Still, by stateside measures, wages are very low. A maid will work for as little as $8 a day, and a gardener for $70 a week. Electricity costs from $12 to $50 a month, depending how economical you try to be. If you use an air conditioner during the summer, expect to top that $50 figure.

To sum up, San Felipe is a different kind of Mexican retirement: one that is basically part-time, and is an alternative to the usual Brownsville-McAllen or the Lake Havasu kind of winter escape.

Baja California Sur

The peninsula is broken into two political entities, north and south, with the territory of *Baja California Sur* only recently elevated to statehood. The first time this writer visited Baja California Sur was in 1963 via 4-wheel-drive locomotion. Driving the unpaved trails of Baja was true adventure in those days, with many hard days of bouncing through clouds of dust and climbing rocky ledges from top to bottom of the peninsula. Baja fans formed a sort of cult in those days, with adventurers who actually made it all the way to La Paz or Cabo San Lucas awarded the highest honors. I remember cursing myself many a time during the drive (it took about three weeks to make it), but the sense of adventure and exploration made it all worth while. An overnight ferry from La Paz to the mainland avoided the return trip, and probably saved a marriage.

Since 1973, a fairly good asphalt highway links the northern and southern parts of Baja, so driving there is easy today. A long expanse of almost uninhabited country separates the population centers of the north from the south. The drive is long, but worth it; it's liberally endowed with spectacular and unforgettable scenery. Scattered along the way are some tiny settlements, an occasional town, and always friendly, helpful people. They seem quite shy, but if you practice your Spanish with them, you'll find them warming up very quickly.

The people in the middle of Baja interact with Americans differently here than do people who live nearer the border, and for good reason. Here, they see a different *type* of American tourist. The "ugly" gringos in search of boisterous weekends, gaudy souvenirs, cheap thrills and hell-raising usually don't stray very far from Tijuana or Mexicali. Obviously, people who travel this far appreciate Mexico and the fascinating Baja scenery, or they wouldn't be here. The local people sense this and they treat you differently.

As in other parts of Mexico, you'll see the Green Angels (*Angeles Verdes*) at least once or twice a day, as they patrol for motorists in trouble. They carry a truckload of spare parts and gasoline. The drivers are excellent mechanics, speak some English, and the services are free (except for parts and gasoline, all available at cost). The trucks are all equipped with two-way radios, so they can be reached either by CB, or by calling their "hotline" number, 5-20-6123.

Incidentally, along this stretch of highway are some of the most innovative automobile mechanics in the world. Just because there are few or no parts for repairs doesn't stop them. They perform miracles by recycling parts from old hulks, reworking them, and fitting them into automobiles that aren't even closely related. So, when driving the highway south, don't worry because there are no dealer agency repair shops. Still, don't let this lull you into venturing into the open country of Baja without a vehicle in good repair, any more than you would cross Nevada or Arizona driving a lemon.

The highway is paved, and although pock-marked in places, is in fairly good shape. Signs posted along the way proclaim that the highway was not intended to be a "high-speed" highway, and caution you to drive carefully. Good advice. Many stretches have no shoulders, so wide vehicles, such as RVs and travel trailers should use special caution. Fortunately, traffic is so light that you seldom encounter tensions about this. Plenty of RVs travel this highway. Sometimes it seems as if every other vehicle on the road is an RV.

San Ignacio and Mulegé

The highway south of Ensenada is picturesque, with many interesting sights and side trips. Occasionally you'll find some North Americans settled into one of the villages. San Ignacio and Mulegé (two of the prettiest towns in Baja) have a few North Americans living there. I suspect these places will increase in popularity in the near future.

San Ignacio was founded in the seventeenth century by Jesuit missionaries who discovered abundant water from the Río San Ignacio naturally irrigating the soil. It was a marvelous place for growing date palms and citrus fruits. Even before the church and mission were completed, groves of oranges and lemons, grapevines and date palms were thrusting roots into the damp soil. The Jesuits were expelled from Baja over two centuries ago, but dates, citrus and grapes survived fabulously. Today they grow like weeds, sometimes like a jungle. (The dates, citrus and grapes, *not* the Jesuits!). Not only here, but farther south in Mulegé as well, the trees and vines grow lushly. You will understand the meaning of the word *oasis* if you ever visit these two towns.

Mulegé was one of my most favorite places in all of my travels, *anywhere* (before the paved highway, that is). An old, *old* town, with buildings that defy centuries of weathering, with tall palm trees and tropical flowers in profusion, Mulegé was in itself fascinating. But the interesting thing was, that before the new highway, it was a penal colony! On a hill overlooking the town, sits a large pastel-colored building: the territorial prison. Convicts who were judged non-violent and who could be trusted to be part of society, yet legally couldn't, were exiled to places like Mulegé to serve out their sentences.

To my way of looking at it, this was not only a very humane practice, but wonderfully practical. Instead of placing a prisoner into a cage with the taxpayers spending $40,000 a year to keep him there (U.S. style), Mexico sent non-dangerous prisoners into "exile." (They may still do this, I'm not sure.) The convict's family then joined him, and together they managed some way to earn a living. Remember, Mexican taxpayers are very much against pampering convicts by paying board and room for them. The family either found jobs or started a business, much the same as if they were still on the mainland. The children went to school, the parents worked and the family lived normal lives as responsible members of the community. The prison on the hill was reserved for someone who occasionally misbehaved, perhaps appearing intoxicated in public, or quarreling with neighbors. If a convict misbehaved too often, he was shipped back to the mainland and tossed into a regular prison. As you can imagine, few people ever misbehaved! If you were looking for a crime-free environment, you couldn't have found any safer place than Mulegé!

However, in the interests of tourism, the government closed the "prison" (which almost never had prisoners in the first place). Today, the children and grandchildren of convicts might be the owners of the stores or restaurants in town. Today, serious crime is almost nonexistent, but no different from almost any small town in Mexico.

A river, slow-moving and tropical, runs through town and down to the gulf. It's fringed with bamboo, tall trees and massive date palms. A half-dozen trailer parks face the river. These parks are very popular with winter retirees. Although we're getting farther south, toward the cooler Pacific Ocean, the summers here are still not particularly livable.

Even so, there are plans for a 300-unit condo and a marina on the river. Just south of town is a development called, Villas de Mulegé. Houses there can be built to your specifications. Without electricity, this development features solar energy. With about

98% sunshine, this doesn't seem to be such a bad idea! Our guess is that Mulegé is in line for development before long.

South of Mulegé are some interesting RV locations. Look to the section on RVs for more information on Bahía de Concepción.

Loreto, a New Boomer

The oldest permanent Spanish settlement in Baja—founded in 1697—Loreto is in the early stages of a potentially big tourist development sponsored by the Mexican government. For years, the attraction here was fishing, but lately more and more retirees are focusing their attention on the town. There is an international airport going in at Nópolo Cove, and a some rather ambitious facilities are underway here, particularly at Puerto Escondido, 16 kilometers to the south. This area is growing from a sleepy fishing resort into a bustling complex with more and more North Americans coming every day.

Some believe that when all of the projected facilities in the area are completed—including a European-styled village, somewhat like Manzanillo's Las Hadas, with red tiled roofs and sparkling white walls—this will make Loreto as popular as anywhere on the mainland. A new Cancún, perhaps. Maybe. The problem here, as with all of Baja California Sur, is the fierce summer heat. As soon as the temperatures begin climbing in May, the gringos begin packing. Another problem is the water supply; some say it isn't adequate to support a large population.

A little south of Loreto, about 25 miles, is a fairly new and modern trailer park at Puerto Escondido which is popular with the "snowbirds." A nice feature here is that the water is good to drink. There's also a restaurant, a swimming pool, and large *palapas* to shade your RV. Occasionally someone will stay the summer, but not too often. Many respondents have given this place (Tripui) rave reviews.

La Paz and Points South

It isn't until you get as far south as La Paz that you begin to encounter any considerable number of North Americans. Then, from La Paz south, you'll find several interesting places. Here, the summers can be warm, but nothing like the fiery temperatures farther north. Year-round living is clearly possible from here on south to "Los Cabos." Rainfall is scanty, with as long as two years between a drop of rain, only to suffer torrential downpours that turn the arroyos into raging rivers. By the way, be very careful when driving in one of the infrequent rain storms. Slight dips in the road can quickly become deep, swirling currents of water. Best wait for someone else to splash through before trying to ford what looks like a shallow pool across the highway! Okay, so it only comes half-way up on the ducks; wait anyway.

La Paz (pop. 150,000) is the largest city in Baja California Sur, and it seems to be growing larger by the day. It's a fairly clean place, and attracts a number of North American residents, some of whom choose to live here all year around. There are four well-kept trailer parks here, and some of the RV buffs regularly haul their rigs back and forth on the ferry boats that connect La Paz with the mainland. But most northern residents choose to go farther south, toward the tip of the peninsula. Some RV and boating enthusiasts claim La Paz is one of the best places in Baja for winter retirement. From here on south, the summers are livable as opposed to the oven-like June through August on the northern part of the gulf.

If, later on, you plan on crossing from Cabo San Lucas to Puerto Vallarta on the ferry (an overnight trip highly recommended by this author), be sure to get your automobile papers in La Paz, if you haven't already obtained them in the U.S. before crossing the border. The *Registro Federal de Vehículos* is near the intersection of Calle Belisario Domínguez and Calle 5 de Febrero on Calle Belisario Domínguez. The papers are free, but if you don't have them, you can't get on the ferry, and you'll have to drive back to La Paz to get them. Also, if for some reason your tourist card hasn't been stamped by this time, go to the immigration office at Paseo Alvaro Obregón and Calle Muelle; you can't cross to the mainland without it, and you aren't legally in Mexico until this is done. (Occasionally people inadvertently drive past the immigration post up north.)

Cost of Living

In our first edition of *Choose Mexico* in 1985, we remarked on the low cost of living in Baja Sur. Good hotel rooms were going for as low as $4 a night. Swordfish steaks cost $3, and an icy margarita 75 cents. It was one of the best buys in Mexico, according to our research.

Things have changed! Don't look for low prices any more. The $4 room? Today it costs $26 (luxury places, $150). That swordfish dinner is $10 and the margarita close to $3. Even a lowly beer is $1.50 in most bars. Very few prices are lower than you'd find back home.

Housing prices are shocking, with many condos selling for over $300,000. Most houses, particularly along the beaches, command prices that would be expensive even in California or Florida. We understand that some places with a view are commanding one million dollars, possibly more! But still, North Americans seem to be buying them as fast as the Mexicans can build them. The tip of the peninsula is in the midst of a real boom.

Why the boom? We really don't understand it at all. When interviewed, the new residents insist that this is the best place in all of Mexico to retire. "I wouldn't even consider living on the mainland," is the typical reply. "We love Baja and we don't care if it costs *more* to live here than it does back home!" They point to the astonishingly blue ocean, the rugged cliffs with surf frothing against the rocky shore, and the crystal-clear skies. "Where else in the world could I have a view like this from my living room?" The eye of the beholder.

This economic boom has had an effect upon the cultural atmosphere of Baja. With higher prices, the wages have naturally risen for the natives, and employment is at an all-time high. Many laborers earn $300 a month, whereas they would only be earning $100 or less on the mainland. However, even though wages are high and unemployment nil, prices are so high for tourist facilities that Mexicans seldom patronize them. Nice restaurants and bars are exclusively gringo. After all, a worker making $13 a day can't really afford to lift a beer with the gringos, not when the beer costs almost two hours of his daily salary or a meal for him and his wife costs two days' pay. There are two economic realities in Baja, one for Mexicans and one for North Americans.

Bahía de Palmas

About halfway between La Paz and Cabo San Lucas, on your way south, is an interesting, fast-growing North American colony spread along the Bahía de Palmas. This is on the Sea of Cortés side of the peninsula, although it's just about open ocean at this point. Some rather fancy homes have been built by the beaches as well as some ordinary places and RV lots. Homes aren't cheap around here, with selling prices as high as $200,000. Of course, it all depends on what you're prepared to spend. Several trailer parks accommodate the RV drivers. Nothing is crowded, and if you're looking for isolated beaches, beautiful ocean water and quiet, then you've found it.

Los Barriles and Buena Vista are the larger communities along the bay. But neither is really large enough to be called even a village. From here on south runs a dirt and gravel road that follows the coast for some really spectacular scenery, all the way to San José del Cabo. Very, very few people live here, but you'll find RVs and gringo houses scattered along the way, taking advantage of the view.

From April through August, you'll find ecstatic fishermen camped here and filling the hotels. The striper, blue and black marlin fishing is reputed to be the best in the world!

This area is reputed to have the best windsurfing in the world, because of the way the wind blows across the bay. It seems that high velocity thermal winds swoop down from the high mountains inland, sending winds of 20 to 25 knots to really speed the windsurfers along! Better know what you're doing, though. There are several really nice hotels in the area that cater to the windsurfers as well as tourists who want someplace different to visit.

Just south of here is one of the most interesting towns in Baja Sur, a place called Santiago. It sits in a broad canyon that is watered by volcanic springs of pure water year-round, and not affected by drought and low rainfall. The result is a lush oasis of trees, greenness and flowers. Some of the streets are lined with flowering trees with brilliant red blossoms that look almost surrealistic. The Palomar Hotel there has one of the best chefs in Baja, and it's worth a detour just to taste one of his soups. But, according to the local people, not one North American resident has ever chosen to live here. I don't understand this.

Todos Santos

Todos Santos, directly west from Bahía de Palmas, on the Pacific side of the peninsula, is reached by an excellent new highway from La Paz. (If you're going directly to Cabo, this is the highway to follow, even though it looks like a secondary road on most maps.) Todos Santos is an area that obviously doesn't suffer from water shortage, because there are numerous orchards and vineyards in the area. It isn't much of a tourist center, which may be a plus, and it has attracted a few American families. Some are into farming and avocado production.

The attraction here is the beaches, which some people claim are the prettiest in Baja. At this point they are quite isolated and unpopulated. They are away from town by a kilometer or so, and may possibly become popular in the near future. Until a paved highway was built in 1985, few people ever visited here. This is changing. Todos Santos is growing daily. With Los Cabos becoming so expensive, this is the place to watch in the future. FONATUR, the development arm of the Mexican government, is responsible for the growth of Baja Sur, just as they developed Cancún, Ixtapa and other resort areas of Mexico.

San José del Cabo

In our first edition we hinted that San José del Cabo was a well-kept secret in Baja California. About 30 miles north of Cabo San Lucas, San José del Cabo was my favorite town in all of the peninsula. In the book, we described it as "an old town with sparkling white houses, dressed in flowers, neat as an old maid's bedroom, and it has escaped much of the Americanization suffered by Cabo San Lucas, although we can't imagine why." Well, it's still neat and clean, but North Americans have certainly discovered San José del Cabo. Its population has tripled since we reported on it in the original version of *Choose Mexico*.

A restaurant owner and his bartenders all insisted that 40 percent of the residents there now are North American. I doubt this seriously, but there are easily 10 to 20 times the number than back in 1985. Some "well-kept secret!" FONATUR is doing its work well here.

The center of town doesn't look as if it's changed a bit, with substantial looking, century-old buildings and nicely landscaped squares. But many of the houses have been converted into gringo residences. On the edge of town, several impressive condo developments are under way, with some of them looking like something out of the Arabian Nights. Impressive, they are; inexpensive, they're not.

If you're reading this book because of it's "$600 a month" subtitle, you can forget about Los Cabos area. However, it isn't impossible to live on far less than in the United States. One lady we interviewed—a widow from Tacoma—reported that she paid $350 a month for a small apartment near the main square, and that her food costs seldom topped $200 even though she ate at a restaurant almost every night. "My social security is around $900 a month," she reported, "and I have no problem saving a little of that every month."

There is one trailer park here (Brisa del Mar) for you RV fans. It's usually full all winter with retired and semi-retired gringos.

The beaches are a couple of kilometers from San José del Cabo. Oddly enough, they aren't fully developed as yet. At a little village called La Playa, there's a store and a couple of restaurants, and that's about it. But there are numerous RV sites there, places where North Americans have leased land and constructed shelters for their RVs and seem to be in the process of building more substantial housing. This is a very quiet, low-key place that appeals to those looking for this kind of ambiance.

Cabo San Lucas

There seems to be something magical about the name *Cabo San Lucas*. This writer has never understood the fascination that many North Americans have for Cabo. It's a sprawling place without a real "downtown" section. Not unless you count a concentration of souvenir shops and incredibly loud gringo bars as "downtown." (For some reason, many tourists feel it obligatory to patronize Cabo bars to scream, jump up and down and shout at the top of their voices. I'm sure they don't do that at home, because any bar I know would "86" them within a matter of ten seconds.) Most of Cabo San Lucas' streets are dirt and often are lined with dejected-looking houses that border upon being shacks.

Nevertheless, many North Americans have fallen in love with Cabo, and seem to be standing in line to buy the next house or condo. Tourists fly down from everywhere in the United States and Canada for the incredible sailfish and marlin sport and are happy to pay $595 a week for a one-bedroom apartment that would cost $595 for *three months* on the mainland. One development offers luxury homes and condos starting at $250,000 for a small one, and who knows how much for a "big" one? We've heard rumors that a million bucks isn't out of range! But the views are gorgeous, and the landscaping and construction spell class.

Scattered throughout the area are apartment developments, sometimes off on a dirt road somewhere, where you can buy something cheaper than the $250,000 figure. We've seen some smaller ones starting at $35,000. Nothing is cheap in Baja Sur any more.

Baja vs. the Mainland

As pointed out earlier, those who love Baja wouldn't consider living anywhere else. There's something special about the desert that attracts some people, but repels others. Of course, the fishing there is marvelous, and for many Baja residents, that is reason enough to love Baja.

At the risk of making enemies of some Baja-lovers, we have to question the inflated prices in the lower tip of the peninsula. Is it worth the extra investment to live in Baja Sur? Obviously, the answer to the question by many who live in Cabo San Lucas and environs is a resounding "yes!"

This writer admits a certain bias against full-time desert living, since he spent some time laboring in Death Valley (Calif.) under the blazing sun attempting to wrest a fortune from his lead-silver claim. The fortune turned out to be elusive, but the starkness of the desert remains as crisp reality. Other people, with more pleasant memories of the desert, and particularly of the desert panorama of Baja, won't understand this at all, for indeed, there is a certain romance, beauty and mystery about the desert that isn't to be found elsewhere. The way nature balances life and environment with delicate perfection reveals some deeply miraculous secrets of the universe. But when you're driving a jarring, chattering air hammer into solid dolomite in 116 degree temperatures, the fascination quickly fades.

Again, the only answer seems to be found within your own personality. You have to go and "try it before you buy it."

If you do decide to do extensive traveling, and/or living in Baja, let us again remind you of the travel clubs which specialize in Baja and west coast mainland travel.

CHAPTER SEVENTEEN

Oaxaca and the Yucatán

Oaxaca

At slightly over 5,000 feet, Oaxaca's climate is a bit warmer than Mexico City's and, without the latter's industrial development, it boasts much cleaner air. Oaxaca's population is passing 300,000, but its large, spread out area and the absence of steel and concrete skyscrapers and other visible hallmarks of twentieth-century life effectively conceal that fact.

Oaxaca is easy to reach from Mexico City by air, bus or rail. The west coast beaches of Puerto Angel, Puerto Escondido and Huatulco are close by and are easily accessible by plane, automobile or bus.

The great majority of residents, both of the city and the surrounding state of which it is the capital, are Indians. They are proud of their heritage and its resistance to assimilation into the politically, culturally and economically dominant cultures of the last five centuries—first Aztec, then Spanish, and now Mexican. Oaxaca was the birthplace of both Benito Juárez, "Mexico's Abraham Lincoln," and Porfirio Díaz, an iron-fisted president for many years, and was the home of numerous accomplished artists. It is conscious of its colonial and Indian past, and has preserved much of its architectural history. Oaxaca is as different in appearance and atmosphere from cities in northern Mexico as Tucson, Arizona is different from Portland, Maine.

On Saturdays, handicrafts flood in from neighboring villages and spill out of the huge Juárez market onto the surrounding streets. Black and green glazed pottery, innumerable baskets in a

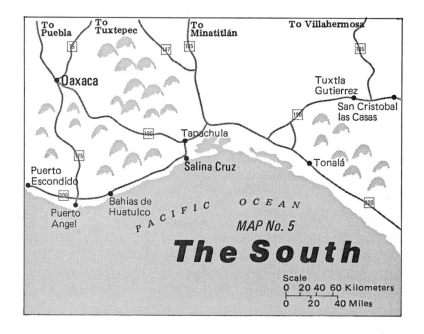

great variety of shapes and sizes, handloomed textiles and many skillful copies of the Monte Albán idols and jewelry beguile even the most apathetic shopper. On other days of the week, there is a market or *tianguis* in one or the other of the many surrounding towns. A trip to these towns can also provide the opportunity to visit the studios of the many talented artisans whose work is sold in the shops of Oaxaca.

Every Mexican town of any size has its zócalo or town square, but few are more sumptuous or lively than Oaxaca's twin plazas. Filled with tall, handsome trees and countless wrought iron benches where locals and foreigners alike while away many sunny hours, and ringed by sidewalk cafes, it *is* the heart of Oaxaca.

Because of his long, dictatorial rule, Porfirio Díaz would win few popularity contests in Mexico today, even in his home town, (although Oaxaca does have a street named after him). Nevertheless, he did give his birthplace an unusually handsome bandstand on which a variety of instrumental groups play several evenings a week. Almost the entire town turns out for these concerts, and parents sit around the zócalo gossiping while children play on the grassy parts of the park. The stream of peddlers—whose wares include carved, painted wooden animals, bird-shaped ceramic whistles, hammocks, baskets, serapes, belts, and even elaborate carpets—could become annoying after a while, were it not for the fact that a polite but firm refusal is usually sufficient to send them on their way. Then one can listen to the music, chat with friends, or just enjoy the passing parade.

In the second edition of *Choose Mexico* we reported that the beauty and unspoiled antiquity of Oaxaca was beginning to attract more tourists, particularly those interested in exploring the Zapotec (Monte Albán) and Mixtec ruins nearby. At that time this mountain city still had only a small colony of North American residents. Most of those who had chosen to live there seemed to indicate that they rather like it that way. One reason may be that food and housing prices have remained somewhat lower in Oaxaca than in many other parts of Mexico. Another reason may be what a retired resident described as "freedom from pressures for conformity."

By early 1992 the number of full- or part-time foreign residents, mostly from the United States and Canada had grown in number to what some there estimate to be 500 or more. It is hard to be precise because Oaxaca seems to attract retirees who are more interested in experiencing Mexican life close up than in becoming part of a foreign enclave. Certainly there are opportunities to meet and socialize with fellow *Norteamericanos*. One is the lending library on Calle Alcalá just a few blocks from the town center (which is said to have one of the best collections of English-language books outside of San Miguel de Allende). It is the place to go when you want to get together with fellow expatriates to get news from home, to exchange local gossip and to get current information on such practical matters as where there is a particularly attractive house or apartment for rent at a reasonable rent. We also found that there tends to be a daily early-morning cluster of English-speaking residents and tourists in one of the outdoor cafes on the *zócalo*. Three language schools serve the many foreign residents who want to get beneath the surface of this magical city.

Because Oaxaca does offer reliably comfortable winter temperatures, it attracts many part-year residents from the United States and Canada. Year after year, they desert the cold and damp of their home communities for the warmth and stimulation of Oaxaca for periods ranging from one to three months.

Most foreign residents, whether living in Oaxaca full or part time seem to choose rooms, suites or cottages on the grounds of the numerous small affordable hotels, scattered throughout the city. Some are able to negotiate monthly rates lower than the $10 dollars a day that seems to commonplace for accommodations more than a few blocks from the center of town.

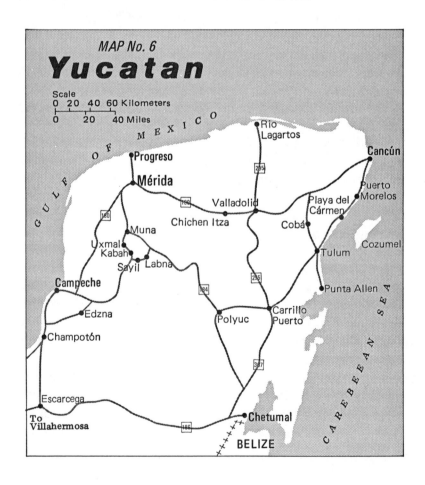

MAP No. 6

Yucatan

Oaxaca is certainly an increasingly viable choice in the Mexico retirement sweepstakes and a wonderful place to visit, even if you have only a few weeks to spend in Mexico.

The Yucatán

The Yucatán peninsula is easily accessible from the east coast of the U.S. and Canada—in fact it is only a couple of hours' flight from Miami or New Orleans. The Caribbean coast from Cancún south has some of the most delightful beaches in the world. Long stretches of sand and coral are fringed with low jungle and an occasional coconut plantation or farm.

Although much of the beach-front land is tantalizing as a site for that dream home, be warned against potential legal pitfalls. Often, people who "own" this land don't realize that they are only there because possession is that well-known percentage of the law. When they try to sell, they discover that "their" land belongs to someone else. Don't let this discourage you, however: you may always rent land, and you can even build—provided you find a reliable lawyer. Away from the beaches, land ownership is more available and more reliable but, alas, less desirable. Most of the Yucatán peninsula is thinly soiled limestone, fit only for scrub jungle and heniquen plantations. Unless you are into tropical agriculture—or isolation—you may be better off with one of the population centers such as Cancún or Mérida.

Cancún

Cancún has become one of the hemisphere's most popular beach resorts. New hotels and condo developments are being built at an alarming rate. Prices in the tourist areas bear a much closer resemblance to those elsewhere in the Caribbean than to those in most of Mexico. Condos are being marketed aggressively, but before you sign up for one—in Cancún, Acapulco, Lake Tahoe, or any resort town—figure out what your weekly and daily costs will be. A popular ploy is to sell condos on a two-or three- week time-share basis. This is for tourists, not for anyone who seriously wants to live in Mexico. There are many small houses being built in downtown Cancún that are far less expensive than housing in the beachfront hotel area and look very comfortable.

Many Americans buy or rent south of Cancún as far south as Tulum. Then, when they want to mingle with compatriots, they have only to drive the excellent road north. Playa del Carmen, where condo construction is booming, and the island of Cozumel are only 35 miles from Cancún and attract many Americans for retirement living.

Mérida

Mérida is another popular spot. It has managed to maintain much of its colonial charm, and if it weren't for unmuffled motorcycles and trucks, it could be described as a sleepy paradise. One problem here is the summer weather. Without a tempering ocean to keep it cool, Mérida can become an oven, as bad as St. Louis or Cincinnati in the summer. In fact, it's even hotter than they are but, fortunately, it doesn't have their oppressive humidity. Modern housing is rather scarce in Mérida. Unless you are willing to buy an old house and fix it to your tastes, your only alternative seems to be a rental. There just isn't the condo boom as there is on the Caribbean coast.

Another point to consider is the relatively high prices on the Yucatán Peninsula. There are several reasons for these, such as its distance from the rest of Mexico and the cost of shipping goods there. Of course, in tourist centers like Cancún, an additional factor is the influx of easy tourist dollars.

Since so many North Americans visit the peninsula's resorts and ruins, some are bound to make it their retirement home, overcoming all the obstacles we have mentioned. Perhaps some of them will take the time to let us know how they are doing. In the meantime, we suggest that you think of it as wonderful place to visit, particularly after you are living elsewhere in Mexico and know how to get the most out of all your travels in that country.

CHAPTER EIGHTEEN

RV Travel in Mexico

Many readers have written to ask about taking motorhomes, trailers and mobile homes to Mexico. We originally skipped this aspect of Mexico living in the belief that RVs are not practical for long-term living or retirement in Mexico. After doing more research and interviewing many RV devotees, we've changed our opinion somewhat. RV travel in Mexico is quite popular, and many RV enthusiasts return year after year. And we must admit, for part-time retirement in Mexico, there are some positive aspects of RV living.

First, let's dispense with the idea of *mobile homes* in Mexico. With few exceptions, dragging one of those monsters into Mexico for retirement living is highly impractical. The exceptions we've found are mainly in Baja California, and only just a short distance from the U.S. border. Because mobile homes contain wiring and plumbing, all set up and ready to use, they have the advantage of being installed on a lot for immediate occupancy. Getting them to some sites in northern Baja is relatively easy, because there's an excellent four-lane highway going as far as Ensenada. However, according to Mexican law, anything over 40 feet long or eight feet wide requires special permits, which could mean lots of red tape! There's good reason for this law: Mexican highways are simply not designed for 12-foot wide packages. When you try to haul that wide box through some of the towns where the streets were laid out 400 years ago for horse and carriage, you could learn what trouble is all about. Your mobile home may bend in places where it wasn't designed to bend.

Once the mobile homes are there, owners tend to disguise the origins by enclosing them with an attractive masonry facade, complete with Spanish-looking arches. Still, it's a mobile home, and not a "real house." Furthermore, as long as you are going to the trouble of building a stone or brick shell around the mobile home and then constructing a roof over the whole thing, you might as well have built a real house in the first place.

Construction costs are so low that you can build a new two- or three-bedroom home to your specifications for far less than what you would have to pay for a modest-sized mobile home and having it carted down to Mexico. This means you have a real house, with brick walls, a fireplace or two and a solid floor (instead of a tin box on wheels) for your residence.

Recreational Vehicle Living

I personally wouldn't bother taking an RV to live in for long periods of time. From my perspective, there is no advantage to dragging an RV around, not when hotels, motels, apartments and restaurants are so cheap. I'm not saving a thing, and the extra aggravation and gasoline isn't worth it to me. For vacations or short-term retirement living—that's a different story.

RV facilities aren't all that great in many retirement places in Mexico and are non-existent in others. Too often, the trailer parks are located way out on the edge of town, so you end up living somewhere because that's where the trailer park is rather than where you might like to stay.

A curious thing is that often you'll pay as much to stay overnight in a RV park as you would pay in the United States. Many parks charge $10 to $15 a day for little more than a space, including electricity and water you may or may not trust to drink. Of course, there's a discount for staying a month or more in a trailer park, but you could end up paying as much as if you had rented an apartment near the town square.

Other problems with RV travel: when highways don't have shoulders for emergency stops, and something happens, you are going to be sitting in the highway while you make repairs to your vehicle. Another caution: RV tires are often non-standard sizes in Mexico, so be sure and stock a good spare. As we mentioned earlier, streets are quite narrow in many Mexican cities, so caution is required when whipping around town to do your shopping. Most people just park their rigs and rely on public transportation or shank's mare.

Our final objection to long-term RV living in Mexico is that it separates you from the everyday life of the community. You'll be staying in an enclave of U.S. or Canadian RV fans, and will have few Mexican neighbors to interact with. You will be insulated from many everyday happenings that you encounter in ordinary Mexican neighborhoods. Instead of living near the *zócalo* where you can stroll around every evening or lounge on a bench while reading the morning papers, you could be on the outskirts somewhere, and have to make a special effort to get into town.

Now the Good News . . .

Having said all of these negative things about RV living in Mexico, let us examine the positive side for a minute. Many, many RV people travel in Mexico, and wouldn't consider any other style of travel. They counter my objections to RVs quite effectively. They point out the many advantages in RV living in Mexico, and the advantages are much the same as RV travel in the States. "If RVs are fun in Kansas, why not in Mexico?" is a pertinent question.

The most often mentioned advantage of using an RV to visit Mexico is having your own kitchen at your disposal. Not having to depend on Mexican restaurants means a lot to some people. "Most RV people eat out occasionally," said one woman, "but the rest of the time, we want to eat just as we do back home."

Some RV enthusiasts counter my major objection by saying they *enjoy* living in a closed, U.S.A. style community. "We don't want to learn another language," reported one woman. "We didn't come here to absorb another culture. We just want to spend a pleasant winter with our friends, then return home when things thaw out in our home town." One couple we met drive to Guaymas every winter, park their rig in the enclave and never once set foot outside the protected walls of the trailer park for the entire season. That's a little extreme, but that makes them happy.

Others disagree that they are isolated from the Mexican community. One woman told of a Halloween party held in San Carlos Bay. "We informed a few taxi drivers in Guaymas that we were having a 'trick or treat' party for kids, and could they find some kids to attend. Comes Halloween night, and the taxi drivers brought over 250 children to the party! Most were dressed in costumes, and we gave out 150 pounds of candies and treats! What a wonderful night!" Halloween has become an annual event, looked forward to eagerly by both gringo adults and Mexican kids in San Carlos Bay.

Another advantage to RV living that several people emphasized is that they can often find a park where they can camp on the beach and enjoy having the surf to lull them to sleep in the evening. One couple we interviewed, regularly bivouacs next to the Seri Indian camp on the mainland side of the Sea of Cortés. "The Indians came to expect us for a visit every winter," they said, "and we brought them old clothes and toys for the children. They treat us with love and respect that's truly heartwarming."

Snowbirds Flock Together!

RV people tend to return to the same parks every year, just as in the United States for their "winter retirement" and eagerly look forward to meeting their friends of last season. Many parks hold holiday celebrations with parties and dinners for the RVers. Many long-term friendships have been forged in Mexican RV parks.

Just as in the United States, the RV people tend to organize and plan activities, from pot lucks to dances. RV owners probably aren't any more friendly than other Mexico travelers, but perhaps because they are quartered so close together, they have more opportunity to be friendly.

Is RV Travel Safe in Mexico?

All of the RV owners we interviewed maintain that driving a rig in Mexico is no more hazardous than in the United States, providing you exercise common sense. Several people told of the extreme helpfulness of local people when they did have some problems. "Truck drivers are especially helpful," said one man. "Once we ran out of gas on a lonely stretch of desert highway. Immediately, two truckers stopped to see what was the matter. Since they didn't have any gasoline in their diesel rigs, one flagged down a passing pickup, and they siphoned enough fuel to get us to the next town. The pickup driver wouldn't accept payment for the gasoline, insisting that it was a gift. The trucker seemed embarrassed when we offered him a tip for his help. He finally accepted when we suggested that he use it to buy Christmas presents for his children." (Incidentally, this is a good way to reward someone for a service without insulting them with a tip: say that you want to buy a gift for the children.)

Mechanical breakdowns seem to be a magnificent challenge to Mexican mechanics. I'm convinced they can fix anything, and they charge almost nothing. A friend once blew a piston on his new Dodge van in El Rosario (Baja). Resigning himself to waiting for the Los Angeles dealer to come down and make good on the guarantee, my friend was surprised when a local shade-tree mechanic offered to get the car going.

"I guarantee it will get you at least to the border," said the mechanic. "If it doesn't make it there, forget it. If it does, send me $100."

What a deal! The mechanic found a piston from a Ford, and a connecting rod from an Plymouth, and he proceeded to work with files, sandpaper and welding torch though the night. In the morning my friend started the engine, and drove it all the way to the dealer in Los Angeles. To this day, the dealer has the engine on display—with the side of the block cut away to show the Ford piston in the Dodge engine—as a tribute to Mexican mechanics doing the impossible!

As far as RV driving being safe in Mexico, it seems apparent that it is, or else the insurance companies would charge a higher premium to insure RVs. On the contrary, because of the good driving records of RV people, insurance companies actually give them discounts (through travel clubs). This is understandable, because generally, RV owners have a higher sense of safety in the first place. You tend to be constantly aware of what is happening ahead of you and behind you, simply because you are driving a much larger vehicle. True, some roads are pitted with potholes and sometimes curves aren't marked, but these hazards cease to be hazards if you simply drive carefully, just as most RV operators do anywhere. As an aside, I've asked every RV operator I've met who has traveled in Mexico about insurance problems in case of an accident. To date, none has reported or heard of any bad experiences. (We'd welcome hearing your personal encounters, good or bad.)

Winter Retirement in Baja

Although RV retirement in Mexico hasn't nearly the attraction of retiring in houses and apartments, there is one exception, and it's a *major* exception. Baja California, both the Pacific side and on the Sea of Cortés, is the fastest-growing winter retirement destination of all. At last count, there are over 100 RV parks in Baja that cater exclusively to North American RVers. Also growing in popularity are mainland winter retirement places, such as Bahía Kino and San Carlos Bay.

As an alternative to Arizona's Yuma, Tucson or Phoenix winter retirement, RVers have discovered San Felipe, on Baja's Sea of Cortés coast. About a two-hour drive south of the border—over a lightly-traveled, good highway—San Felipe is attracting snowbirds away from the Yuma-Lake Havasu area for winter. Well-equipped parks—right on the beach—host several thousand people every winter. San Filipe offers complete facilities, even visiting mechanics who will perform maintenance and repairs on your vehicle while you lounge in the sun or fish for dinner.

A trailer space costs about $240 to $300 a month in most parks—about what you would pay in the United States. "We don't save money by spending the winter here," said one couple, "but we don't spend any more than we used to spend in Yuma, but we have a lot more fun!"

Boondockers' Heaven

In most parts of Mexico, boondocking isn't very common. Unless they are part of a large caravan, most RVers feel uneasy about boondocking, just as they do in most parts of the United States. However, in Baja, boondocking has become an art form, one engaged in by most RV travelers at some time or another. Only, it doesn't seem like boondocking when you back your rig up to the surf and have several hundred boondocking *Norteamericanos* for companions. Ninety percent of them are retired, by the way.

Most boondocking is done in the most beautiful parts of the peninsula, where non-RVers cannot stay. This is because the Baja Peninsula is so dry that much of it is all but uninhabitable. Without fresh water supplies, the best beaches can have no hotels or tourist accommodations. If you cannot camp, no matter how rich you might be, you can only glimpse these beautiful sights as you drive past. Just park your rolling home, and you enjoy beaches and scenery that those poor rich folks must forego. A trip to the nearest town every week to replenish the drinking water and buy extra groceries is all that's needed.

Like birds flocking together, winter retirees cluster along the shores and congregate wherever fishing and scenic attractions beckon. Our favorite string of beaches are located just south of Mulegé, about halfway down the Peninsula. Santispac, El Coyote, Requesón and several others string out along the blue waters of the Sea of Cortés. Hundreds of RVs arrive here every October and stay until the weather begins heating up in April. With their rigs lined up along the beach, campfire pits in front, and sometimes a palm thatch *palapa* built for shade, these Americans and Canadians enjoy a bountiful season of companionship, fishing, swimming, boating, hiking and just plain loafing.

Not unexpectedly, as more and more "Winter Mexicans" crowd the beaches, natives are beginning to see commercial possibilities and they naturally want their share. Beaches usually belong to an *ejido*, or Indian communal lands, and nominally are under tribal or communal control. And, even though all Mexican beaches are open to the public, the ejido is permitted to charge for overnight parking. That's why some beaches today are no longer totally free, although they might as well be free because camping charges are so low. Typically, a caretaker makes the rounds every evening and asks for a dollar or so to park overnight—depending on the beach. In return, the caretakers make sure things are tidy and keep their eye out for anyone suspicious.

The ejido beach caretakers also keep their eyes on trailers and palapas left throughout the summer when Baja sunshine makes Death Valley seem cool. From the reports we get, theft is rarely a problem. "We leave our trailer, trail bikes and boat here all summer," said one couple. "We put small things inside, and chain the bikes to the boat for safety. Yet we've never had anything stolen, not even when we've forgotten to secure things."

Traditional RV Parks

Going down the west side of Baja, you'll find numerous regular RV parks with a very large one at Estero Beach, south of Ensenada. There is even a KOA camp with 200 spots in Tijuana! However, we don't recommend retirement in Tijuana; Californians might snicker at the idea.

San Quintín has some good beach camping, as well as two parks with a total of 85 spots. Guerrero Negro, San Ignacio, Santa Rosalía and Mulegé, all have facilities with over 300 RV spaces and lots of beach camping. These towns are covered in our chapter on Baja California.

Bahía de Los Angeles has always been a popular place with fishing enthusiasts and those who love desert solitude. There are three RV parks here, all near town, with boat ramps, and one at the junction. The last time we were there, they charged $4 a night for electrical hookup and a cement pad, with the water just feet from our door. A water truck passes through with drinking water, and will fill your tanks for about $1.50. The sea provides a bountiful harvest of clams and scallops, not to mention fish for those willing to toss a line in the water. Kids knock on the door every evening to see if you want to buy their freshly-caught fish or live pin scallops, still in the shell. Can't get fresher than that. A nearby restaurant serves excellent meals of fish, lobster and tough but tasty Mexican steaks.

Two little markets in the village supply rudimentary foods such as chickens, coffee and sterilized milk. Folks on tight budgets depend on the sea for much of their food, with clam chowder, sauteed scallops and rockfish fillets *a la Veracruzano* providing wonderful gourmet dinners. "We load up our cabinets with canned goods and such before we leave San Diego," said one lady in Bahía de Los Angeles. "We seldom have to buy any groceries here other than fresh eggs and tortillas from the *tienda* and veggies from local gardens. We feel as if we are eating for free."

Farther south is Loreto, where there are three parks, one of which has purified drinking water. There are about 150 spaces in this area. Talking about the newest park in Puerto Escondido (just south of Loreto), a friend says: "One of the nicest in Mexico. You can pay a yearly rental and build your own *palapa*" (a *palapa* is one of those palm-thatched roofs that are so effective in the tropics in providing shade.) We understand that there is even a market there, so you don't have to run into town for shopping.

Tourism is just starting to take off in this area, and you can expect some spiffy things to come in the future. (See the chapter on Baja for more details.)

La Paz has six parks with a total of 411 spaces. Most of them have good water. Respondents have raved over a couple of the parks here. Not only are they topnotch, but the personnel are extremely helpful. "We came in with a blown tire," one couple reported. "The owner of the park said, '*No hay problema!*' And before we knew what was happening, we had two men replacing the hard-to-find radial tire, which they had to run into town to locate. 'No charge for the labor, just for the tire!' said the owner. We tipped the workers, and they were delighted."

Then, farther south are two interesting places, Los Barriles and Buena Vista with four parks, three of them on the beach (Vardugos, Playa de Oro and La Capilla). There are 110 spaces in Los Barriles, and 43 in Buena Vista.

Los Cabos

At the lower end of the Baja Peninsula are the towns of Cabo San Lucas and San José del Cabo. A three-day drive from the border doesn't discourage many RVs. All of the trailer parks report that winters mean a full house.

In San José del Cabo there is only one park, Brisa del Mar, situated on the south edge of town. There are 100 spots here. The rates are about the same as other places in Los Cabos, about $240 a month for long stays. If you want to stay for the winter, you need to get there about the first of November to make sure you have a spot. All the other parks in the area report the same.

At La Playa, near San José del Cabo, there are many RVs that are obviously there permanently. The lots are leased from villagers, and many RVs have been enclosed by a roof to keep the sun from baking them in the warmer seasons. If you have a motorhome, you'll need a car to get back and forth into town, because there's little here except a store and a couple of restaurants.

A word of caution about park rents that you might read in many guidebooks on Mexico, but particularly about Baja: Most books are hopelessly out of date. It makes for some misunderstandings when a guidebook states that the price of overnight parking is $3.00 when it's really $15. Prices have gone up very fast in Baja, so don't take it out on the park owner if the guidebook is wrong. Believe the manager, not a book!

In Cabo San Lucas, there are six parks with a total of 295 spaces. That's not many, considering the number of people who make the trek each winter. One park, the San Vincente, is strictly for retirees and full-time living. But openings don't happen all that often, so getting there early is recommended.

On the Mainland

The very closest RV facilities that we are aware of are at a place called El Golfo de Santa Clara, just a few miles south of Yuma. There are three very rustic camps, primitive and only for self-contained units. But the fishermen love it. Incidentally, this writer's (John Howells) claim to immortality is in El Golfo. Thirty years ago, before there was a highway, I met a developer who wanted to build a resort on an isolated beach south of town. I drove him and his crew to the beach in my jeep and helped him survey the property. He was so appreciative that he named the beach after me: *Johnny's Beach*. He named the resort *Las Aventuras de Juanito* (Johnny's Adventures). But unfortunately he ran out of money (the story of my life, as well) and he didn't finish more than a bar-restaurant, which is still called "Johnny's Place."

Next is the town of Puerto Peñasco. For people from Arizona, this is the closest access to a real town (El Golfo is more of a village) on the Sea of Cortés, and there have been some rather fancy homes built there. There are five trailer parks along the beach, most with boat ramps and laundromats.

Kino Bay is the next logical stop for RV retirement living. This is a popular place for well-heeled Hermosillo farmers to build beautiful, bougainvillea-covered mansions. Apparently, many North Americans are buying leases on villas as well. We receive reports that lots of retired U.S. military are spending winter retirements there. Kino is divided into two sections: Old Kino, and New Kino. The old part is basically a fishing village, holding little attraction for tourists or retirees. It's in New Kino where the retirees head. The town spreads out for nine miles along the beach, and there are several impressive condominium developments underway.

Here's where you'll meet the Seri Indians, a semi-nomadic tribe who formerly lived on Tiburon Island in the Gulf. A few years ago, the Mexican government moved them to the mainland. Existence on the island had become too precarious. The Indians brought with them their skills at carving driftwood, and you'll see them often, offering you beautiful sculptures at irresistible prices. One couple we know regularly boondocks near the Seri Indian village. They bring clothing and toys for the children and are welcomed every year.

Five trailer parks in Kino accommodate visitors, one large one with 200 spaces. Space rental in New Kino is as little as $4 a day (during our last visit), which puts it in the economical category. If you travel in the summer, you can be assured of plenty of space, because most "snowbirds" go home for June, July and August.

San Carlos Bay

The most popular place, and the mecca for many, many RV fans is San Carlos Bay, 256 miles from Nogales, Arizona. Just north of Guaymas, this section of beach has seen an astounding boom in recent years.

With a backdrop of rugged mountains and gentle beach at your doorstep, it's small wonder that RV fans love this area. The same people come back year after year, having reunions with friends of last year. "We've met the same people here every year for the last ten seasons," reported one couple.

There are ten restaurants, grocery stores, a drug store, shopping, two marinas, and everything you might need for a winter's retirement. There's even a branch bank there for converting dollars into pesos. You don't have to be continually running into town. This is fortunate, since the city of Guaymas is rather unexciting.

There are several RV parks in San Carlos, including one particularly nice one with over 300 spaces, right on the water. Sometimes you can make arrangements to keep your boat there during the summer while you do your retirement thing somewhere cooler. The retiree organizations are quite active here. They offer Spanish lessons, dancing and art lessons for their members. They engage in orphanage support and buy school supplies for the local kids.

RVing in the Tropics

As long as you've traveled this far, you might as well haul your rig on down to Mazatlán and points south along the Gold Coast. Here you'll find a few year-round retirees living in motorhomes and trailers, but plenty of winter retirees. By June, the parks are all but empty. This is a little odd, because the summer climate along the west coast of Mexico is pretty nice, at least compared to summers in most of the United States. The summer temperatures and humidity are always lower than Miami, just about the same as Chicago summers.

Summer is the rainy season south of the tropic of Capricorn, so things are nice and green, and the tourist rush is long over. The summer climate from Mazatlán on south is much more livable because the coast faces the Pacific Ocean rather than the Sea of Cortés as you find farther north. We checked several RV facilities around Mazatlán and found them to be adequate, priced about the same as in Baja with the better parks about $225 to $275 a month. This may not sound expensive, except when you consider that for that same amount you could rent an apartment or possibly even a house.

Another drawback is that most of the parks along the Gold Coast sit far from the beach and a long walk to town. One notable exception is in Bucerias, about 20 miles north of Puerto Vallarta. Run by an American (as are most Mexican RV facilities) the park is the only one in town and fronts on a lovely beach.

In between Mazatlán and Puerto Vallarta is the little town of San Blas (described elsewhere in this book). The trailer park a few blocks from the town's center is pretty well-filled in winter and, like the rest of parks, it's totally empty in the summer. But there are some really attractive parks near San Blas that look like interesting places for RVs.

Matachen and Playa los Cocos are about ten minutes' drive from San Blas, and have very rustic, but picturesque camping spots. The view of the mountains and Matachen Bay are marvelous. Then, along a road that follows the ocean to a village called Santa Cruz, you'll find some great places to park your rig. Most of these are next to a store or somebody's house, and the rates are negotiable. You have the surf at your door and pretty tropical vegetation all around. We've met several people who regularly haul a fishing boat there and spend several months with the surf lapping at their beach.

For some reason or other, this part of the coast always seems to be green and lush while the rest of the west suffers from lack of rainfall during the winter season. Even during the severe drought of 1988, this stretch of beach looked marvelously tropical and verdant.

RVs in Puerto Vallarta? Acapulco?

Yes, of course. The largest in Puerto Vallarta is a nice, U.S.-style trailer park, complete with rec rooms and laundry facilities. None of these parks is close to the beach, and it's a good taxi trip to the center of town. Acapulco has four parks, with a total of 240 spaces, none near town, and two about eight miles away, at Pie de la Cuesta (on the beach). This isn't so bad though, because there are buses that run into town quite regularly.

For the dedicated RV explorer, the adventure of going so far south is a major attraction. It must be, because most parks on the coast seem to fill up during the winter.

RVs in Other Parts of Mexico

Almost anywhere you go in Mexico you are likely to encounter someone driving or hauling an RV. One of our favorite places (we camped in a tent, but there were many RVs) was near the Mayan ruins at Palenque. The park is called Nututún. It's next to a small river and has a great restaurant.

All along the Caribbean coast south from Cancún are magnificent RV discoveries to be made. Often you can make arrangements to stay on private land, with a Mayan family, parked next door to their thatched roof house. We camped at one place where one of the owner's sons took us out fishing for barracuda and showed us a pool which reputedly housed a 14-foot crocodile!

What if there Are No Parks?

Most towns along the West Coast have a park or two, but as you go farther east, parks are scarcer and not as well equipped. This is no problem, however, since almost any motel will be happy to find a place for you to park, and probably give you an electric line and water if you need it. (Be careful of loading questionable water into your drinking water tanks, however, it could contaminate everything.) The motel will no doubt charge you something. Another place to stay is by a gasoline station. Most Pemex stations stay open all night, so the only problem is the noise of trucks and cars coming and going. They don't charge, but for a tip they will allow you to plug into the electricity.

Most books and pamphlets we read warn against parking alongside the road in Mexico, or in isolated areas. That is probably good advice even for RVs in the United States. However, we must report that many people tell us that they camp anywhere they please in Mexico and enjoy this more than staying in regular RV parks. Of course, these are the same people who "boondock" anywhere they please in the United States. My own personal opinion is that I would feel much safer parking my motorhome overnight on a Mexican beach or residential neighborhood than in similar locality in the United States. Understand, this is my conviction, not my recommendation! I've done my share of camping in isolated areas of Mexico and have never felt the slightest apprehension.

I know of one family from Dallas who drives their motor home every year to visit an Indian family in the mountains above Mazatlán. They bring presents, clothing and a Polaroid camera to take pictures of all the neighbors who look forward to the visit with great joy. This is a different type of RV travel than staying in U.S.-style trailer parks, but it might be worth a try.

Travel Clubs

There are two major RV travel clubs that specialize in Mexico travel: *Vagabundos del Mar*, which also does caravans, mostly into Baja, and has its own trailer park in La Paz; the other is Mexico West Travel Club. Both clubs sell insurance at group rates and can score fishing licenses and boat permits for you. These clubs are located in California, and concentrate on Baja more than the mainland, but they can be valuable to anyone interested in Mexico.

RV Insurance

Don't believe the guidebooks when they say all Mexican insurance rates are the same. Insurance rates are pretty much set by the Mexican government, so it might seem that you aren't going to save a whole lot by shopping around. That's not really true. You can save a bundle, depending on where you buy and how you buy. See Appendix for details.

RVs in Mexico?

To sum up, you folks who love RVs, and don't mind pulling or pushing them into Mexico, are in for a great time. The fraternity and neighborliness you are used to back home among fellow RV folks, is even more vibrant in Mexico. Yes, there are lots of RVs in Mexico. No, it isn't any more dangerous than RV living back home. Yes, there are some adventures to be enjoyed. But before you hook up and head for Mexico, may we suggest that you consult the book *RV Travel in Mexico* by John Howells (Gateway Books, 1989).

Cesar mendoza   1992   "SAN ANGEL"

CHAPTER NINETEEN

20 Questions & Answers

We have received many letters from readers asking for more information about living in Mexico. We answer every letter, but cannot always provide an individual reply to every query. Many of the questions were already answered in the book; the readers simply didn't look carefully. But we discovered many areas of information that we overlooked and/or didn't stress enough in the first two editions. We'll try to remedy this by including this chapter of answers to the 20 most frequently asked questions.

QUESTION: What effect will the proposed new trade agreements between the United States and Mexico have on retirees living there?

ANSWER: In the short-run, very little, if any. The agreements are not yet a reality and are unlikely to be implemented in the immediate future. In the long-run they will probably mean lower prices for imports and somewhat higher prices for domestic products in Mexico. This may lead to a gradual overall increase in the cost of living, but the most important effect will be an improvement in the standard of living of the average Mexican citizen. It is hard for anyone who values the country and its people to see that as negative.

QUESTION: Can a couple really live well on $600 a month?

ANSWER: Yes, definitely. We have checked prices in communities all over Mexico and in many (but not all) of them we have found retired North American couples who are living comfortably on that income.

Maintaining a car will bring the minimum figure a little higher than that, but public transportation is excellent and even the frequent use of taxis will not add substantially to your expenses.

Of course a larger income will broaden your options and will enable you to enjoy more luxuries. Although in *Choose Mexico* we have not confined ourselves to writing exclusively about places where one can live on $600 a month, we have tried never to lose sight of the fact that some of our readers need to know where that can be done.

Recently, readers have been asking, "I have an income of only $400 a month. Can I get by on that?"

Well, as we've said before, $400 a month is a lot more than most Mexicans have to live on, but a lot less than most gringos have to live on. Figure your position from there. If you were fluent in Spanish, and were willing to live on a very low standard of living, you might manage.

Personally, we would recommend against trying to live there on that amount of money, but if you are into the culture, don't mind forsaking gringo luxuries, well... it could be a rather dreary living experience by our standards, but an ordinary experience by Mexican standards. On the other hand, we would be hard pressed to find a place in the U.S. where you could live on $400 a month with any measure of dignity.

Basically, we do *not* recommend that anyone move to Mexico because they are indigent. In the long run, a poor person might be much better off in the United States, given the social services and welfare grants available. In Mexico, nothing of the sort exists. Furthermore, the Mexican government dislikes the idea of someone entering the country who cannot afford to live there. People who can't support themselves often find deportation as the remedy.

And don't expect the local North American community to come to your aid. This is one area where they are definitely not very friendly, not when it comes to people they feel are freeloaders.

QUESTION: Hasn't the tremendous change in the relative values of the peso and the dollar affected the amount of money you need to live on in Mexico?

ANSWER: Soon after the first edition of *Choose Mexico* was published in 1985, we started to get letters from readers asking if the changes in the exchange rate (which seemed to be occurring daily) weren't making the book and all the prices it listed out-of-date.

If you read any edition of our book carefully, however, you'll see that we've avoided stating prices in pesos. It isn't a catastrophe, therefore, if an item that used to cost 100 pesos now costs 3,000 as long as you are living on dollars. That is because inflation and devaluation have taken place in tandem. If inflation had run way ahead of devaluation, Mexico today would be prohibitively expensive. On the other hand, if there had been only devaluation and no inflation, that 100 peso item that translated to about 65 cents five years ago would now cost you only four cents today and a room in a comfortable hotel less than one dollar. As attractive as that might sound, you don't need to be an economist to recognize that it would not be a stable situation.

As things stand, prices seem to have reached an equilibrium at a somewhat higher level than when the first two editions of *Choose Mexico* were published and we have seen little change in recent years. The principal exceptions are tourist and border areas and facilities that cater almost exclusively to foreigners. Their proprietors seem to be catching on that people who are on vacation and have little idea of the "other Mexico" we write about in Chapter Three will not balk at prices that are way out of line, as long as they are about what they are used to paying.

QUESTION: Can I get a job in Mexico?

ANSWER: It's not altogether out of the question, but probably not, at least until you have achieved Inmigrado status (at least five years).

Unless you are an Inmigrado, it is illegal to work in Mexico without a work permit which is obtained from the Department of Immigration, with its central office in Mexico City and some branch offices elsewhere around the republic. These permits aren't easy to get. Unless you can do some kind of work that no Mexican citizen can perform, you aren't likely to get permission. The restrictions have relaxed somewhat over the years, particularly in real estate sales and promotion, teaching English and so forth.

If you are caught working without a permit, you take a big risk. According to the director of immigration in Baja California Sur (Lic. Gabriel Cuervo), "Working without papers in Mexico is a very serious crime and comes with a generous jail sentence of 18 months or deportation." Another point is that if you do obtain papers, they are good only for the employer specified. Should you decide to change employers, you need to apply for another permit. If you don't, you face the same serious charges as if you didn't have papers in the first place.

Finally, wages are so low in Mexico that you would have to have some kind of special talent that no one else has to demand any kind of decent salary. Real estate and condo salesmen working on commission may do well, however, depending upon their ability and their luck.

None of these rules applies to an artist or a writer. If their works are sold to foreign companies or citizens, there is no competition with Mexican workers.

QUESTION: Can I bring my pets with me?

ANSWER: Dogs and cats can be brought into Mexico if they are healthy and have received the required immunizations and you have a veterinarian's certificate to prove it. Birds, however, cannot be brought across the border in either direction. We advise you to check with the nearest Mexican consulate on the details of how recent your immunization certificate should be and what information it must contain.

QUESTION: How about moving my furniture there?

ANSWER: You can legally move your furniture and other household goods to Mexico once you have FM-2 (Inmigrante) status. You cannot do so when you first enter Mexico as a tourist. Whether it pays to transport your property there rather than selling and replacing it with new purchases in Mexico is something you will have to decide for yourself when you have been there for a while.

You may be surprised at the bargains on furniture that are available to you there.

QUESTION: Do American appliances work on Mexican electrical current?

ANSWER: Yes, the current is the same as in the U.S. No adapters are needed and anything that works at home will work there (although we have heard reports that electric clocks do not keep good time).

QUESTION: Can a single woman be safe and comfortable in Mexico?

ANSWER: Although young women alone in Mexico are sometimes annoyed by the attentions of the men and the culture there gives them less freedom to go where they want, when they want, than at home, it is not usually an issue for those who are beyond their thirties. In communities where there are large numbers of North Americans, the problem is far less likely to arise. You see single women all the time in Mexico, traveling on buses, trains, walking around town or reading books in the town square.

Since age is respected in Mexico to a greater extent than in our youth-accented society, residents have reported that the older the woman, the nicer local people seem to be. We've met many elderly ladies, some in their 70s and 80s, who have lived in Mexico for years with no problems.

Of course, the opposite can be true: The younger and prettier the woman, the more attention she will attract. Most of the attention will be in the form of sly whistles or double-entendre remarks made for the amusement of bystanders. The best thing to do is to ignore it; they seldom say anything insulting, and you probably won't understand, anyway.

It seems that young, pretty American ladies have the reputation of being "hot," or "sexy." In a sense, this is relatively true, since Mexican girls rarely engage in pre-marital sex. Living together casually with a member of the opposite sex—as is common in the U.S.—is slightly scandalous in Mexico, so you can see why Mexican men can have mistaken ideas about gringo girls' morals. So when a girl dresses provocatively, in clinging clothes, she can have all sorts of panting men following behind her, hoping to change their luck.

We once met a stunning blonde in Puerto Escondido who solved the problem of beach romeos trying to date her. She simply rolled up some newspapers, and wrapped the bundle in a blanket to look like a baby, and presto: no more hassle! "I'm going to get a patent on an inflatable baby doll you can carry in your purse," she said. "Then when you want some peace, you simply blow it up."

Here are some other tips that younger single women have passed along to us. First of all, try not to give strangers casual eye contact. In Mexico, this can be interpreted as a "come-on." If you see someone you would like to know better, arrange for someone to introduce you. Otherwise they think you are "loose." Next, if someone tries to come on strong, *never* show fear. Culturally, Mexican women often pretend to be frightened when actually they are being coy; this turns some men on. Boredom, anger or haughty amusement are among your most devastating weapons. Finally, if someone touches you when you don't want to be touched, make your anger known. If this doesn't cure the situation, get loud about it, very loud if necessary.

QUESTION: What income taxes do retirees in Mexico have to pay?

ANSWER: If they have income in the United States, they have to continue filing returns and paying taxes there. They do not pay any taxes to Mexico on their U.S. income. As we have stated before, they cannot be employed in Mexico, so the only taxable income they are likely to have there is on the interest on their deposits in Mexican banks. It is withheld.

QUESTION: How about golf and tennis in Mexico?

ANSWER: Tennis is a very popular game among the upper classes in Mexico. It's a sort of status symbol, and you'll find many courts in larger cities. Many, however, are private clubs or at private homes. If you are a real tennis buff, you might look for a condo-type rental with its own courts.

Golf is another thing entirely. While golf also carries an upper-class connotation, there aren't many courses available outside the exclusive country clubs in the larger cities. Prices tend to be higher than on public courses at home, although not as expensive as at private clubs in the U.S. Puerto Vallarta, for example, until recently had only one golf course for the entire area. Palm Springs in California, on the other hand, with about as many residents, has over 60 golf courses.

There are several reasons for this non-popularity of golf. One is that Mexico has a perpetual water shortage in the winter, when most people would be playing golf. To expend enormous amounts of water keeping a course in playable condition would be terribly wasteful; the government hates to give well permits to golf courses when farmers anxiously wait for their own permission to drill for water. So, Mexican fairways are often so dry and hard that they might as well be in cement. In the summers, when regular rainfall keeps the grass green, the golf-playing tourists are all at home in the United States playing golf there.

Another reason for the scarcity of courses is that golf is a middle-class game in the United States and Canada. It's a moderately expensive pastime requiring greens fees and equipment, plus considerable spare time to devote to the game. But Mexico has a very small middle-class population. Most people work six days a week, sometimes 12 hours a day, and can spare neither the time nor the money to take up golf.

Don't get us wrong. There is golf in Mexico. Guadalajara alone has five courses. We just don't want to give our readers the mistaken impression that the country is a golfer's paradise or that the sport fits easily into a $600 a month lifestyle there.

QUESTION: Are insects a problem?

ANSWER: There are few unpleasant bugs in most of the areas where North Americans have chosen to retire. The only insects we have seen much of are flies and they are much more likely to be found in outdoor markets than in screened kitchens. There are occasional scorpions to be seen in dry climates, especially in hot weather, but we've never heard retirees refer to them as a serious problem.

QUESTION: Isn't Mexican automobile liability insurance very expensive?

ANSWER: It is, if you buy it by the day. I paid about $18.00 to cover my car for three days on a recent short trip to Baja. But just as in the U.S., it becomes far less costly when you are insured for a longer period. The annual liability premium for an older car is about $150. If you have an expensive new U.S. car and want collision as well as liability insurance on it, you may well have to pay more than you do in the U.S., unless you join a club with insurance benefits (See Appendix).

QUESTION: How can I get in touch with Americans living in Mexico to correspond with them?

ANSWER: This is the question that gives us the most trouble. Are there many people in your hometown who would be willing to spend a lot of time writing to strangers? If so, there must not be many better ways to spend your time there. Most people who have retired in Mexico seem to be too busy enjoying life to develop extensive correspondences with people they don't know. In our section on resources we've listed some people who offer information services. Their newsletters and orientation packages may be your best hope of getting current and individualized answers to your questions.

QUESTION: What will my legal status be?

ANSWER: This question is answered in great detail in Chapter Six. The most important thing to understand is that becoming a legal resident of Mexico does not impair your U.S. citizenship in any way.

QUESTION: Are there schools for English-speaking children and adolescents?

ANSWER: Every large city in Mexico (and some smaller ones, too) has at least one bilingual school to which many Americans (as well as some Mexicans) send their children. Since this is primarily a book for retirees, we do not list these schools, but advise readers with young children to visit the community they are thinking of moving to and check personally.

QUESTION: What happens if I die while I am in Mexico?

ANSWER: Your spouse or friends can get a certificate from the local authorities allowing your remains to be flown back to the U.S., if that is what you wish. It is not a problem.

QUESTION: Can U.S. television programs be received in Mexico?

ANSWER: Yes, with a satellite antenna. They are becoming increasingly popular in Mexico. A recent newspaper ad offers antennas of various sizes for between $475 and $700 U.S. There are also English-language cable stations in some of the larger cities. A less expensive way to see U.S. programs is on videotapes rented or traded back and forth with friends.

QUESTION: Can you recommend a real estate broker who can help me buy or rent a house or apartment in Mexico?

ANSWER: We don't feel that dealing with a real estate broker long-distance is a wise way to shop for a home in Mexico. Also, the ownership and personnel of real estate firms can change during the life of a book. As we discuss at greater length in the chapter on housing, we strongly urge you to visit a community before you make any commitments. It is also a good idea to study the real estate listing in English-language newspapers of the communities you are considering (see Appendix for names and addresses). These papers will also contain the names of real estate brokers of whom you may want to make preliminary inquiries. However, please remember not to be discouraged by high prices, since you can almost always do much better on the spot.

QUESTION: How are the hunting and fishing in Mexico?

ANSWER: Fishing in Baja and along the Pacific Coast varies from good to fantastic, and licenses are usually provided by the people who rent you the boat, or can be purchased in town. Companies like Mexico West Travel Club or Vagabundos del Mar (See Appendix for addresses and telephone numbers) can help you get a license before you enter Mexico. Inland communities like Guadalajara often have lakes and streams nearby where fresh-water species abound. Bringing your fishing tackle into Mexico is not a problem.

Hunting, however, is somewhat more complicated. The Mexican government is very cautious about people toting guns or bringing them into the country. (Don't even *think* about bringing a handgun! The best advice we've heard concerning handguns is: If you feel you can't travel without one, then better visit somewhere else.) Shotguns are about the only firearms permitted across the border. The red tape involved is incredible. Besides proof of citizenship, a character reference in duplicate from your police department, the serial numbers, calibers and makes of your guns, you will need up to 14 passport-size photos, and several days of running around to the Mexican consulates, Military Commandante and Mexican Game Department offices. Fees, stamps and papers will cost about $120, plus *mordidas* and a doozy of a headache.

There are people who you can pay to do all this for you. Contact Mexican Hunting Association, 3302 Josie Ave., Long Beach, CA 90808, for more information. Or, you can book a package tour with guns, permits and guides included. It's our understanding that heavier caliber weapons can be rented once you are in the country.

QUESTION(S): I am a divorced woman, age 54. What are my chances of meeting eligible men, either American or Mexican?

My wife died several years ago, and I'm thinking of getting married again. Are there any single women retiring in Mexico? What about marrying a Mexican lady?

ANSWER: As far as finding companionship among other retirees and residents is concerned, our observation is that the chances can be excellent. There are several good reasons for this. First of all, there are a lot of single North Americans going to Mexico to live. When people become separated, divorced or widowed, they often think of changing their lifestyle completely, and Mexico is a great place for that. Secondly, because of the accepting nature of the English-speaking society, it's much easier to become acquainted than back home. You don't need singles bars or introduction services. Simply join in the social groups, volunteer activities, or take language lessons in a school, and you will come in contact with just about everyone in the foreign colony before long. And finally, there are certain personality types that seem to gravitate toward foreign living. They tend to be adventurous, open to new ideas and to change, perhaps brighter, and certainly more alert and active than average. When you have people with similar interests together in a setting where friendship is highly prized, you can see how odds go up as to finding compatible companions.

As regards cross-national marriages, there are some factors that should be taken into consideration. Yes, *machismo* exists in Mexico, although not to the extent that cliché would have you think. But it's definitely a man's world in Mexico. It's only in the modernized societies like the United States where women can compete with men on a more equal level. A woman can drive a tractor or a truck as well as a man and she can operate a computer equally well. But in Mexico where mules and oxen are used in the fields instead of tractors, and where they have far fewer computers, women are not so equal. Women's lib is a foreign concept here.

For this reason, an American woman, before considering marriage with a local man, should make certain she knows how he stands on many issues, and how he is likely to treat her after the initial euphoria of the romance fades. Men should also know what kind of marriage they are getting into when marrying a local woman instead of one from the foreign colony. There are a lot of

cultural differences that could cause problems, particularly since many Mexican women view sex differently than American women. For one thing, sex is often looked on as a necessary evil just to conceive children, not something to enjoy or for recreation.

In any event, there is one big advantage in marrying Mexican citizens, that is you immediately gain the right to become a resident, to own businesses, work, or do anything a Mexican citizen can do, except vote. This can be important in some cases, others think of nothing but love, true love!

CHAPTER TWENTY

Will You Love It?

Most foreigners either love Mexico or hate it. This phenomenon is so well known that just about every guidebook to the country, after listing the numerous reasons for the author's deep affection for the land and its people, finds it necessary to warn that "Mexico is not everybody's cup of tea." (Someone should offer a prize for an alternative to that cliché— "cup of tequila" would not qualify.) No doubt the principal reason for these strong feelings is that Mexico, like many of its favorite foods, is highly spiced. Nothing is muted, neither the colors nor the sounds. Mexico does not sneak up on you. It confronts you immediately and totally.

The shock is particularly intense for the American who has gone right next door to find himself in a country vastly different from his own. Mexico quickly shatters the illusion that foreignness is a function of distance. More than one traveler, familiar with every part of Europe including Russia, has observed that Mexico is the most foreign country he has ever visited.

Are Mexico's differences from the U.S. good or bad news? I know my answer to that question, but I do not know yours. Even if I knew you very well, I am not at all sure that I could predict which it would be. Yes, there are some people about whose reaction to the country I could make a confident guess. Most of them are so rigid, impatient or demanding that I cannot imagine them tolerating the inefficiencies and delays of Mexican life. I'm proud that, after a number of months in Mexico, I have learned to sit in a restaurant for twenty minutes before the waiter takes my order and another twenty until the food arrives without any knotting of my insides. (I'm doubly proud that I can even do it back in the U.S.) I am not, however, sufficiently unreasonable to expect or demand that everyone master this trick. Would you be outraged or amused by the fact that, each time postage for an airmail letter to the U.S. goes up, it is many months before stamps are available for the new amount or that often envelopes and packages have to be mailed with wall-to-wall small denomination stamps because no larger ones are available? Trivial? Of course, but if your answer is "outraged," or even if you would merely find that situation annoying, it is quite possible that Mexico is not your "c.o.t." There are just too many little things like that which, if you let them, could add up to constant annoyance.

Somewhat more serious are the seemingly arbitrary and unpredictable shortages that plague Mexico for months at a time. Several years ago it was toothpaste, reportedly because of some difficulty in manufacturing the tubes. Unlike the U.S. where many brands of almost every product are available, Mexico usually has only one and anything that interrupts its manufacturer's operations cuts off the supply altogether. Mexicans and longtime foreign residents there learn to deal with these shortages in a variety of ways. A friend who is traveling north of the border is often asked to pick up a couple of extra tubes of toothpaste or whatever to bring back. The Indian women street vendors in Mexico City often seem to have mysterious sources of supply and can furnish the scarce item when none of the shops has it. Approached in the right spirit, obtaining the seemingly unobtainable becomes a game. But, of course, it may not be the kind you enjoy playing.

Most Americans are deeply offended by the sight of people spitting in the street. In the days when spittoons were a ubiquitous feature of the American domestic landscape, the esthetic aversion to that practice was probably much weaker. However, a very effective anti-spitting campaign by the Tuberculosis Association succeeded in sensitizing our grandparents and we continue to view it with an intense distaste that Mexicans do not seem to share. To be comfortable in Mexico you do not have to enjoy the sight, but it does help to be able to ignore it.

Drinking only bottled or boiled water is a nuisance. How much more convenient it is to place your glass under any tap and enjoy, without any trace of concern, the clear liquid that pours out. It is also pleasant to pick up a piece of fruit in the market and eat it as you find it, or, if you are fastidious, after running some cold water over it. It is usually some time after you have returned from Mexico before you are able to resume those practices without a moment of hesitation. Water in Mexico is not safe and one must learn while there to avoid everything (uncooked) with which it may have come in contact.

Are these serious enough inconveniences to spoil your enjoyment of the country or are they somewhat like the necessity to retrain your reflexes before you can drive or even cross streets safely in England? You may not know what your reaction will be until you have been in Mexico for a little while. Part of the initial strain is fear that you will forget and inadvertently expose yourself to danger. That worry soon fades as the required new behaviors become second nature.

Many Americans are appalled by what they see as the pervasive corruption of Mexican political life. Indeed, it is true that few Mexican presidents have left office without arranging for themselves and their friends to live in luxury for the rest of their lives. However, to see this as contrasting sharply with universal probity north of the border requires that one forget the "sleaze" factor that has figured so prominently in the history of just about every U.S. presidential administration in our time. Of course every scandal on the federal level has many counterparts in the statehouses. Less visible but far more widespread are the abuses of power routinely encountered in the world of commerce.

It is all too easy to jump from the unquestionable fact that American customs inspectors are much less likely to take bribes than their Mexican counterparts to the dubious conclusion that Americans are honest and Mexicans are crooked. It is not even a question of degree, but rather of different culturally approved manifestations of what, sadly, appears to be a universal weakness. However, most American do take a while to become comfortable with the idea of "tipping" minor public officials.

This brief recitation of some things Americans find to dislike about Mexico is far from exhaustive. It does, however, include many of the most frequently heard complaints. For those who allow them to, they constitute ample reason for choosing other places in which to spend time. For many others—the author included—they are part of the price one must pay for sharing in the riches of Mexican life.

We mailed a questionnaire to Americans, most of them retired, living in cities, towns and villages from one end of Mexico to the other. One of the questions was, "What do you like most about Mexico?" I was not surprised by the most frequent answer, since it was the one I would have given, only by the near unanimity with which it was offered. That answer was, "the people." Every other response—"the climate," "the natural beauty," "the low prices"—lagged far behind.

What is it about the Mexican people that appeals so strongly to Americans? What qualities can transcend the barriers of language, class, ethnicity and culture to evoke this response so universally? First, it is their friendliness. Most of the time you are treated with the warmth and curiosity that all strangers receive in Mexico. The fact that you are a foreigner as well as a stranger seems to be incidental. Second, it is their happiness. It may be anomalous, but poverty in Mexico is much more common than misery. The people seem to have the ability to enjoy life, no matter how grim its circumstances. It is a gift that, as a people, we Americans do not appear to possess.

Related to their friendliness, but separate from it, is their helpfulness. Mexicans are almost always willing to stop whatever they are doing to be of assistance to a friend, a neighbor or a stranger. They even seem to welcome the opportunity to be helpful (or perhaps to stop what they are doing). Another related quality is courtesy. Politeness is not enough to make an individual or a people good and, perhaps as a reaction to our belated recognition of that fact, we in American have given it up. Mexicans, however, are too deeply steeped in a tradition of courtesy that goes back centuries to have acquired the knack of rudeness. They still ask to be excused when they must squeeze by you in a crowd and they still preface every request or order with "*por favor*" (please).

Then there is the love the Mexicans so obviously feel for their children. Much has been said and written about *machismo,* but there is no more common sight in Mexico than a father carrying his baby or small child. A sensitive observer of the Mexican scene has noted that Americans are often distressed by the callousness with which the Mexicans treat animals, but that Mexicans are equally scandalized by the verbal brutality American parents visit on their children. Perhaps if Mexican children were not so extremely well behaved the sight of a parent screaming at his offspring might be more common, but as it is, I have never seen it.

As one spends more time in Mexico and learns more Spanish, his understanding of Mexicans is likely to undergo many changes. It will become clear, for instance, that easy friendliness will not usually evolve into deeper friendship. Nevertheless, even when the contradictions of Mexican character are realized, for the American who has been in the country for decades, as much as for the newcomer, the appeal of the people remains uppermost as a reason for wanting to be there.

It is tempting to look for explanations. Do Europeans experience the same reaction to Mexicans as we do? Do our southern neighbors embody some impulses that we North Americans lack or suppress? It seems likely that memories of a gentler era that has vanished in the United States do contribute to our response.

It would be a severe distortion to suggest that Mexico appeals only to those who are sympathetic to the policies of its government. Americans and other foreigners have fallen in love with the country under regimes that have covered the full spectrum from right to left, and often their affection has been very much in spite of the ideology and behavior of the party in power. Even today, Mexico is full of Americans who deplore everything about the government's foreign and domestic policies, would love to see them become carbon copies of ours, but would not think of moving back to the U.S. where they can enjoy the originals. Very few, by any means, are too poor to afford the higher prices in their homeland, so there must be something else about Mexico that holds them.

Of course there are other attractions in addition to the Mexican people. One is the climate. The weather may not be perfect everywhere in Mexico at any given time, but chances are that it is some place and usually not too far from where you are.

The residents of Mexico City discovered at least five centuries ago that when, as occasionally happens, the winters there are a bit too nippy its easy to find temperatures a dozen degrees warmer in nearby Cuernavaca. In Guadalajara they know that in January descending to the Pacific Coast only a few hours away takes you from the fifties to the balmy eighties. In San Miguel, Morelia and dozens of other cities and towns of the Central Plateau, spring is "eternal." If you live in a climate that is bearable year-round, it may be hard to understand the thirst for warmth and sunshine that historically has made Italy the symbol of Paradise on earth for Northern Europeans from England to Russia and draws such flocks of sun-starved Scandinavians to Spain every winter. Unless you have gasped for air in a New York, Washington or Houston summer, the annual exodus to the mountains and the beaches may seem inexplicable. If, on the other hand, you suffer either extreme heat or cold in the course of your year, it may not be necessary for me to tell you much more about why the Mexican climate draws so many refugees from the extremes of U.S. winters and summers. Yes, parts of Mexico can be hot, but the bulk of the population lives in, and visitors flock to, places where altitude or sea breezes provide year-round moderation.

It is difficult to avoid sounding crass when discussing how reasonable living in Mexico can be. Compulsive bargain hunting is an illness and, many would say, one of the least attractive characteristics of Americans abroad. Perhaps, though, the retiree who is trying to make a limited income provide the comfort we have been encouraged to expect as the reward for a lifetime of work can be viewed a little differently from the tourist who is looking for a cheap vacation. In Mexico, I discovered Americans who would be barely making it at home living comfortably. I freely admit that the hope this experience gave me for my own future colors my perception of the country as a place to retire. Certainly, I would not advise anyone to move there for the low prices alone. Nothing is a bargain if you do not enjoy it. Nevertheless, the stretch it gives to a modest income must be counted as one of the major advantages of Mexico as a place to visit or live.

In the end, although I hope that these observations may help you make some guesses about whether you will love or hate the Mexico experience, you will not know for sure until you have tried it. If you go expecting to find a replica of U.S. living, but with palm trees and mariachis in the background, you will be disappointed. Some things you may value highly are not considered important there. On the other hand, you may learn to appreciate some qualities, such as patience, courtesy and simplicity, that our culture often slights. Even if you decide, after you have seen it for yourself, that you cannot love Mexico as I do, I doubt that you will regret having tried.

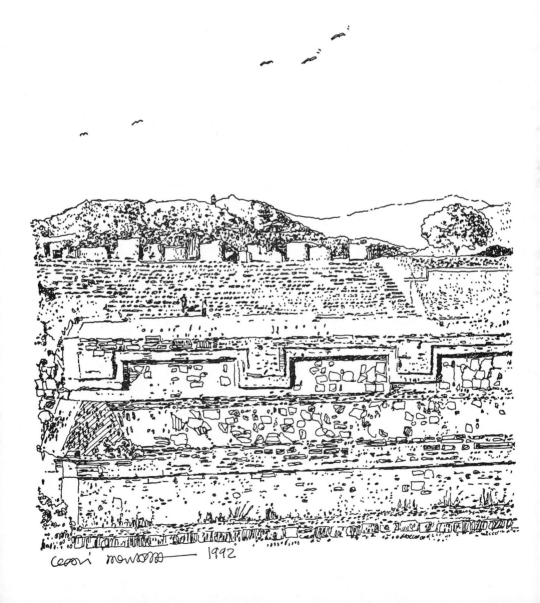

Appendix

English Language Newspapers

The News
Balderas 87—3rd Floor
06050 Mexico , DF, Mexico
    (A daily sold throughout Mexico)

The Colony Reporter
Duque de Rivas 254
45050 Guadalajara, JAL, Mexico

Atención San Miguel
Apdo 119
San Miguel de Allende, GTO, Mexico

Ensenada News and Views
Blvd. Costero 22800
Ensenada, BCN, Mexico

Baja Times (Rosarito Beach)
P.O. Box 755
San Ysidro, CA 92073

Newsletters

AIM
(Adventures in Mexico)
Apdo 31-70
45050 Guadalajara,JAL, Mexico
    A newsletter on retirement and travel in Mexico.

Retiring in Guadalajara
Apdo 5-409
Guadalajara, JAL, Mexico
    This newsletter covers only Guadalajara but covers it in
    great detail.

Resources:

American Canadian Club
Hotel Plaza del Sol
Lopez Mateos y Mariano Otero
45050 Guadalajara JAL Mexico
Attn: Len or Nellie Friedman
Tel: 47-87-90 (until noon)
> For $1.00 to cover the cost of printing and mailing, they'll send you a very current update on living costs.

Mr. and Mrs. F.G. Furton
Apdo 5-409
Guadalajara, JAL, Mexico
> They offer many services to newcomers to Guadalajara.

Automobile Insurance

For long-term residents of Mexico, insurance is not only essential, but can be expensive. But we've found a way to beat the high rates. The secret is to join a travel club and take advantage of their group rates. The two clubs we know about are Mexico West and Vagabundos del Mar. They have been able to negotiate substantially reduced rates for their members with Mexican insurance companies.

You can join these clubs for about $40. Then you are eligible to purchase, for $143, full-coverage insurance on a car worth about $12,000 (slightly more for a more expensive vehicle). This policy covers you in Baja and on the West Coast of Mexico about as far south as Mazatlán. If you want coverage for the rest of Mexico, it will cost you an additional premium of about $50 for a total of $223 for full coverage for a full year. This is considerably lower than the rates normally charged by Mexican companies. Know, however, that no part of the premium is returned if you cancel the insurance in less than a year.

Mexico West Travel Club, Inc.
P.O. Box 1646
Bonita, CA 91908
(619) 585-3033

Vagabundos del Mar
P.O. Box 824
Isleton, CA 95641
(707) 327-5511

Health Insurance

ClubMex
Guadlaljara—Escuela Militar de Aviación No. 60
(phone 52-29-92)
Lake Chapala—Hidalgo 79-F in Máskaras shopping center
on Chapala-Ajijic highway (phone 5-25-92)
U.S.—3450 Bonita Road, Suite 103
Chula Vista CA 95010

Banking

California Commerce Bank
615 S. Flower
Los Angeles, CA 90017
(213) 624-5700
Guadalajara information number: 25-32-58.

Mexican Government Tourism Offices

Washington
1911 Pennsylvania Ave. NW
Washington, DC 20006
Chicago
233 North Michigan, Suite 1413
Chicago, IL 60601
New York
405 Park Avenue
Suite 1203
New York, NY 10022
Houston
2707 N. Loop West, Suite 450
Houston, TX 77006
Los Angeles
10100 Santa Monica Blvd.
Los Angeles, CA 90067

Montreal
One Place Ville Marie, Suite 2409
Montreal, Quebec H3B 3M9
Toronto
181 University Avenue, Suite 1112
Toronto, Ontario M5H 3M7

Citizens Emergency Center—U.S. State Department

Situation reports on any destination around the world: Locates travelers abroad to deliver emergency messages.
(202) 647-5225
Available: 8:15—5:00 p.m. weekdays; 9:00—3:00 p.m. Saturdays (Eastern Time)

Books

American-Canadian Club. *Retiring to Mexico*. Indianapolis, IN:ACC Books, 1991.

Cassell's Colloquial Spanish, New York: MacMillan, 1980

Chase, Stuart. *Mexico: A Study of Two Americas*. New York: Macmillan, 1931.

Flandrau, Charles Macomb. *Viva Mexico!* Champaign, IL: University of Illinois Press, 1964.

Franz, Carl. *The People's Guide to Mexico*. John Muir Publications, Sante Fe, New Mexico, 1992

Gilmore, Betty and John. *A Guide to Living in Mexico*. Toms River, NJ: Capricorn Books, 1972.

Johnson, William Webber. *Heroic Mexico: The Violent Emergence of a Modern Nation*. New York: Doubleday, 1968.

Kennedy, Diana. *The Cuisines of Mexico*. New York: Harper & Row, 1972.

Lincoln, John. *One's Man Mexico*. New York: Hippocrene Books, 1983.

Miller, Tom. *The Baja Book III*. Huntington Beach, CA: Baja Trail Publications, 1987.

Reavis, Dick J. *Conversations with Moctezuma: Ancient Shadows Over Modern Life in Mexico*. New York: William Morrow, 1990.

Riding, Alan. *Distant Neighbors: Portrait of the Mexicans*. New York: Knopf, 1985.

Rodman, Seldon. *Mexico Journal: The Conquerers Conquered*. Carbondale, IL: Southern Illinois University Press, 1964.

Sierra, Justo. *The Political Evolution of the Mexican People*. Austin, TX: University of Texas Press, 1975.

Simon, Kate. *Mexico: Places & Pleasures*. New York: Harper & Row, 1984.

Simpson, Lesley Byrd. *Many Mexicos*. Berkeley, CA: Univerity of California Press, 1967.

Strode, Hudson. *Timeless Mexico*. New York: Harcourt Brace Jovanovich, 1944.

Zamba, Michael. *Living in Mexico*. Chicago, IL: Passport Books, 1991.

NOTE: There are numerous excellent guidebooks for travelers in Mexico, most of them updated annually. They are your best source of information on hotels, restaurants, museums, ruins and other attractions to enjoy while you explore the country in search of the retirement site that is just right for you. It will be worth your while to look at many of these in your library and pick up some at the bookstore before you go. Among those to consider are:

AAA Travel Guide to Mexico

Birnbaum, Stephen. *Mexico*

Fodor's *Budget Mexico*

Frommer's *Mexico on $45 a Day* 1992.

Insight Guides. *Mexico*

Harvard Student's Agencies, Inc.*Let's Go Mexico 1992*

Lonely Planet Guides. *Mexico*

Sunset. *Mexico: Travel Guide*

About the Authors

John Howells was born in New Orleans and grew up in suburban St. Louis. His teen years, however, were spent in Mexico City and he has been returning to Mexico as often as possible ever since. Now a resident of California, he has worked on newspapers from coast to coast – 40 in all. He has been a Linotype operator, English teacher, silver miner and a travel and feature writer. John earned a B.A. in Anthropology and a M. A. in Mexican-American Graduate Studies from San Jose State University. He is the author of seven travel-retirement books.

Don Merwin is a native New Yorker who now lives in the San Francisco Bay Area. He began his career in communications as a writer for Edward R. Murrow in the early 1950s and spent the next three decades as publicist, administrator and planner in health and human service organizations. Don and his wife, Judith, are the publishers of Gateway Books. They look forward to eventual retirement in Mexico. Meanwhile, they explore new south of the border locations every chance they get.

Index

O ur books are available in most bookstores. However, if you have difficulty finding them, we will be happy to ship them to you directly. Mail us this coupon with your check or money order and they'll be on their way to you within days.

Foreign Retirement

Retire on $600 a Month
CHOOSE MEXICO: $10.95 _____

Exploring the Travel/Retirement Option
ADVENTURES ABROAD   12.95 _____

Leisurely Vacations or Affordable Retirement
CHOOSE SPAIN   11.95 _____

Retirement in the U.S.

Strategies for comfortable retirement on Social Security
RETIREMENT ON A SHOESTRING   6.95 _____

Detailed information on America's 100 Best Places to Retire
WHERE TO RETIRE   12.95 _____

Travel

The Complete How-to-do-it Book
RV TRAVEL IN MEXICO   9.95 _____

A Guide for the Mature Traveler
GET UP AND GO: 10.95 _____

Subtotal: _____

Add $1.90 for postage and handling for the first book,
.50 for each additional one.
(Canadian orders: $ .75 additional postage)   _____

California residents add 7.25% sales tax   _____

Total Enclosed: _____

| Credit Card Orders Only • Call our FREE number: 1-800-669-0773 |

Name_____

Address_____

City/State/Zip_____

Books should reach you in two or three weeks. If you are dissatisfied for any reason, the price of the books will be refunded in full.

Mail to: Gateway Books • 13 Bedford Cove • San Rafael, CA 94901